W9-AMX-646

American Revolution
Primary Sources

American Revolution Primary Sources

Linda Schmittroth

Lawrence W. Baker and
Stacy A. McConnell, Editors

U·X·L®

AN IMPRINT OF THE GALE GROUP

DETROIT · SAN FRANCISCO · LONDON
BOSTON · WOODBRIDGE, CT

American Revolution: Primary Sources

Linda Schmittroth

Staff

Lawrence W. Baker, *U•X•L Senior Editor*
Stacy A. McConnell, *U•X•L Editor*
Carol DeKane Nagel, *U•X•L Managing Editor*
Thomas L. Romig, *U•X•L Publisher*

Rita Wimberley, *Senior Buyer*
Evi Seoud, *Assistant Manager, Composition Purchasing and Electronic Prepress*
Dorothy Maki, *Manufacturing Manager*

Tracey Rowens, *Senior Art Director*
Margaret Chamberlain, *Permissions Specialist (Text and pictures)*
Kelly A. Quin, *Editor, Imaging and Multimedia Content*
Pamela Reed, *Imaging Coordinator*
Leitha Etheridge-Sims, *Image Cataloger*
Robert Duncan and Dan Newell, *Imaging Specialists*
Randy A. Bassett, *Image Database Supervisor*
Barbara J. Yarrow, *Imaging and Multimedia Content Manager*

Linda Mahoney, *LM Design, Typesetting*

Library of Congress Cataloging-in-Publication Data

American Revolution : primary sources / [compiled by] Linda Schmittroth; edited by Lawrence W. Baker and Stacy McConnell.

p. cm.

Includes bibliographical references and index.

Summary: A collection of annotated documents relating to the American Revolution, including speeches, autobiographical text, and proclamations.

ISBN 0-7876-3790-4

1. United States—History—Revolution, 1775–1783—Sources—Juvenile literature. [1. United States—History—Revolution, 1775-1783—Sources.] I. Schmittroth, Linda. II. Baker, Lawrence W. III. McConnell, Stacy A. IV. Title.

E203.A577 2000
973.7—dc21   99-046940

Copyright © 2000
U•X•L, an imprint of The Gale Group
27500 Drake Road
Farmington Hills, MI 48331-3535

Cover illustration of stamp burning is reproduced by permission of Archive Photos; King George III, reproduced by permission of The Granger Collection, Ltd.; and George Washington, courtesy of the Library of Congress.

Printed in the United States of America

10 9 8 7 6 5 4 3 2 1

Contents

Advisory Board. ix

Reader's Guide. xi

Timeline of Events in Revolutionary America xv

Words to Know. xxv

Primary Sources

Chapter 1: British Actions, Colonial Reactions. 1

The Stamp Act. 7
George Washington Reacts to
the Stamp Act (box) 12

The Declaratory Act. 19

The Townshend Revenue Act 25
Charles Townshend (box). 26
Samuel Adams, Committee-Man
and Son of Liberty (box) 32

The Intolerable Acts. 37
   The Boston Port Act 44
   The Quartering Act. 45
   Arthur Lee, Forgotten Revolutionary (box) 42

Edmund Burke 49
   Edmund Burke, British Supporter
   of the Colonies (box) 51
   "On Conciliation" 52

King George III 55
   Proclamation of Rebellion 58
   George III, Benevolent Monarch or
   "Royal Brute"? (box) 58

John Dickinson 63
   Letters from a Farmer in Pennsylvania
   to the Inhabitants of the British Colonies 66

Benjamin Franklin 71
   Benjamin Franklin, Man of
   Many Talents (box). 74
   "An Edict by the King of Prussia" 75

Thomas Jefferson 81
   *A Summary View of the Rights
   of British America* 83

Patrick Henry. 89
   Patrick Henry, Orator and Statesman (box) 92
   "Give Me Liberty, or Give Me Death!" 93

Thomas Paine. 97
   Thomas Paine, a Lover of Mankind (box). 98
   Common Sense. 101

Chapter 2: Great Congressional Documents 107

The Continental Association 111
   Virginia Delegates to the First
   Continental Congress (box) 114
   John Adams, Founding Father (box) 123
   John Adams's Writings (box). 125

Wartime Proclamations 127
   Declaration of the Causes and Necessity
   of Taking Up Arms 129

Olive Branch Petition 130
John Dickinson, Man of Contradictions (box) . . 131

The Declaration of Independence 135
Thomas Jefferson, Foremost Spokesman
for Freedom (box) 137
"Remember the Ladies" (box) 145
John Hancock, Patriot (box) 148

Articles of Confederation 151
Revolutionary War Documents on
the World Wide Web (box) 154
Native Americans in the Revolution (box) . . . 164

Chapter 3: Scandal and Betrayal 169

Thomas Hutchinson 171
Thomas Hutchinson (box) 173
Letter of Thomas Hutchinson,
June 18, 1768 175
Letter of Thomas Hutchinson,
January 20, 1769 177

Benjamin Franklin 183
Letter to Massachusetts Speaker of
the Assembly Thomas Cushing 185
The Hutchinson Letters (box) 187
Resolves of the House of Representatives,
Respecting the Letters of the Governor,
Lieutenant Governor, and Others. 191

Benjamin Franklin 197
Public Statement on the
Hutchinson Letters 198

**Americans' Reactions to Benedict
Arnold's Treason** 203
Comments of Lieutenant John Whiting
on Arnold's Treason 205
General George Washington's
Announcement to the Continental
Army of Arnold's Treason 206
"An Acrostic on Arnold" 207

Closing Lines of George Washington's
Summary of the Treason Story 207
Benedict Arnold, American Traitor (box) 208

Chapter 4: Notes from the Battlefronts 211

Lord Dunmore 217
Declaration of Martial Law in Virginia 218

Joseph Plumb Martin 221
Joseph Plumb Martin, Proud Yankee
Soldier (box) 222
A Narrative of Some of the Adventures,
Dangers, and Sufferings of a
Revolutionary Soldier 224

Thomas Paine 229
The Crisis 231

Eliza Wilkinson 235
Account of the Looting of Her Sister's
Home by British Soldiers 237

Horace Walpole 241
Letter to the Earl of Strafford about the
Surrender of Cornwallis at Yorktown 243

George Washington 247
Farewell Address to the Armies of
the United States 250

Where to Learn More 255

Index 259

Advisory Board

Special thanks are due to U•X•L's American Revolution Reference Library advisors for their invaluable comments and suggestions:

- Mary Alice Anderson, Media Specialist, Winona Middle School, Winona, Minnesota

- Jonathan Betz-Zall, Children's Librarian, Sno-Isle Regional Library System, Edmonds, Washington

- Frances Bryant Bradburn, Section Chief, Information Technology Evaluation Services, Public Schools of North Carolina, Raleigh, North Carolina

- Sara K. Brooke, Director of Libraries, The Ellis School, Pittsburgh, Pennsylvania

- Peter Butts, Media Specialist, East Middle School, Holland, Michigan

Reader's Guide

American Revolution: Primary Sources presents thirty-two excerpts from documents, narratives, satirical pieces, pamphlets, and letters that explore events surrounding the American Revolution. The book begins with the hated 1765 Stamp Act, continues through the great documents of the Continental Congresses, and ends with General George Washington's 1783 farewell address to the Continental Army. Along the way, students can sample the words of ordinary people living in extraordinary times, such as Joseph Plumb Martin, who was a teenage soldier, and Eliza Wilkinson, who recalls when British soldiers looted her sister's Southern home. Both lived to write lively accounts of their wartime adventures.

American Revolution: Primary Sources is divided into four chapters that focus on specific themes: British Actions and Colonial Reactions; Great Congressional Documents; Scandal and Treason; and Notes from the Battlefronts.

Enlightening, easy-to-understand commentary accompanies the excerpts. American Revolution: Primary Sources includes the following additional material:

- An **introduction** places the document and its author in a historical context.

- **"Things to remember while reading . . ."** offers readers important background information and directs them to central ideas in the text.

- **"What happened next . . ."** discusses the impact of the document on both the speaker and his or her audience.

- **"Did you know . . ."** provides significant and interesting facts about the excerpted document, the author, or the subjects discussed in the excerpt.

- **"Where to learn more"** lists sources for more information on the author, the document, or the subject of the excerpt.

Other features of *American Revolution: Primary Sources* include short biographies of featured authors, illustrations depicting the personalities and events discussed in the excerpts, and sidebars presenting additional information on unusual or significant aspects of the issue or event under discussion. In addition, a glossary running alongside each primary document defines unfamiliar terms, people, and ideas contained in the excerpted material. Finally, *American Revolution: Primary Sources* provides a timeline, which lists significant dates and events of the Revolutionary era, and a cumulative subject index.

American Revolution Reference Library

American Revolution: Primary Sources is only one component of the three-part American Revolution Reference Library. The other two titles in this multivolume set are:

- *American Revolution: Almanac:* This work presents a comprehensive overview of the Revolutionary era. The volume's twelve chapters describe in narrative form the events leading up to the war and the major events of the era.

- *American Revolution: Biographies:* This two-volume set presents profiles of fifty-nine important figures from the American Revolution era. The essays cover such key people as patriots John Adams, Thomas Jefferson, and Thomas Paine, as well as less celebrated people such as poet and former slave Phillis Wheatley; Frenchman Pierre Charles L'Enfant, who designed the city of Washington, D.C.; and

Frederika von Riedesel, a German who chronicled the Revolution while traveling throughout the colonies with her young family as her husband fought for the British.

- A cumulative index of all three titles in the American Revolution Reference Library is also available.

Comments and suggestions

We welcome your comments on *American Revolution: Primary Sources* as well as your suggestions for other topics in history to consider. Please write: Editors, *American Revolution: Primary Sources,* U•X•L, 27500 Drake Rd., Farmington Hills, Michigan 48331-3535; call toll-free: 800-877-4253; fax: 248-414-5043; or send e-mail via http://www.galegroup.com.

Timeline of Events in Revolutionary America

1754 The French and Indian War begins, pitting the French and their Indian allies against the British for control of North America.

1760 George III becomes king of England.

1763 French and Indian War ends with a British victory. To satisfy Native Americans, King George III forbids colonial settlement west of the Appalachian Mountains.

1765 In March, King George III approves the Stamp Act, which taxes the American colonies to pay for the French and Indian War. Horace Walpole, British Member of Parliament, opposes the Stamp Act before Parliament and speaks out for the rights of American colonists.

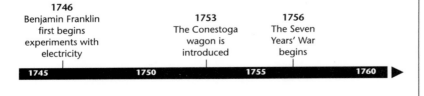

1746
Benjamin Franklin
first begins
experiments with
electricity

1753
The Conestoga
wagon is
introduced

1756
The Seven
Years' War
begins

| 1745 | 1750 | 1755 | 1760 |

In July, Boston patriots ("Sons of Liberty") unite in opposition to the Stamp Act. In August, a mob destroys the house of Massachusetts lieutenant governor Thomas Hutchinson to protest the act.

In October, delegates at a Stamp Act Congress adopt John Dickinson's Declaration of Rights and Grievances, protesting the Stamp Act.

1766 The British government repeals the Stamp Act and replaces it with the Declaratory Act, asserting England's right to make laws that colonists must obey.

British politician William Pitt makes a famous speech in Parliament, declaring his opinion that Britain "has no right to lay a tax upon" the American colonies.

1767 Thomas Hutchinson and other Massachusetts government officials begin writing a series of letters to people in England, describing unrest in the colonies. The letters will explode into the Hutchinson letters affair (1773).

In June, British politician Charles Townshend pushes through Parliament the Townshend Acts, imposing new taxes on American colonists.

In December, John Dickinson's *Letters from a Farmer in Pennsylvania* appear in colonial newspapers, protesting Parliament's power to tax the colonies.

1768 Arthur Lee writes a series of weekly essays to the *Virginia Gazette* newspaper under the name "Monitor." The essays mostly restate Dickinson's ideas as expressed in *Letters from a Farmer* but in a more excited style.

In February, Samuel Adams writes a letter opposing taxation without representation and calls for the colonists to unite against British oppression.

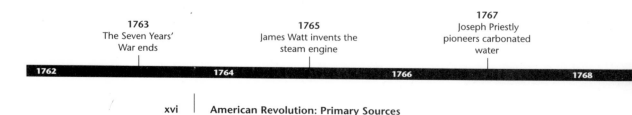

1763
The Seven Years'
War ends

1765
James Watt invents the
steam engine

1767
Joseph Priestly
pioneers carbonated
water

1762   1764   1766   1768

In May, British troops arrive in Boston to enforce the Townshend Acts.

In June, British tax collectors seize John Hancock's ship, *Liberty,* and sell its cargo.

1769 George Mason's *Virginia Resolves,* which opposes British taxation and other policies, is presented to Virginia lawmakers.

1770 In March, during the Boston Massacre, five colonists are killed by British soldiers.

In April, most of the Townshend Acts are repealed by Parliament, except the tax on tea.

In October, John Adams and Josiah Quincy successfully defend British soldiers on trial for firing shots during the Boston Massacre.

In November, at the urging of Samuel Adams, a committee of correspondence is formed in Boston, Massachusetts; it issues a declaration of rights and a list of complaints against British authorities.

1773 Benjamin Franklin's "An Edict by the King of Prussia" is published; it is a piece of satirical writing about relations between England and the colonies.

The Hutchinson letters affair becomes an international scandal.

In May, the Tea Act, a new tea tax, takes effect.

In December, patriots protest the Tea Act by throwing crates of tea into Boston Harbor. The incident becomes known as the Boston Tea Party.

1774 Thomas Jefferson publishes *A Summary View of the Rights of British America,* a pamphlet blaming King George III for the breakdown in relations between England and the colonies.

1771
The first *Encyclopaedia Britannica* is published

1773
Phillis Wheatley's first book of poems is published

1768   1770   1772   1774

In March, Parliament passes the Intolerable Acts to punish Boston for the Boston Tea Party.

In May, British general Thomas Gage replaces Thomas Hutchinson as royal governor of Massachusetts.

In September, the First Continental Congress meets in Philadelphia to discuss the tense situation with Great Britain. The Congress adopts several documents, including The Continental Association.

In October, Massachusetts lawmakers begin war preparations.

1775 In March, British politician Edmund Burke gives his speech "On Conciliation" before Parliament, urging the British government to settle differences with colonists. His proposal to reconcile with the colonies is voted down. Patrick Henry delivers his famous "Give me liberty or give me death" speech in front of the Virginia legislature. An angry royal governor, Lord Dunmore, declares martial law in Virginia.

In April, Massachusetts governor Thomas Gage is told to put down the "open rebellion" of the colonists using all necessary force. Paul Revere rides to Concord and Lexington, Massachusetts, to warn the patriots that British soldiers are on the way. The first shots of the Revolutionary War are fired between Minutemen and British soldiers at Concord. The British retreat to Boston.

In May, Governor Thomas Gage imposes martial law in Massachusetts. The Second Continental Congress meets in Philadelphia and appoints John Hancock its president. The Congress adopts several documents, including the Declaration of the Causes and Necessity of Taking Up Arms and the Olive Branch Petition. Congress also prepares an address to Native Americans, asking that they forget past grievances against the

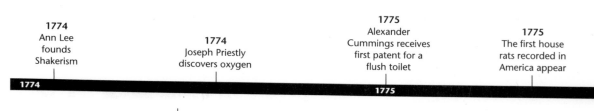

1774
Ann Lee founds Shakerism

1774
Joseph Priestly discovers oxygen

1775
Alexander Cummings receives first patent for a flush toilet

1775
The first house rats recorded in America appear

1774   1775

colonists and remain neutral in any conflict between the colonies and Great Britain. Mary Katherine Goddard becomes publisher of *Maryland Journal* and keeps colonists informed about events in the fight for independence.

In June, George Washington is appointed commander-in-chief of the new Continental Army. Before he arrives in Boston, Massachusetts, patriots are defeated by British at the Battle of Bunker Hill.

In July, George Washington takes command of the Continental Army outside Boston, Massachusetts. The Continental Congress approves John Dickinson's Olive Branch Petition, which calls for King George III to prevent further hostile actions against the colonists until a reconciliation can be worked out.

In August, King George III declares the colonies in open rebellion against Great Britain.

In December, Continental Army soldiers under Benedict Arnold fail in an attempt to capture Quebec, Canada.

King George III proclaims the closing of American colonies to all trade effective March 1776.

1776   In January, Thomas Paine's *Common Sense* is published, in which he urges independence from England.

In March, British general William Howe and his troops abandon Boston, Massachusetts, for Canada; patriots reclaim Boston. Abigail Adams writes her famous "Remember the Ladies" letter to her husband, John Adams.

In May, the Continental Congress tells each of the thirteen colonies to form a new provincial (local) government.

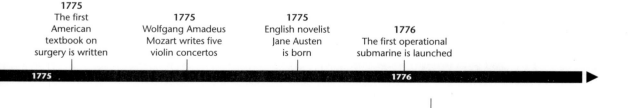

1775
The first American textbook on surgery is written

1775
Wolfgang Amadeus Mozart writes five violin concertos

1775
English novelist Jane Austen is born

1776
The first operational submarine is launched

1775   1776

In June, George Mason proposes a plan for a state government to Virginia lawmakers. Betsy Ross of Philadelphia is believed to design the first American stars and stripes flag.

In July, Congress adopts the Declaration of Independence. A massive British force lands in New York City to crush colonial rebellion.

In August, General William Howe defeats George Washington at the Battle of Long Island, New York. King George issues the Proclamation of Rebellion.

In September, Benjamin Franklin is one of three men appointed by Congress to go to Paris to seek French assistance in the war. Nathan Hale is executed by the British for spying.

In October, the American Navy is defeated at Battle of Valcour in Canada, in which Benedict Arnold commands a fleet of American ships.

In December, George Washington's troops flee to Pennsylvania; fearing attack, the Continental Congress abandons Philadelphia for Baltimore, Maryland. The Continental Army defeats Great Britain's hired German soldiers in a surprise attack in Trenton, New Jersey.

1777 Young Joseph Plumb Martin joins the Continental Army. He will later write a book describing his wartime experiences.

In June, British general John Burgoyne's troops capture Fort Ticonderoga from the Americans. George Washington loses at Brandywine and Germantown near Philadelphia, Pennsylvania; the British seize Philadelphia.

In July, France's Marquis de Lafayette is appointed major general of the Continental Army.

1776
George Washington asks Betsy Ross to design a flag for the new United States

1777
Vermont prohibits slavery

1777
Joseph Bramah patents the water closet

1776   1777

In November, the Continental Congress adopts the Articles of Confederation, America's first constitution. The articles propose a loose union of the states with no strong central government.

In December, George Washington's troops set up winter quarters at Valley Forge, Pennsylvania. France's King Louis XVI recognizes American independence, paving the way to openly assist the war effort.

1778   In February, France and the United States sign treaties of trade and alliance.

In March, the British fail at an attempt to make peace with the Americans.

In June, General Sir Henry Clinton (who replaced William Howe) abandons Philadelphia and heads for New York. On the way, he is attacked by Americans at the Battle of Monmouth, New Jersey.

In July, France declares war on Great Britain.

1779   Spain declares war on Great Britain.

1780   In May, Charleston, South Carolina, falls to British troops.

In June, sixteen-year-old Eliza Wilkinson is at her sister's home in South Carolina when it is looted by British soldiers. She will later write about her wartime experiences.

In September, Benedict Arnold openly goes over to the British side, thereby committing treason against the colonies.

1781   In March, the Articles of Confederation are ratified by all the states.

In October, British general Charles Cornwallis surrenders his troops at Yorktown, Virginia; Great Britain loses all hope of winning the Revolutionary War.

1778
The sandwich
is invented

1779
Jan Ingehousz
studies
photosynthesis

1779
War of Bavarian
Sucession ends

1780
London's first Sunday
newspapers appear

1778   1779   1780   1781

1782   Benjamin Franklin, John Adams, John Jay, and Henry Laurens travel to France to draw up a peace treaty.

1783   In April, Congress declares the Revolutionary War officially ended; Loyalists and British soldiers pack up their headquarters in New York City and depart for Canada or England.

In November, George Washington delivers a farewell speech to his army; he resigns his military commission.

1784   In January, the Treaty of Paris is ratified by Congress, bringing the Revolutionary War to an official end.

In March, Thomas Jefferson's plan for dividing the western territories is adopted by Congress.

1785   In January, Congress relocates to New York City.

In February, John Adams becomes the first U.S. ambassador to England.

1786   In September, the Annapolis Convention meets; Alexander Hamilton proposes and Congress approves his plan for a 1787 convention to replace the Articles of Confederation with a Constitution.

1787   In May, convention delegates meet in Philadelphia to rewrite the Articles of Confederation.

In July, Congress adopts the Northwest Ordinance, based on one written earlier by Thomas Jefferson, that prohibits slavery in U.S. territories and provides a method for new states to enter the union.

In October, Alexander Hamilton, James Madison, and John Jay publish the *Federalist* in defense of the new American Constitution.

1788   In February, in Massachusetts, Samuel Adams and John Hancock agree to support the new Constitution, but only if amendments will be added that guarantee civil liberties.

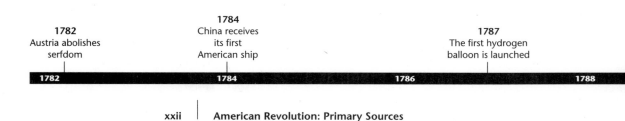

1782
Austria abolishes
serfdom

1784
China receives
its first
American ship

1787
The first hydrogen
balloon is launched

| 1782 | 1784 | 1786 | 1788 |

In June, in Virginia, James Madison and his followers succeed in getting the ratification of the Constitution despite opposition by Patrick Henry and George Mason. The U.S. Constitution is adopted by all of the states. Congress is granted land for a new federal capital.

In July, Congress formally announces that the Constitution of the United States has been ratified and is in effect.

In September, New York City is named the temporary seat of the new U.S. government.

1789 In April, George Washington is sworn in as the first U.S. president.

In July, the French Revolution begins in Paris. King Louis XVI will be beheaded in 1792 during this revolution.

In September, the U.S. Army is established by Congress.

1791 The Bill of Rights, written by James Madison, is passed by the U.S. Congress.

1797 John Adams becomes the second U.S. president.

1801 Thomas Jefferson becomes the third U.S. president.

1790
Benjamin Franklin dies

1794
Eli Whitney patents
his cotton gin

1800
Washington, D.C.,
becomes U.S. capitol

1789   1793   1797   1801

Words to Know

A

Abolitionism: The belief that measures should be taken to end slavery.

Absolutism: A system in which one person—usually a king or queen—rules without any kind of restrictions on his or her actions.

Agent: A person who conducts business on another's behalf.

Allegiance: Loyalty to king, country, or a cause.

Articles of Confederation: An agreement among the thirteen original states, approved in 1781, that provided a loose form of government before the present Constitution went into effect in 1789.

Artillery: The science of using guns; a group of gunners in an army; or the weapons themselves, especially cannons that throw bombs across a battlefield.

Assemblies: One of the names used by the colonies for their lawmaking bodies.

B

Boston Massacre: An encounter between British troops and townspeople in Boston, Massachusetts, in 1770, before the Revolutionary War. The British fired into a crowd and five Americans were killed.

Boston Port Act: One of four laws of the Intolerable Acts passed by the British government in 1774 to punish Boston for the Boston Tea Party. According to this act, the Boston port would not be opened until Boston paid the East India Company for the tea that Bostonians dumped into the harbor. The act closed the harbor even to fishing boats; the idea was that eventually Boston's citizens would be starved into paying for the tea.

Boston Tea Party: An incident on December 16, 1773, in which Boston patriots dumped 342 chests of English tea into Boston Harbor to protest British taxes.

Boycott: A refusal to buy, sell, or use certain products from a particular company or country, usually for a political reason.

Brigadier general: A military position just below major general.

Bunker Hill, Battle of: The first great battle of the Revolutionary War, fought near Boston, Massachusetts, in June 1775. The British drove the Americans out of their fort at nearby Breed's Hill to Bunker Hill; the Americans gave up only when they ran out of ammunition, proving they were willing to take on trained British soldiers.

Burgesses: An old term for members of the British Parliament; the lawmaking body of Colonial Virginia called itself the House of Burgesses.

C

Cavalry: Soldiers on horseback.

Coercive Acts: The British name for the Intolerable Acts.

Colonel: A military rank below brigadier general.

Colonial: Relating to the period before the United States declared independence.

Colonial agents: Men appointed by lawmaking bodies in the colonies to live in London, circulate among important people, and report back on what was happening in Parliament.

Colonialism: The extension of the power of a nation beyond its own borders.

Colonies: Territories that are settled by emigrants from a distant land that remain subject to or closely connected with the parent country.

Committees of Correspondence: Colonial groups that shared information, coordinated the activities of colonial agitators, and organized public opinion against the British government.

Committees of Safety: One of many colonial committees that had the authority to call up militias (groups of volunteer soldiers) when they were needed.

Common Sense: A pamphlet written by Thomas Paine in 1776 in which he urged the colonies to declare independence immediately.

Confederation: A group of states united for a common purpose.

Conservatives: People who wish to preserve society's existing institutions.

Constituents: People represented by elected officials.

Continental Army: The army of American colonists formed during the American Revolution.

Continental Association: A document produced by the First Continental Congress that stated the colonists' complaints against Great Britain and described a boycott of British imports and exports that would remain in effect until their complaints were addressed.

Continental Congress: An assembly of delegates from the American colonies (later called states) that governed before and during the Revolutionary War and under the Articles of Confederation. The Continental Congress first met in 1774.

D

Declaration of Independence: The document establishing the United States as a nation, adopted by the Continental Congress on July 4, 1776.

Declaration of the Causes and Necessity of Taking Up Arms: The Second Continental Congress' response to King George III's statement that war was required now that "the New England governments are in a state of rebellion."

Declaratory Act: A law stating that the British government had the power to make laws that would bind the colonists "in all cases whatsoever."

Delegates: Representatives.

Democracy: A system of government in which power belongs to the people, who rule either directly or through freely elected representatives.

Duties: Taxes on imported or exported goods.

E

"An Edict by the King of Prussia": A humorous piece written by Benjamin Franklin that compared the settlement of England in the fifth century by Germans with the settlement of America during the Revolutionary Era.

F

Federalist: One who supports a strong central government instead of a loose organization of states.

Founding Fathers: A general name for male American patriots during the Revolutionary War, especially the signers of the Declaration of Independence and the drafters of the Constitution.

French and Indian War: A series of military battles between Great Britain and France (and France's Native American allies) that took place on the American frontier and in Canada between 1754 and 1763.

G

Gazette: Newspaper.

"Give me liberty, or give me death" speech: Famous lines uttered by Virginia representative Patrick Henry during a speech in which he expressed his support for American military action.

Great Britain: The island off the western coast of Europe made up of England, Scotland, and Wales. Also called Britain or England.

Grievances: Complaints.

I

Infantry: Men with handguns.

Intolerable Acts: Four laws passed by the British government in 1774 to punish Boston for the Boston Tea Party.

L

Letters from a Farmer in Pennsylvania to the Inhabitants of the British Colonies: Letters written by John Dickinson which were some of the earliest objections to British policies.

Levy: Impose.

Lexington and Concord, Battle of: The first battle of the Revolutionary War, a minor skirmish fought in Massachusetts on April 19, 1775.

Loyalists: Colonists who remained loyal to England during the Revolution; also known as Tories.

M

Martial law: Temporary rule by military authorities imposed upon regular citizens in time of war or when civil authority has stopped working.

Mercenaries: Soldiers for hire.

Militia: A military force consisting of citizens rather than professional soldiers.

Minutemen: Armed American citizens (nonmilitary) who promised to be ready to fight alongside regular soldiers at a moment's notice.

Monarchy: Rule by a king or queen.

N

Neutral: Not committed to either side of an issue.

New England: The region in the northeastern United States that includes present-day Connecticut, Maine, Massachusetts, New Hampshire, Rhode Island, and Vermont. The name was probably given by English explorer John Smith, one of the original settlers of Jamestown, Virginia (1607), because the region resembled the coast of England.

New World: A European term for North and South America.

"No taxation without representation": A popular phrase of the Revolutionary War era. The colonists were not allowed to choose representatives to Parliament, which passed laws taxing the colonists. This offense against colonial rights is one of the main grievances against Great Britain listed in the Declaration of Independence.

O

Olive Branch Petition: A document adopted by the Second Continental Congress that proposed to King George III that he end hostile actions until a reconciliation between Great Britain and the colonies could be worked out.

"On Conciliation:" A speech by Edmund Burke, a member of Parliament who was a champion of colonial rights, which described his views on what ought to be the relationship between England and America.

P

Pamphlets: Reading material with paper covers.

Parliament: The British lawmaking body.

Patriot: A person who loves, supports, and defends his or her country.

Petition: A formal document making a request.

Plantations: Newly established colonies or settlements.

Privateer: A sailor on a privately owned ship who is authorized by the government to attack and capture enemy vessels.

Proclamation of Rebellion: A declaration by King George III that said that *all* the colonies were in a state of rebellion. This was the same thing as an official declaration of war against America.

Propaganda: Biased or distorted information spread by persons who wish to present only their point of view and thus further their own cause.

Q

Quaker: A member of the Religious Society of Friends, a group that opposes all violence and warfare.

R

Radical: A person who favors revolutionary changes in a nation's political structure.

Rebel: A person who resists or defies ruling authority.

Redcoats: British soldiers, who wore red uniforms.

Repeal: Do away with.

Republic: A form of government in which people hold the power and exercise it through elected representatives.

Resolution: A formal statement of a decision or expression of opinion put before or adopted by a lawmaking assembly.

Revenue: Money collected to pay for the expenses of government.

Revolution: A sudden political overthrow; a forcible substitution of rulers.

Revolutionary War: The conflict lasting from 1775 to 1783 in which American colonists gained independence from British rule.

S

Saratoga, Battle of: A major battle of the Revolutionary War, fought in northern New York. The battle is often called the turning point of the war because the American victory there convinced France to send aid.

Satirical writing: Writing that ridicules individuals or groups by pointing out their stupidities or abuses.

Sedition: Acts or language leading to rebellion.

Self-evident: Something requiring no proof or explanation.

Skirmish: A minor encounter in war between small bodies of troops.

Sovereignty: Complete independence and self-government.

Stamp Act: A law passed by the British government in 1765 that required the payment of a tax to Great Britain on papers and documents produced in the colonies.

Statute: Law.

A Summary View of the Rights of British America: A pamphlet by Thomas Jefferson that directly blamed King George III for the breakdown in relations between England and the colonies.

T

Thirteen colonies: The colonies that made up the original United States upon the signing of the Declaration of Independence in 1776: Connecticut, Delaware, Georgia, Maryland, Massachusetts, New Hampshire, New Jersey, New York, North Carolina, Pennsylvania, Rhode Island, South Carolina, and Virginia.

Tories: Colonists who remained loyal to England during the Revolution; also called Loyalists.

Townshend Acts: Laws passed by the British government in 1767. They included a Quartering Act, which ordered the colonies to house British troops, and a Revenue Act, which called for taxes on lead, glass, paint, tea, and other items.

Treason: Betrayal of king and country.

Tyranny: Absolute power, especially power exercised cruelly or unjustly.

U

Unalienable rights: Rights that cannot be given away or taken away.

V

Valley Forge: A valley in eastern Pennsylvania that served as quarters for the Continental Army in the winter of 1777–78. General George Washington had been forced to leave the comfort of Philadelphia, and his soldiers suffered from cold and lack of supplies.

W

West Indies: A group of islands between North and South America, curving from southern Florida to Venezuela. Much trade was carried on between colonial America and British-owned islands in the West Indies. The French, Spanish, and other nations owned islands in the West Indies, too. Some Revolutionary War battles were fought there between the French and Spanish navies and the British navy.

Y

Yankee: Once a nickname for people from the New England colonies, the word is now applied to anyone from the United States.

Yorktown, Battle of: The last battle of the Revolutionary War, fought in 1781 near the Virginia coast. General Charles Cornwallis surrendered his army to General George Washington.

British Actions,
Colonial Reactions

The Stamp Act
. . . 7

The Declaratory Act
. . . 19

The Townshend Revenue Act
. . . 25

The Intolerable Acts
. . . 37

Edmund Burke
. . . 49

King George III
. . . 55

John Dickinson
. . . 63

Benjamin Franklin
. . . 71

Thomas Jefferson
. . . 81

Patrick Henry
. . . 89

Thomas Paine
. . . 97

By the late 1500s, after centuries of petty fighting among the many noble families of Europe, four nations had emerged that were stable and wealthy enough to turn their attention to overseas exploration. These nations were Spain, Portugal, France, and England (also known as Britain or Great Britain). They all looked to the vast and unknown wilderness of the North American continent as an exciting opportunity for exploration. For the most part, their motive was profit.

The English (also called British) focused their early efforts on the Atlantic Coast. It was English businessmen, not the nation of Great Britain, who paid for the settlement of Roanoke (1585) and Jamestown (1607) in Virginia, and Plymouth Colony (1621) in Massachusetts. By the time the American Revolutionary War began in 1775, there were thirteen such settlements, or colonies. For more than 140 years, the colonies and Great Britain, the "mother country," shared strong bonds of friendship and business, based on a common language and customs and a profitable trade relationship. The colonies sent farm products and raw materials to Great Britain and in return got British-manufactured goods. Everyone seemed to be happy with the relationship.

But in the 1760s, some discontented voices began to be heard in the colonies. The unhappiness grew and grew and finally erupted in war in 1775. Why did the American colonies rebel against England? John Adams (1735–1826), a Founding Father of the new American nation that was formed while the two countries fought, said the Revolutionary War began only after a revolution took place "in the minds and hearts of the people." Sometimes "revolution" means the overthrow of a government. Another meaning for "revolution" is a momentous change in any situation. In the momentous change that took place in their minds and hearts, the people of colonial America began to look hard at their relationship with Great Britain.

The American colonies were three thousand miles from Great Britain. Over the years, far from their homeland, colonists had developed their own system of looking after their own affairs. People in the colonies began to question whether there was any need to be ruled by a distant king and country, or whether it was possible to break away from an unsatisfactory relationship and rule themselves. This was revolutionary thinking.

Gradually, the colonists became convinced of the rightness of a system of government in which everyone had a say. But to achieve this goal, they were finally forced to go to war against England, then one of the most powerful nations in the world.

The first rumblings of colonial resentment started in 1763, when the French and Indian War (1754–63) ended and colonists were told they could not buy land west of the Appalachian Mountains. (In the modern-day United States, the Appalachians stretch from Maine in the north to Alabama in the south.) Two years later, the British government passed the Stamp Act, the first of several acts designed to collect taxes from the colonies. The Stamp Act was followed by the Townshend Acts in 1767 and later by a series of acts the colonists called the Intolerable Acts. What was behind those actions by Great Britain, actions that finally lost them a vast, rich country?

Great Britain's actions seemed harmless enough—the country needed money, and plenty of it, to pay off huge war debts run up during the French and Indian War. And Great Britain expected the colonists willingly to help pay off those debts. After all, the British had been protecting the colonists in that war.

The French and Indian War was fought in America by Great Britain and France to decide who would control North America. Tensions between the longtime enemies had reached a boiling point when British colonists tried to expand westward from the Eastern Seaboard (the colonies bordering the Atlantic Ocean) into territory beyond the Appalachian Mountains. The region was inhabited by Indians and claimed by France. The situation erupted into a war in 1754. The French enlisted the help of their Indian allies but were soundly defeated by the British. With this victory, Britain became the world's leading power, with vast new territories to oversee.

Americans expressed their admiration for the astounding British victory. Americans, who had furnished and paid for twenty-five thousand of their own soldiers to fight the war, congratulated themselves on having been a major factor in assuring victory. Now that the bothersome French were gone, it seemed that a glorious era of peace, prosperity, and westward expansion was about to begin, an era that would benefit both the colonies and Great Britain. But within a dozen years, the loyal and admiring colonists turned into freedom fighters, seeking total independence from Britain.

The French and Indian War was a long and expensive ordeal for the British. They believed they won the war singlehandedly, because they had no respect for the untrained American soldiers who had fought by their side, and they saw the American contribution as minimal. Their contempt was reinforced when angry Indians on the western frontier (the territory west of the Allegheny Mountains, won from France) rebelled against years of being cheated by colonial traders and rose up in Pontiac's Rebellion in 1763. British soldiers had to put down the rebellion.

After Pontiac's Rebellion, English political leaders agreed that British soldiers would have to keep the peace between Indians and colonists. England was not pleased that it had to protect the colonists from the consequences of their own actions. King George III (1738–1820) promised the Indians that his American subjects would stay off Indian lands for a time. At least ten thousand British soldiers would be stationed in forts along the frontier to protect colonial settlements. But King George and his advisers agreed that it was only fair and right that the colonies should help pay for food and other expenses for the soldiers.

The British decided that the colonies' share should be one-sixth of the yearly cost of feeding and housing the soldiers. To raise the money, Parliament, Britain's lawmaking body, passed the Stamp Act in 1765. To Parliament's complete surprise, the Americans strongly objected to the Stamp Act. Americans may have taxed themselves to help support British soldiers during the French and Indian War, but they were totally unwilling to allow an outside body—the British Parliament—to tax them for the same purpose. The Stamp Act was soon repealed. But Parliament did not wish to appear weak in the face of American protests, and Great Britain still needed money. Parliament followed up the Stamp Act with one act after another, including the Declaratory Act, the Townshend Acts, and the Intolerable Acts.

The first acts of Parliament were either taxes on the colonies or declarations of Parliament's right to tax them. As each act of Parliament was passed, Americans grew angrier. At first, only a few men, such as Boston political leader Samuel Adams (1722–1803), urged an open break with Great Britain. Adams formed the Sons of Liberty and staged violent actions to get Americans stirred up against the British.

But to most Americans, the prospect of a complete break remained a fearful one for a long time. Before resorting to war, the colonists tried to persuade King George and Parliament to see reason—as the colonists interpreted "reason." The king and most members of Parliament saw matters differently and stubbornly continued to insist on their right to tax the colonies. Between 1765 and 1776, many pamphlets were written and fiery speeches were made, in America and England, arguing both sides of the issue. In America, words poured from the pens of men such as John Dickinson (1732–1808; author of *Letters from a Farmer in Pennsylvania to the Inhabitants of the British Colonies*), Thomas Jefferson (1743–1826; author of *A Summary View of the Rights of British America*), and Thomas Paine (1737–1809; author of *Common Sense*). The cause of liberty also found expression in the passionate speeches of Patrick Henry (1736–1799; "Give me liberty, or give me death"), and in the humorous writings of Benjamin Franklin (1706–1790; including "An Edict by the King of Prussia"). These men wrote and spoke of the rights of Englishmen (the colonists still saw themselves as Englishmen), and explained how these rights were being violated by Great Britain. Gradually, they convinced many of their countrymen that it was time to form a new nation apart from Great Britain. British statesmen argued otherwise and finally grew impatient with the Americans' words and actions.

In 1774, Great Britain retaliated against the violence and disobedience in the colonies with the Intolerable Acts—acts to punish the colonies for their resistance to British taxes. By 1775, a fever pitch had been reached, with the British loudly asserting their rights over Americans, American political leaders and writers eloquently denying such rights, and Sons of Liberty members resorting to violence in hopes of provoking a war. The colonists were finally convinced that a violent separation from Great Britain was the only possible way to achieve their basic human right to govern themselves as they saw fit. When shots rang out between British and American soldiers at Lexington and Concord, Massachusetts, in the spring of 1775, the Revolutionary War had effectively begun.

The Stamp Act

Issued by British Parliament

**Passed on March 22, 1765; excerpted
from *Documents of American History*, 1958**

In 1764, Great Britain's twenty-seven-year-old king, George
III (1738–1820), had ruled for only four years. (George
became king in 1760 when his father, George II [1683–1760],
died). George III was said to be not very bright—he was eleven
years old before he learned to read. As often happened when a
new king or queen ascended the British throne, George faced
power struggles among the important men who surrounded
him. The struggles would decide who had influence over the
king and would therefore gain power themselves. In his early
days on the throne, George III was more interested in establishing his power and settling on advisers than in dealing with
any restlessness in the American colonies. Unfortunately, he
did not always appoint the most capable people to advise him.

The king's first man in charge of money matters was
George Grenville (1712–1770), regarded by most people, and
especially George III, as a terrible bore who thought of nothing
but work. But King George was a thrifty man, and he did not
disagree when Grenville proposed first the Sugar Act, then the
Stamp Act, to raise money in the colonies to pay for the British
soldiers stationed there.

"There shall be raised,
levied, collected, and
paid unto his Majesty, his
heirs, and successors,
throughout the colonies
and plantations in
America, which now are,
or hereafter may be,
under the dominion of
his Majesty, his heirs and
successors, . . . for every
pack of . . . cards, the
sum of one shilling."

From the Stamp Act

Ever since the establishment of the American colonies, the British government had allowed merchants on the Board of Trade to oversee colonial trade. As long as British merchants were happily and profitably trading with the colonies, that was all that mattered. Grenville knew that some colonists smuggled goods into the colonies from the West Indies, which meant that England was not making any money from the exchange of goods.

Grenville convinced King George that it was time to get control of the American colonies and earn some money from them for government expenses. Grenville pointed out to King George that the colonists were paying only a fraction of the taxes that Englishmen paid, and many colonists enjoyed a far higher standard of living than the average Englishman. (This was only partially true. While fighting in America in the French and Indian War, British soldiers had been entertained by wealthy colonials. From this, the soldiers had gotten the impression that all Americans were wealthy. They returned home from the war and spread the news.)

In 1764, Grenville convinced Parliament to pass small taxes on sugar imported into the colonies. These taxes were paid by merchants and ship captains and so did not fall directly on the colonists. The following year, Parliament passed the Stamp Act. As the tax burden upon the colonists was really rather small, Parliament expected no complaints. However, the colonists saw matters differently.

The Stamp Act declared that as of November 1765, certain documents could only be printed on special paper stamped by the British Treasury Office. Taxes were placed on the purchase of items such as dice and playing cards. Lawyers would have to pay taxes before they could be licensed. Stamp distributors named and paid by Parliament would make sure that the terms of the Stamp Act were carried out. Important colonial men eagerly applied to Parliament for the well-paying job of stamp distributor but lived to regret it.

The Stamp Act also ordered that admiralty courts (courts that tried trade cases) would be in charge of making sure the terms of the act were carried out. Admiralty courts were disliked by American colonists, because they enforced unpopular laws, were considered too powerful, and did not use juries in making decisions.

Before the Sugar Act and the Stamp Act, the British Board of Trade had taken care of tax matters in the colonies, levying taxes on trade goods. The Board was a small organization. Colonial businessmen, or their representatives in London, knew the members of the Board, and if they objected to the Board's policies, they could complain and often persuaded the Board to reverse its policies. Now Parliament, a faraway body of complete strangers who had never had anything to do with taxing the colonies, stepped in and claimed the right. Colonial businessmen had no influence over Parliament, nor did they have any representatives there.

The colonists believed that their lawmaking bodies (usually called assemblies) were the only bodies entitled to collect taxes in the colonies, except for taxes on trade. They believed the assemblies were equal to Parliament. The colonists feared that Parliament would not stop at one tax; one tax would lead to another. Colonial assemblies immediately and flatly denied that Parliament had any legal right to tax the colonies.

The stamp tax would affect everyone sooner or later. Newspaper owners and printers would have to pay for stamped paper. Lawyers would have to use special paper for legal documents. Tavern owners would have to put stamps on bottles of alcohol and would have to pay taxes on the purchase of playing cards and dice. Merchants would have to use stamped and taxed paper for most business transactions. These people would have to charge their customers higher prices to make up for paying the tax.

Dice were among the items that would be taxed as a result of the Stamp Act.
Reproduced by permission of Field Mark Publications. Photograph by Robert Huffman.

Things to remember while reading an excerpt from the Stamp Act:

- Few people in England expected the anger that greeted the passage of the Stamp Act. Certainly members of Parliament did not. Even Benjamin Franklin (1706–1790) did not, although he was employed by several of the colonies to represent them in London on business matters, and he might be expected to know how people would feel about such a tax. Franklin was in London on colonial business in the summer of 1765, unaware of all the uproar that was going on back home.

- After the Stamp Act passed, Franklin's attitude was, what's done is done, and one might as well make the best of it. He suggested to two of his friends, John Hughes and Jared Ingersoll, that they apply for jobs as stamp distributors. In the summer of 1765, Ingersoll's Boston home was attacked by an angry mob, while another mob in Philadelphia came close to destroying the homes of Franklin and Hughes. Friends and supporters of Franklin, including his wife Deborah, stood outside the Franklin home to prevent the mob from carrying out their threats. The mob's anger dissolved at the sight of these defenders, and the homes of the two men were not touched.

Excerpt from the Stamp Act

*WHEREAS by an act made in the last session of parliament, several **duties** were granted, continued, and **appropriated**, towards **defraying** the expences of defending, protecting, and securing, the British colonies and **plantations** in America: and whereas it is just and necessary, that provision be made for raising a further **revenue** within your Majesty's **dominions** in America, towards defraying the said expences: . . . be it **enacted** . . ., That from and after [November 1, 1765,] there shall be raised, **levied**, collected, and paid unto his Majesty, his heirs, and successors, throughout the colonies and plantations in America, which now are, or hereafter may be, under the dominion of his Majesty, his heirs and successors,*

[There followed an extremely long and detailed list of the items that required special paper, and the items for which stamp taxes had to be paid, and how much everything would cost. Here are some examples.]

*For every **skin** or piece of **vellum** or **parchment**, or sheet or piece of paper, on which shall be **ingrossed**,*

*written or printed, any **declaration, plea, replication, rejoinder, demurrer**, or other pleading, or any copy thereof, in any court of law within the British colonies and plantations in America, a stamp duty of three **pence**. . . .*

Duties: Taxes.

Appropriated: Set apart for a specific use.

Defraying: Paying.

Plantations: Newly established colonies or settlements.

Revenue: Income.

Dominions: Nations within the British Empire.

Enacted: Made into law.

Levied: Imposed.

Skin: Short for onion skin, a thin, strong, clear sheet of paper.

Vellum: A fine paper-like substance used for writing, made from lambskin, calfskin, or goatskin.

Parchment: A paper-like substance used for writing, often made from sheepskin or goatskin.

Ingrossed: Engrossed; written or printed in final-draft form.

Declaration, plea, replication, rejoinder, demurrer: Various legal papers.

Pence: A British term for the plural of penny.

For every skin . . . on which shall be ingrossed . . . any licence for **retailing of spiritous liquors,** to be granted to any person who shall take out the same . . ., a stamp duty of twenty **shillings.** . . .

For every skin . . . on which shall be ingrossed . . . any **probate** of a will, letters of administration, or of guardianship for any **estate** above the value of twenty **pounds sterling** money; within the British colonies, and plantations upon the continent of America, the islands belonging thereto, and the Bermuda and Bahama islands, a stamp duty of five shillings.

And for and upon every pack of playing cards, and all dice, which shall be sold or used . . ., the several stamp duties following (that is to say)

For every pack of such cards, the sum of one shilling.

And for every pair of such dice, the sum of ten shillings.

And for and upon every paper, commonly called a **pamphlet,** and upon every news paper . . . and for and upon such advertisements as are **herein after** mentioned, the respective duties following (that is to say)

For every such pamphlet and paper contained in half a sheet, or any lesser piece of paper . . ., a stamp duty of one half-penny, for every printed copy thereof.

For every such pamphlet and paper (being larger than half a sheet), and not exceeding one whole sheet . . ., a stamp duty of one penny, for every printed copy thereof. . . .

For every advertisement to be contained in any **gazette,** news paper, or other paper, or any pamphlet . . ., a duty of two shillings.

For every **almanack** or calendar, for any one particular year, or for any time less than a year, which shall be written or printed on one side only of any one sheet, skin, or piece of paper parchment, or vellum . . ., a stamp duty of two pence.

For every other almanack or calendar for any one particular year . . ., a stamp duty of four pence.

And for every almanack or calendar written or printed . . ., to serve for several years, duties to the same amount respectively shall be paid for every such year.

For every skin . . . on which any **instrument, proceeding, or other matter or thing aforesaid,** shall be ingrossed . . ., in any other than the English language, a stamp duty of double the

Retailing of spiritous liquors: Selling alcoholic beverages.

Shillings: British coins worth one-twentieth of a British pound.

Probate: The process of establishing that a person's will is authentic and legal.

Estate: All of a person's possessions and debts left behind at death.

Pounds sterling: Another name for British money.

Pamphlet: Printed material with a paper cover.

Herein after: Later.

Gazette: Newspaper.

Almanack: Almanac; annual publication that contains general statistical information.

Instrument, proceeding, or other matter or thing aforesaid: Any legal matters already mentioned.

George Washington Reacts to the Stamp Act

George Washington (1732–1799) had an undistinguished childhood that gave no hint of the greatness that he would later achieve. His formal schooling ended when he was fifteen years old, and the only subject he excelled in was mathematics. Although he was not a great writer and composed no pamphlets setting forth the rights of Americans, he left behind hundreds of letters and diary entries that began when he was sixteen years old.

He inherited Mount Vernon, the family estate, on the death of his older half-brother in 1752. In 1759, he married a wealthy widow, Martha Dandridge Custis, and with her property now added to his own, he became one of the richest men in the colonies. He spent the time before the American Revolutionary War overseeing the planting of crops on his estate and serving in the Virginia House of Burgesses (that colony's lawmaking body). His diary entries and letters from the period show him to be a practical man, very interested in his business affairs.

In a letter written on September 20, 1765, to one of his wife's relatives, Francis Dandridge, Washington commented on the recently passed Stamp Act. Washington's comments were of a practical rather than eloquent nature. He saw no advantage to be gained by Great Britain in the measure, because the colonists did not have the money to pay for stamps and would simply have to learn to get along without the items that required stamps. This would, therefore, result in lost income for Great Britain. He wrote:

amount of the respective duties before charged thereon. . . . (Commager, pp. 53–55)

What happened next . . .

News of the March 22, 1765, passage of the Stamp Act reached the colonies in the spring of 1765. Reaction was mild at first. But then, inflamed by newspaper articles, pamphlets, and complaints about "taxation without representation" (the colonies had no representatives in Parliament), the mood

The Stamp Act Imposed on the Colonies by the Parliament of Great Britain engrosses the conversation of the Speculative [thinking] part of the Colonists, who look upon this unconstitutional method of Taxation as a direful attack upon their Liberties, and loudly exclaim against the Violation; what may be the result of this and some other (I think I may add) ill judged Measures, I will not undertake to determine; but this I may venture to affirm, that the advantage accrueing to the Mother Country will fall greatly short of the expectations of the Ministry; for certain it is, our whole Substance [all our money] does already in a manner flow to Great Britain and that whatsoever contributes to lessen our Importation's must be hurtful to their Manufacturers. And the Eyes of Our People, already beginning to open, will perceive, that many Luxuries which we lavish our substance to Great Britain for, can well be dispensed with whilst the necessaries of Life are (mostly) to be had within ourselves.

This consequently will introduce frugality [not wasting things], and be a necessary stimulation to Industry. If Great Britain therefore Loads her Manufactures with heavy Taxes, will it not facilitate [make easy] these Measures? They will not compel us I think to give our Money for their exports, whether we will or not, and certain I am none of their Traders will part from them without a valuable consideration. Where then is the Utility [usefulness] of these Restrictions?

Washington became a major force behind the adoption of nonimportation agreements in the late 1760s. Nonimportation agreements were refusals to accept British goods. Washington argued that "Parliament hath no more right to put their hands into my pocket, without my consent, than I have to put my hands into yours for money."

turned defiant. It was a bad time for Parliament to be trying to collect taxes. The colonies were suffering from a smallpox epidemic. Many people lost their jobs at the end of the French and Indian War. Colonists did not like the idea that stamp distributors were going to collect taxes from them and get paid well by Parliament.

Throughout the summer and fall (the Stamp Act was scheduled to go into effect in November 1765), colonial assemblies up and down the East Coast, from Rhode Island to South Carolina, passed strongly worded resolutions against the Stamp Act. They insisted on their right to tax themselves and declared that Great Britain seemed intent on enslaving Americans. In Virginia, Representative Patrick Henry (1736– 1799) spoke eloquently before the House of Burgesses against the

Stamp Act. His fellow representatives were speechless with admiration, but newspapers in England wondered why he was not tossed in jail.

After Henry's stirring words, the Virginia House passed its resolution declaring: "Resolved therefore, That the General Assembly of this Colony have the only and sole exclusive right and power to lay taxes and impositions upon the inhabitants of this Colony, and that every attempt to vest such power in any person or persons whatsoever other than the General Assembly aforesaid has a manifest tendency to destroy British as well as American freedom. . . . " Furthermore, "any person who shall, by speaking or writing, assert or maintain that any person or persons other than the General Assembly of this Colony, have any right or power to impose or lay any taxation on the people here, shall be deemed an enemy to His Majesty's Colony." These were strong words, indeed, and a direct challenge to Parliament's authority.

In Boston, Governor Francis Bernard (1712–1779), who, like other colonial governors, had been appointed by Parliament, urged the assemblymen to remember that acts of Parliament must be observed. Finally, members of the Massachusetts House of Representatives decided to invite representatives of all the colonies to a Stamp Act Congress to decide on a course of action. Nine of the thirteen colonies responded to the invitation, sending representatives to New York City (October 7–25, 1765). The Stamp Act Congress adopted a Declaration of Rights and Grievances, which denied Parliament's right to tax the colonies and urged repeal of the Stamp Act.

At the same time the assemblies were meeting and debating, a secret anti-British organization called the Sons of Liberty was formed and took violent action to express unhappiness with British policies. The unfortunate men who had accepted jobs as stamp distributors felt the anger of mobs who destroyed their property and hanged or burned images or dummies of them to show contempt. On the cross of one such "hanged" Boston stamp distributor was a paper bearing the words: "What greater joy did New England see / Than a stamp-man hanging on a tree."

In his book *The Reluctant Rebels,* writer Lynn Montross described the disorder following the passage of the Stamp Act: "Mobs of howling Liberty Boys surged through the streets of every town in America. There was a great deal of spectacular hell-raising, which reached a climax when forts occupied by British [soldiers] were attacked in New York and both Carolinas."

American resistance was not limited to words and violence. A nonimportation policy was adopted, in which colonial merchants refused to accept imported British goods. Soon British merchants were crying out for the repeal of the Stamp Act, before it had even gone into effect!

By early November, nearly every stamp distributor in America had been thoroughly frightened into inactivity by the actions of the Sons of Liberty. One by one, they resigned their positions as distributors of stamps and paper.

Some people who should have been obeying the Stamp Act carried on with business as usual, pointing out, rightly, that they had never received an official copy of the Act and could not be expected to obey it. Others did not plead ignorance but acted in a spirit of defiance. In Rhode Island, for example, Governor Samuel Ward (1715–1776) refused to carry out the terms of the Stamp Act. In other colonies, courts closed to protest the required stamps on legal documents, and trading ships set sail without bothering to obtain the proper, stamped papers. Printers continued to print on unstamped paper, and newspapers continued to publish—including many articles on the danger of the Stamp Act to American liberties.

As it turned out, the Stamp Act was put into effect in only one colony—Georgia, and even there it was enforced in only a small way. On April 26, 1766, less than six months after the Stamp Act went into effect, the colonies received news of two Parliamentary actions: Parliament had repealed the Stamp Act, but it had replaced the Act with something that would prove just as bothersome, the Declaratory Act. But America was so busy rejoicing over the repeal of the one that they paid little attention to the other. And Americans learned a valuable lesson from their experience: that Parliament could be forced to back down if the opposition was loud enough.

Did you know . . .

- In January 1765, just as George Grenville was preparing to introduce the Stamp Act for debate in Parliament, King George was stricken for the first time with a major attack of "madness." Although the disease he suffered from was misunderstood in King George's time, it is now believed he had porphyria (pronounced por-FEAR-ee-uh). Porphyria is an inherited chemical abnormality that can produce both physical and mental symptoms. King George became feverish and agitated, but he recovered in time to sign the Stamp Act in March 1765. A 1994 movie, *The Madness of*

King George, explores his bouts with porphyria, which grew increasingly severe until his death in 1820.

- King George once complained about the hardworking but dull Grenville, author of the Stamp Act: "When he has wearied me for two hours, he looks at his watch to see if he may not tire me for an hour more." By the time the Stamp Act was repealed, Grenville had already been replaced by a new man. Grenville never again held public office, and he died in 1770. He holds a reputation as the man who did much to bring on the American Revolution.

- Among the earliest voices speaking out against the Stamp Act was that of Isaac Barré, son of a Frenchman, soldier, and member of Parliament. He had fought for England in the French and Indian War and knew and understood Americans' independent spirits. He is credited with coining the term "Sons of Liberty" to describe the colonists in a passionate speech he made early in 1765. He warned Parliament that people who had "fled tyranny [harshness] . . . [and] exposed themselves to almost all the hardships to which human nature is liable" were not likely to put up with British oppression.

- Samuel Adams (1722–1803), second cousin of future U.S. president John Adams (1735–1826), is credited with founding the Sons of Liberty and inspiring some of their violent deeds. He is not as well remembered as other towering figures of revolutionary times, but his contemporaries appreciated his contributions. Thomas Jefferson called him "truly the Man of the Revolution." Samuel Adams was not very popular in England. John Adams called him "a man of humanity . . . as well as integrity," but he added in his 1782 conversation with an English gentleman: "In England . . . you may have been taught to believe . . . that he eats little children."

Where to Learn More

Commager, Henry Steele. *Documents of American History.* New York: Appleton-Century-Crofts, 1958.

Cornish, Rory T. *George Grenville: 1712–1770.* Westport, CT: Greenwood Publishing, 1992.

Donovan, Frank, ed. *The John Adams Papers*. New York: Dodd, Mead & Co., 1965.

Farley, Karin Clafford. *Samuel Adams: Grandfather of His Country*. Austin, TX: Raintree/Steck Vaughn, 1994.

Fradin, Dennis Brindell. *Samuel Adams: The Father of American Independence*. New York: Clarion Books, 1998.

"George III" in *Encyclopedia of the American Revolution*. Edited by Mark M. Boatner III. Mechanicsburg, PA: Stackpole Books, 1994.

Green, Robert. *King George III*. New York: Franklin Watts, 1997.

Hibbert, Christopher. *George III: A Personal History*. New York: Basic Books, 1999.

Montross, Lynn. *The Reluctant Rebels*. New York: Harper & Brothers, 1950.

Morgan, Edmund S., and Helen M. Morgan. *The Stamp Act Crisis: Prologue to Revolution*. New York: Collier Books, 1962.

The Declaratory Act

Issued by British Parliament

Passed on March 18, 1766; excerpted from *Documents of American History*, 1958

In March 1765, the British Parliament passed the Stamp Act to raise money in America to help pay for British soldiers stationed there. The Stamp Act, scheduled to go into effect on November 1, 1765, taxed printed matter such as newspapers, legal documents, and even dice and playing cards. Much to Parliament's surprise, Americans protested the tax in the strongest terms, in many cases resorting to violence against British officials in America. They also refused to buy British goods.

It became clear that more British soldiers would have to be sent to America to enforce an act that did not promise to raise much money anyway. British merchants suffered from Americans' refusal to buy their goods. Trade between England and America came to a standstill, and merchants protested to Parliament.

Benjamin Franklin (1706–1790), sixty years old in 1765 and internationally known as a scientist, inventor, and writer, was in London at the time everyone there was discussing colonial fury over the Stamp Act. At first he had been in favor of complying with the act, but in September 1765, a vengeful mob in Philadelphia, Pennsylvania, nearly destroyed

"The King's majesty . . . had, hath, and of right ought to have, full power to make laws and statutes of sufficient force and validity to bind the colonies and people of America, subjects of the crown of Great Britain, in all cases whatsoever."

From the Declaratory Act

British prime minister Charles Watson-Wentworth, the marquis of Rockingham, was the mastermind behind the Declaratory Act.
Reproduced by permission of Archive Photos.

Franklin's home. Soon after that, he set to work convincing his friends in Parliament to repeal the Stamp Act.

In January 1766, members of Parliament debated repeal of the Stamp Act. Franklin was called to testify. In response to questioning, Franklin gave his opinion that Americans would never submit to the Stamp Act. He also testified that Americans objected to Parliament imposing "internal taxes" (taxes like the stamp tax, which they would be forced to pay against their will). Franklin said the colonists had no objection to Parliament imposing "external taxes" (taxes on trade items, which they could refuse to buy). This would turn out to be a bad argument. To England's dismay, from the Stamp Act on, the colonists objected to the placing of any kind of taxes on them.

While the debate went on over repealing the Stamp Act, members of Parliament also pondered how a repeal could occur without England appearing weak to the Americans. The Declaratory Act of 1766 was the answer. The Declaratory Act was the brainchild of new prime minister Charles Watson-Wentworth (1730–1782), also known as the Marquis (pronounced MAR-kwis) of Rockingham (pronounced ROK-ing-im). The Declaratory Act affirmed the right of Parliament to make laws that would bind the colonists "in all cases whatsoever." King George III (1738–1820) approved the repeal of the Stamp Act and the adoption of the Declaratory Act on the same day, March 18, 1766.

Things to remember while reading an excerpt from the Declaratory Act:

- The Declaratory Act opened by summarizing the American argument that only colonial assemblies had the right to impose taxes on Americans. The Act countered the American argument by declaring that the colonies were subject to the king and Parliament, who alone had the right to make laws binding on the colonies "in all cases whatsoever." Furthermore, any colonial lawmaking bodies that denied or questioned Parliament's authority had no legal basis for doing so or even any legal right to exist.

- The Declaratory Act did not mention any intention by Parliament to impose taxes. Members of Parliament assumed their right to tax had existed from the beginning of American settlement in the colonies. Parliament did not buy Benjamin Franklin's theory that there was a distinction between internal (forced) and external (trade) taxes. The Declaratory Act set the stage for Parliament to impose nontrade taxes on the colonies.

Excerpt from the Declaratory Act

WHEREAS, several of the houses of representatives in his Majesty's [George III] colonies and **plantations** in America, have **of late,** against law, claimed to themselves, or to the **general assemblies of the same,** the sole and exclusive right of imposing duties and taxes upon his Majesty's subjects in the **said** colonies and plantations; and have, **in pursuance of such claim,** passed certain votes, resolutions, and orders, **derogatory** to the legislative authority of parliament, and inconsistent with the dependency of said colonies, and plantations upon the crown of Great Britain: . . . be it declared . . ., That the said colonies and plantations in America are, and **of right ought to be, subordinate unto,** and dependent upon the imperial crown and parliament of Great Britain; and that the King's majesty, by and with the advice and consent of the **lords spiritual and temporal, and commons** of Great Britain, in parliament assembled, had, **hath,** and of right ought to have, full power to make laws and statutes of sufficient **force and validity** to bind the colonies and people of America, subjects of the crown of Great Britain, in all cases whatsoever.

And be it further declared . . ., That all resolutions, votes, orders, and proceedings, in any of the said colonies or plantations, whereby the power and authority of the parliament of Great Britain, to make

Plantations: Newly established colonies or settlements.

Of late: Lately.

General assemblies of the same: Lawmaking bodies of the colonies and plantations.

Said: Previously mentioned.

In pursuance of such claim: In carrying out the imposing of duties and taxes.

Derogatory: Offensive.

Of right ought to be, subordinate unto: Should be under the control of.

Lords spiritual and temporal, and commons: Religious and civilian members of the upper house of Parliament (House of Lords) and members of the lower house of Parliament (House of Commons).

Hath: Have.

Force and validity: Legal impact.

*laws and statutes as **aforesaid**, is denied, or drawn into question, are, and are hereby declared to be, **utterly null and void to all intents and purposes whatsoever**. (Commager, pp. 60–61)*

What happened next . . .

In America, there was great jubilation over the repeal of the Stamp Act. Wealthy Virginians gathered in Williamsburg, the capital city, for an elegant ball. In Boston, Massachusetts, the Sons of Liberty gathered with other citizens on Boston Common, where wealthy merchant John Hancock (1737–1793) had thoughtfully provided casks of wine for a celebration. New Yorkers voted to erect a lead statue of King George (a few years later, when war broke out, the lead was melted down and made into bullets). Three hundred Philadelphia men agreed to buy new suits made of English cloth to celebrate the resumption of trade between England and America.

Parliament thought it had made a fine bargain with the colonies. It had repealed an unpopular tax but had affirmed what it considered longstanding Parliamentary rights. Americans rejoiced that a wrong had been righted. On top of that, England had been shown what havoc could be caused by an American refusal to buy its goods. Flushed with victory, Americans hardly noticed the Declaratory Act. They expected to continue to pay taxes on trade items; they also expected there would be no more talk of "internal taxes" designed "to raise revenue" (money to pay for British government expenses). But their victory was only temporary. Founding Father and Boston lawyer John Adams (1735–1826) was one of the few who took note of the significance of the Declaratory Act. He wondered whether Parliament would "lay a tax in consequence" of it. He was soon able to read his answer in the Townshend Acts.

Did you know . . .

- Former prime minister William Pitt (1708–1778) became a hero in America for his passionate speech in favor of the repeat of the Stamp Act. In 1765, when the Act was passed, Pitt was sixty-seven years old and suffering from the mental illness that would continue to plague him for the remainder of his life. Some historians believe this condition was manic-depression, a type of mental illness in which a person suffers severe and prolonged mood swings. Pitt was well enough at the time Parliament was debating the repeal of the Stamp Act to speak in favor of it. In his speech, he said: "I rejoice that America has resisted! Were I but ten years younger I should spend the rest of my days in America, which has given the most brilliant proofs of its independent spirit." Pitt died in 1778 without ever visiting America. American towns erected statues to honor their champion.

Where to Learn More

Commager, Henry Steele. *Documents of American History.* New York: Appleton-Century-Crofts, 1958.

Hibbert, Christopher. *Redcoats and Rebels: The American Revolution Through British Eyes.* New York: Avon, 1991.

Scheer, George F. *Rebels and Redcoats: The American Revolution Through the Eyes of Those Who Fought and Lived It.* New York: Da Capo Press, 1988.

The Townshend Revenue Act

Issued by British Parliament

Passed on June 29, 1767; excerpted from
Documents of American History, 1958

The Stamp Act of 1765 was passed by Parliament to help pay for British soldiers on duty in America. It raised money by taxing printed matter such as newspapers, legal documents, and even the sale of dice and playing cards. After the colonies expressed their outrage, Parliament repealed the tax. But England still needed money from the colonies to help pay for the soldiers. Charles Townshend (1725–1767), an adviser for King George III (1738–1820), informed the king and Parliament that he had figured out a way to tax the colonies without their objecting. Not only would his proposals raise money, Townshend said, they would also demonstrate Parliament's power over the colonies. Parliament passed the Townshend Acts on June 29, 1767. They included the Townshend Revenue Act, which is excerpted later; an act setting up a new board of customs commissioners (customs are taxes on imported and exported goods); and an act suspending New York's lawmaking body, the New York Assembly.

A revenue is money collected to pay for the expenses of government. The first Townshend Act, the Townshend Rev-

"There shall be raised, levied, collected, and paid, unto his Majesty, his heirs, and successors, for upon and the respective Goods herein after mentioned, which shall be imported from Great Britain into any colony or plantation in America. . . . "

From the Townshend Revenue Act

Charles Townshend

Charles Townshend was the second son of the third Viscount Townshend. A viscount (pronounced VIE-count) is a member of British royalty who ranks below an earl and above a baron. This is a fairly high rank, but as a second son, Charles would not inherit the title. His mother was an heiress who is said to have been brilliant, witty, and direct. Townshend inherited those positive qualities. On the negative side, he has been described as a man without principles. British author Tobias Smollett (1721–1771) said that Townshend would have been "a really great man if he had had any consistency or stability of character."

Townshend was educated in Holland and England and was elected to Parliament in 1747, where he served until 1761. In 1766, he became Chancellor of the Exchequer, the man in charge of collecting the money needed to run the British government. Almost immediately, he proposed the acts that are associated with his name. The very next year, he died of "an incurable putrid fever," most likely typhus, which is often spread by fleas.

enue Act called for taxes on lead, glass, paint, tea, and other items. The second Townshend Act created a board of customs commissioners to enforce the Townshend Revenue Act as well as other British trade laws that had been loosely enforced up until then. The third Townshend Act, called the Restraining Act, suspended the New York Assembly. It was passed at the request of Thomas Gage (1721–1787), commander in chief of British soldiers in America from 1763 to 1775.

British soldiers were in America for two reasons: to protect colonial settlers on the western frontier (western New York, Pennsylvania, and Maryland) from hostile Indians, and to make sure France did not try to reclaim the land it had recently lost to Great Britain (see Stamp Act entry on p. 7). General Gage was headquartered in New York City, and most of his soldiers were spread throughout New York state. The colonists were supposed to provide housing and food for the soldiers, in their own homes if no other quarters could be found. General Gage had problems getting the colonists to cooperate, so at his request, Parliament passed the Quartering Act in 1765. The Act ordered colonial officials to provide living quarters for Gage's soldiers for a period of two years. New York officials complained because the financial burden fell most heavily on New York state. When the New York Assembly refused to comply with the Quartering Act, Gage asked Parliament to suspend the assembly (prevent it from passing any laws), and Parliament did so by way of a Townshend Act.

Things to remember while reading an excerpt from the Townshend Revenue Act:

- The colonists had objected to the Stamp Act partly because its purpose was to forcibly collect money in the colonies to pay for British government expenses—the expenses of keeping British soldiers in America. The colonists called the Stamp Act an "internal tax," the kind of tax they said could only be imposed by colonial assemblies, made up of representatives chosen by American colonists. If England needed money to pay for English government expenses, the colonists believed that England had to collect tax money from Englishmen in England.

- The Townshend Revenue Act proposed that Britain would collect small taxes on certain products that were shipped to colonial ports. Parliament thought the colonies could have no objection; this was a tax on trade items, an "external tax," the kind of tax the colonies had always paid. When he testified before Parliament about repealing the Stamp Act, Benjamin Franklin (1706–1790) told Parliament that the colonists would have no objection to paying taxes on imports and exports. But Parliament underestimated the growing anti-tax mood in the colonies. After their experience with the Stamp Act, the colonies were prepared to resent any kind of tax imposed by Parliament.

- The Townshend Revenue Act also expanded the powers of the hated admiralty courts. Anyone who tried to avoid paying the new taxes—smugglers, for instance—would be tried in admiralty courts. Under the terms of the Townshend Revenue Act, admiralty court judges, as well as governors and other royal officials, would now be paid out of the tax money collected. This meant they would depend on England for their salaries, not on the colonial assemblies, as before. Townshend meant to ensure that angry colonists could not stop British officials from performing their jobs by withholding their paychecks. In the long run, Townshend meant to tighten British control over the economy and the governing of the colonies.

- In a further crackdown on smugglers, the concept of writs of assistance was revived under the Townshend Revenue Act. Writs of assistance were documents that allowed British customs officials to enter and search any warehouse

Duties: Taxes.

Plantations: Newly established colonies or settlements.

Drawback of the duties of customs: A refund for taxes paid on imported goods that will be re-exported.

Said: Previously mentioned.

China earthen ware: Porcelain.

Effectually: Effectively.

Clandestine running of goods: Secret smuggling.

Expedient: Proper.

Dominions: Nations within the British Empire.

Defraying the charge of the administration of justice: Paying court costs.

There shall be raised, levied: Taxes shall be established and collected.

Herein after: Later.

Hundredweight avoirdupois: (Pronounced AV-or-da-POIZ) A British unit of weight equal to 112 pounds when a pound equals 16 ounces.

Crown, plate, flint: Types of glass.

Shillings: Coins worth one-twentieth of a British pound.

Pence: British term for the plural of penny.

or private home at any time to look for smuggled goods. The customs officials could order colonial officials to assist them in the searches. Such writs had been legal since 1755 but were seldom used. The Townshend Revenue Act promised to make the unpopular searches common, in violation of the deeply held belief that a man's home was his castle.

Excerpt from the Townshend Revenue Act

*An act for granting certain **duties** in the British colonies and **plantations** in America; for allowing a **drawback of the duties of customs** upon the exportation from this kingdom, of coffee and cocoa nuts of the produce of the **said** colonies or plantations; for discontinuing the drawbacks payable on **china earthen ware** exported to America; and for more **effectually** preventing the **clandestine running of goods** in the said colonies and plantations.*

*WHEREAS, it is **expedient** that a revenue should be raised, in your Majesty's **dominions** in America, for making a more certain and adequate provision for **defraying the charge of the administration of justice,** and the support of civil government, in such provinces as it shall be found necessary; and towards further defraying the expenses of defending, protecting and securing the said dominions; . . . be it enacted . . . That . . . **there shall be raised, levied,** collected, and paid, unto his Majesty, his heirs, and successors, for upon and the respective Goods **herein after** mentioned, which shall be imported from Great Britain into any colony or plantation in America which now is or hereafter may be, under the dominion of his Majesty, his heirs, or successors, the several Rates and Duties following; that is to say,*

*For every **hundredweight avoirdupois** of **crown, plate, flint,** and white glass, four **shillings** and eight **pence.***

For every hundred weight avoirdupois of green glass, one shilling and two pence.

[The Act continues with a list of other taxed items. It then declares that the monies raised will be used to pay for "defending, protecting, and securing, the British colonies and planta-tions in America" and can also be used for other expenses. The Act describes steps that would insure that the new taxes could be collected.]

*It is lawful for any officer of his Majesty's customs, authorized by **writ of assistance under the seal of his Majesty's court of exchequer,** to take a constable, headborough, or other public officer **inhabiting** near unto the place, and in the daytime to enter and go into any house, shop, cellar, warehouse, or room or other place and, in case of resistance, to break open doors, chests, trunks, and other package there, to seize, and from **thence** to bring, any kind of goods or mer-chandise whatsoever **prohibited or unaccustomed,** and to put and secure the same in his Majesty's storehouse next to the place where such seizure shall be made. . . .*

[It is also made legal] that the officers for collecting and manag-ing his Majesty's revenue, and inspecting the plantation trade, in America, shall have the same powers and authorities to enter houses or warehouses, to search or seize goods prohibited to be imported or exported into or out of any of the said plantations, or for which any duties are payable, or ought to have been paid. . . . (Commager, pp. 63–64)

Writ of assistance under the seal of his Majesty's court of exchequer: Authority given to customs officers to seek assistance from local officers, granted by the British government department that manages and collects money.

Inhabiting: Living.

Thence: That place.

Prohibited or unaccustomed: Forbidden, or not paid for with import fees.

What happened next . . .

At first, most of the colonists reacted cautiously to the Townshend Acts. But Samuel Adams (1722–1803), a member of the Sons of Liberty, a Massachusetts assemblyman, and a man with a longstanding bitterness against Great Britain, took action. Shortly after the new customs officers arrived in Boston in November 1767 and prepared to open for business, Adams wrote the Massachusetts Circular Letter (so called because it was addressed to a large number of people). The letter pointed out that Parliament's attempt to raise a revenue was contrary to the colonists' rights, because they were not represented in Parliament. (Remember that Parliament believed it had the right to make laws binding on the colonies "in all cases what-soever," according to the Declaratory Act.) The Circular Letter

Customs officials who attempted to search homes for smuggled goods sometimes were tarred and feathered by angry Bostonians.
Reproduced by permission of Archive Photos.

was adopted by the Massachusetts Assembly in February 1768, and copies were sent to all the colonies.

While the other colonies discussed the Circular Letter and pondered what to do, King George created a new American Department and named Wills Hill, the Earl of Hillsborough, head of it. Hill believed he should show the colonies who was boss. One of his first moves in his new job was to compose his own circular letter and send it to all colonial governors (who were appointed by Great Britain). In his circular letter, Hill advised the governors to treat the Massachusetts Circular Letter "with the contempt it deserves." He informed the governors that any assembly that approved the Circular Letter was to be dissolved. Hills did not intend it, but his action had the effect of uniting the colonies in sympathy for Massachusetts.

Massachusetts proceeded to become the center of colonial defiance. The Sons of Liberty staged a wave of sometimes-violent protests in Boston. Customs officials who tried to carry out their jobs were tarred and feathered (a painful procedure in which a person is covered with hot tar and coated with feathers). Finally, they asked Governor Francis Bernard (1712–1779) for protection. He proved unwilling to act—he said that Boston's citizens would never stand for him calling in British soldiers to patrol the streets; in fact, he feared for his life if he did it. So the commissioners called upon the British Royal Navy in Halifax, Nova Scotia (Canada), and a British warship sailed into Boston.

Made bold by the presence of the British Navy, customs commissioners singled out John Hancock (1737–1793), one of Boston's wealthiest and most popular citizens, to teach Boston a lesson. In June 1768, Hancock's boat *Liberty* was seized by customs officers for an alleged violation of the Town-

shend Acts. In turn, the customs officers found their own boat set on fire. As tempers flared, Governor Bernard suspended the Massachusetts Assembly in June 1768. From London came orders to British general Gage to move some of his soldiers from New York to Boston. On October 1, the British Army took control of Boston Common.

With British soldiers camped on Boston's doorstep, the spirit of defiance spread. One by one, nearly every assembly expressed its approval of the Massachusetts Circular Letter and was suspended. The assemblies met in secret, and by the end of 1768, most had adopted agreements not to import British goods until the Townshend Acts were repealed. Over the next few months, British imports to America fell by nearly half.

Parliament had expected the Townshend Revenue Act to bring in about 9 percent of the total yearly cost of paying for soldiers to protect the colonies. With customs officials unwilling to carry out their duties for fear of mob action, in 1768, the

Five people were killed during fighting between Bostonians and British soldiers on March 5, 1770. The event became known as the Boston Massacre. *Chromolithograph by John Bufford. Courtesy of the National Archives and Records Administration.*

Samuel Adams, Committee-Man and Son of Liberty

Samuel Adams was born on September 27, 1722, in Boston, Massachusetts, the son of Mary Fifield Adams and Samuel Adams. The elder Adams made his living as a beer brewer but also acted as a church assistant, tax assessor, and town official. The young Samuel was educated at the Boston Latin School, the first public school in the American colonies. In 1736, he went away to Harvard College (later Harvard University) with the intention of becoming a minister. But when the younger Adams was eighteen, a bank founded by his father was declared illegal and the elder Adams lost all his money, a situation young Samuel blamed on the British-appointed governor of Massachusetts, Thomas Hutchinson (1711–1780). The loss of the family fortune forced the younger Adams to take a job as a waiter to pay his way through college. He became bitter towards the British over this issue.

Adams gave up the idea of being a minister, and when he graduated from Harvard College in 1743, he engaged in a variety of business ventures. But his heart was not in any of them, and they all proved unsuccessful. The young man preferred to spend his time in political discussions. Over time, he hardened in his opinion that America should become free of Britain and what he considered its corrupt ways.

By 1764, it might have seemed to observers that the forty-two-year-old Adams was something of a failure. He was poor and had lost several businesses and most of the money he inherited from his father. He was just beginning to show his political skills, however, and his real successes still lay ahead.

Adams was becoming known as an agitator who stirred up political resistance to Britain. More and more of his time was spent talking with anyone who would listen about the rights and liberties of the American colonists. Adams first spoke out in taverns and at informal meetings around Boston. In 1772, at Adams's request, the town of Boston appointed a Committee of Correspondence. Its twenty-one members met to state the rights of the colonists and work to have them widely publicized throughout the colonies. In a short time, many such letter-writing networks were set up, and the move toward colonial unity advanced.

actual amount collected was about 4 percent of the total cost, and in the next two years, the Townshend Revenue Act brought in even less than that—not a lot of money for all the trouble it was causing.

Sons of Liberty leader Samuel Adams.
Painting by John S. Copley. Courtesy of the National Archives and Records Administration.

Adams also headed a secret organization in Boston, the Sons of Liberty. This group took its name from a speech given in Parliament by a man who opposed the Stamp Act of 1765. He had called the colonists "these sons of liberty." Adams's Sons of Liberty sometimes called themselves Committees of Correspondence to cover up their secret activities. It was they who were responsible for many of the acts of mob violence against people who remained loyal to Great Britain. The Sons burned homes and tarred and feathered stamp agents, forcing all such agents to resign even before the Stamp Act was supposed to go into effect.

Perhaps Adams's greatest triumph was the Boston Tea Party (1773). British government in Massachusetts collapsed afterward, and the Committees of Correspondence served for a time as the colonial government. Some people say Adams provoked the incidents at Lexington and Concord in 1775 that resulted in the first shots of the war being fired. Throughout the war, Adams kept constantly busy, keeping patriots inflamed, counseling colonial leaders, and writing countless newspaper articles. By the war's end in 1783, he had burned himself out. He seemed unable to do anything constructive; his talent had been in destruction of British rule. He died in Boston on October 2, 1803. This Founding Father, whom many historians say was largely responsible for American independence, was called by President Thomas Jefferson (1743–1826) "the Man of the Revolution."

British merchants complained loudly about the financial losses they were enduring because Americans were not buying their goods. In England, people were being thrown out of work because there was no market for the goods they produced.

British merchants told Parliament it was foolish to risk profits from trade in a quarrel over a small amount of tax money.

In Boston, tension was thick. Samuel Adams and his Sons of Liberty complained loudly and often about the presence of British soldiers. Everything finally came to a head with the Boston Massacre of March 5, 1770, when five people were killed in a clash between British soldiers and townspeople. Parliament and colonists alike were shocked by the violence in Boston. Parliament once again backed down, and on April 12, 1770, the Townshend Acts were repealed. Only the tax on tea was kept. In the end, what was good for British merchants won out over Parliament's desire to show the colonies who was boss.

After the shock of the Boston Massacre, a period of calm fell over the colonies and England. The *New York Gazette* offered this opinion: "It's high time a stop was put to mobbing . . . . God knows where it will end." With British merchants happily trading once again, and distracted by problems with Spain, Parliament was almost silent on the question of the American colonies for the next three years—until the Tea Act was passed in 1773.

Did you know . . .

- Charles Townshend was clever and witty, loud and amusing, and his nickname was "Champagne Charlie" (pronounced sham-PAIN; a sparkling wine). His personality traits were apparently good enough qualifications for King George, who listened to Townshend's advice and supported the Townshend Acts. Within months after the Acts went into effect, Townshend died at the young age of forty-two. There are different stories of how Townshend got his nickname. According to one version, he gave an important speech while apparently drunk. According to another version, some of his speeches had the effect of making his listeners feel as lightheaded as if they had been drinking champagne.

- Samuel Adams's dislike for the British dated back to at least 1741. Adams was eighteen and attending what is now Harvard University in Cambridge, Massachusetts, when the British-appointed governor of Massachusetts, Jonathan

Belcher (1682–1787), declared illegal The Land Bank founded by Adams's father. The Adams family lost all its money, and Samuel had to take a job as a waiter to pay his way through college. He thought it wrong for the governor to have so much power over the colonists.

- Benjamin Franklin had a close friend, William Strahan, who was a member of Parliament. In November 1769, as the time drew near when Parliament would be discussing colonial outrage over the Townshend Acts, Strahan wrote a letter to his friend. He asked Franklin to give his views on the situation so Parliament might better understand what was going on. Franklin told Strahan that a partial repeal (keeping a tax on tea, for example) would not satisfy the colonists. Franklin said it was not the tax they objected to but its purpose—"the better support of [British] government. . . . This the colonists think unnecessary, unjust, and dangerous to their most important rights." Franklin warned Strahan that if Parliament did not modify its hard line against the colonies, there was likely to be more violence and loss of affection for England.

- Parliament was not inclined to listen to Franklin's warnings. Members were getting firsthand information from Thomas Gage, commander in chief of British troops in America from 1763 to 1775. Gage witnessed the turmoil that began with the Stamp Act in 1763 and escalated with the Townshend Acts. He reported his concerns in letters to Parliament. In March 1768, he warned that Americans were moving toward "a struggle for independency." Gage could see that his soldiers were unpopular with Bostonians. He warned Parliament in a letter written before the Boston Massacre in 1770 that his soldiers were suffering "assaults upon their persons till their lives were in danger," and it was only a matter of time before they resisted and defended themselves. His reports hardened the hearts of King George and his advisers against any sort of compromise with the colonists.

- It was probably Samuel Adams who gave the name "massacre" to the March 5, 1770, incident in which five citizens were killed by British soldiers. British Captain Thomas Preston and eight of his men were arrested and charged with manslaughter (taking the life of another without the intention of doing injury). A trial was held, but little evidence was produced that Preston ordered his men to fire, nor was it known who actually fired. Preston said that in all the confusion, it was impossible to know "who said fire, or don't fire, or stop your firing." Preston and six others were finally let go; two others were found guilty, were branded (burned with a hot iron) on the hand, and released. Founding Father and Boston lawyer John Adams (1735–1826) defended the soldiers in court. He said it was only right that the men receive a fair trial.

Where to Learn More

Clark, Dora Mae. *British Opinion and the American Revolution*. New York: Russell & Russell, 1966.

Commager, Henry Steele. *Documents of American History*. New York: Appleton-Century-Crofts, 1958.

Draper, Theodore. *A Struggle for Power: The American Revolution*. New York, Random House, 1996.

Farley, Karin Clafford. *Samuel Adams: Grandfather of His Country*. Austin, TX: Raintree/Steck Vaughn, 1994.

Fradin, Dennis Brindell. *Samuel Adams: The Father of American Independence*. New York: Clarion Books, 1998.

Rinaldi, Ann. *The Fifth of March: A Story of the Boston Massacre*. San Diego: Harcourt Brace, 1993.

The Intolerable Acts

Issued by British Parliament

Passed on March 31, 1774, and June 2, 1774; excerpted from *Documents of American History*, 1958, and *American Journey* (CD-ROM), 1995

The Tea Act of 1773, which was soon followed by the Intolerable Acts, was passed because Parliament was trying to save the British-owned East India Company from going out of business. The company was ailing because Americans were refusing to import British tea (instead, it was being smuggled in from Holland). Parliament decided to impose small, secret taxes on East India tea (the taxes would be paid in London before the tea reached the colonies). Parliament thought that even with the secret tax, the tea would still be so cheap Americans would prefer to buy it rather than the more expensive tea they were smuggling in from elsewhere.

But Americans saw through this trick. They still objected to paying taxes of any kind "without representation" in Parliament. What was to stop the British from trying this same trick with other goods, the colonists wondered? American merchants would be left out in the cold, while British merchants reaped big profits. This threat to American interests brought angry colonists together in a way not seen since the Stamp Act. (The Stamp Act was a 1765 attempt to raise money in the colonies to help pay for British soldiers stationed there.

". . . dangerous commotions and insurrections have been fomented and raised in the town of Boston, in the province of Massachuset's Bay, in New England, by divers ill-affected persons, to the subversion of his Majesty's government, and to the utter destruction of the public peace, and good order of the said town. . . ."

From the Boston Port Act, one of the Intolerable Acts

Boston patriots dressed as Indians dumped 342 chests of tea into Boston Harbor to protest the Intolerable Acts. The incident became known as the Boston Tea Party.
Reproduced by permission of Archive Photos.

It taxed printed material, legal documents, and even dice and playing cards.) All the colonies refused to accept East India tea, but Boston's defiance of the British proved the most dramatic. On December 16, 1773, a group of Boston patriots disguised as Indians dumped 342 chests of tea into Boston Harbor, an act known to history as the Boston Tea Party.

The dumping of the tea was considered by Parliament to be a wicked and totally illegal act. In London, British prime minister Sir Frederick North (1732–1792) went before an outraged Parliament with several proposals designed to punish the colonists. The proposals included the Boston Port Act, the Massachusetts Government Act, the Administration of Justice Act, and the Quartering Act. Together these measures came to be known by the colonists as the Intolerable Acts.

As England's prime minister, North was the highest-ranking member of Parliament. He also acted as an adviser to King George III (1738–1820), but unlike many of the king's other advisers, North was a capable man. However, in order to stay in the king's good graces, North often argued in favor of measures of which he did not approve. One such measure was the tax on tea that remained after the Townshend Acts were repealed in 1770. North's first act after he became prime minister in 1770 was to argue in favor of keeping the tea tax. He wanted peaceful relations with the colonies, but after the Boston Tea Party, he went along with King George's desire to teach Bostonians a lesson. He hoped to accomplish this with the Intolerable Acts of 1774. Of all the Intolerable Acts, the Boston Port Act was the most hateful to Bostonians.

Lord North declared that the inhabitants of Boston deserved punishment, even if the innocent suffered along with the guilty. According to his Boston Port Act, the port would not be opened until Boston paid the East India Company for the dumped tea. The Act closed the harbor even to fishing boats; the idea was that eventually Boston's citizens would be starved into paying for the tea. British soldiers were sent by King George to occupy Massachusetts's largest city, to keep its unruly citizens in line.

Parliament also passed three other Intolerable Acts aimed at punishing Boston: the Massachusetts Government Act, the Administration of Justice Act, and the Quartering Act.

The Massachusetts Government Act gave the British-appointed governor of Massachusetts (1) the power to appoint members of the Massachusetts Council (they had always been elected by the Massachusetts Assembly) and (2) complete control of town meetings. To the citizens of Massachusetts, this takeover of their form of government, which they had held sacred since 1691, was even worse than taxation without representation.

The Administration of Justice Act declared that British officials who committed major crimes would be tried in another colony or in Great Britain. So, if another incident similar to the Boston Massacre took place, for example, British soldiers would stand trial far from the scene.

The fourth Intolerable Act was the Quartering Act of 1774. In 1765, General Thomas Gage (1721–1787), commander in chief of British soldiers in America, had requested that Parliament pass a Quartering Act because the colonists were refusing to provide living quarters and supplies for Gage's soldiers (see Townshend Revenue Act entry on page 25). The first of the colonial Quartering Acts had gone into effect in 1765. It required the colonies to provide buildings for British troops and to supply them with free bedding, firewood, cooking utensils, cider, and other items. A second Quartering Act followed in 1766 and required the colonies to put up troops in public buildings such as inns, taverns, and unoccupied dwellings. The Quartering Act of 1774, an Intolerable Act, required that the colonists put up troops not only in public buildings but also in dwellings belonging to private citizens. This meant that citizens were required to feed and house an enemy soldier on their private property. The Quartering Act was cruel punishment, indeed; it treated Boston as though it were a captured enemy city.

Things to remember while reading excerpts from the Boston Port Act and the Quartering Act of 1774:

- With the adoption of the Boston Port Act, the struggle between Great Britain and America took on a new meaning. It was no longer a struggle over trade regulations or taxes; now it was about making Americans submit to "the supreme authority of Great Britain"—in the words of Lord North—or face the consequences. But the American colonists considered such submission to be slavery. According to David Ramsay (1749–1815), who would serve as a doctor in the Revolutionary War and publish his *History of the American Revolution* in 1789: "The people of Boston alleged . . . that the tea was a weapon aimed at their liberties, and that the same principles of self-preservation which justify the breaking of the assassin's sword uplifted for destruction, equally authorized the destruction of that tea." Boston was sure to suffer dreadfully from the closing of its harbor, and clearly the city would need help from the other colonies. It remained to be seen whether this would happen.

- It is hard to imagine what a serious effect the harbor closing would have on Boston. The Boston economy depended on shipbuilding and trade. The sea supplied

Bostonians with a large part of their diet, because the Massachusetts soil was too poor and rocky to farm. With the closing of the harbor, Boston's population would have to look elsewhere for food. The food would have to be carried over long distances, over inadequate roads.

- The years of calm between the repeal of the Townshend Acts (April 12, 1770) and the Boston Tea Party (December 16, 1773) were frustrating ones for Sons of Liberty member Samuel Adams (1722–1803). He kept busy sending letters to newspapers calling for American independence. But most of the colonists felt secure from further unfair treatment by the British, and they began calling Adams and his ideas "old-fashioned." When news of the passage of the Boston Port Bill reached Boston in May 1774, Adams's views found more sympathetic listeners for the first time in years. On May 18, 1774, Adams wrote to his friend and fellow radical Arthur Lee (1740–1792) that the people of Boston, with the help of its "sister Colonies" would "sustain the shock with dignity and . . . gloriously defeat the designs of their enemies." Adams and his followers drew up a proposal asking all the colonies to cut off all trade with England until the Boston Port Bill was eliminated. Many people feared that such a move would harm America more than England.

- On the eve of June 1, 1774, when the Boston Port Act was scheduled to go into effect, less radical colonial voices still urged a nonviolent, reasoned response. One such voice was that of Benjamin Franklin (1706–1790), who recommended that Bostonians pay for the dumped tea. Merchants feared that mob actions by groups like the Sons of Liberty would result in widespread destruction of property. There were wide differences of opinion as to what should be done.

- Francis Bernard (1712–1779) served as the British-appointed governor of Massachusetts from 1760 to 1769. He served during the Stamp Act Crisis of 1765, when violent protests broke out in Massachusetts over England's attempts to tax the colonies to raise money to pay for British soldiers in America. British tax collectors could not carry out their duties and appealed to Governor Bernard to call out British soldiers to help and protect them. Bernard said his council would never approve of calling

Arthur Lee, Forgotten Revolutionary

The Lee family of Virginia produced many famous figures in American history, including Henry "Light-Horse Harry" Lee (1756–1818), a hero in the Continental Army of the American Revolution; and Henry Lee's son, Robert E. Lee (1807–1870), whose surrender to General Ulysses S. Grant (1822–1885) in 1865 would end America's Civil War (1861–65). Some Lees made important contributions but are not so famous. One of those was Arthur Lee (1740–1792), the last of the eleven children of Thomas and Hannah Ludwell Lee. Two of Arthur's brothers—Francis Lightfoot Lee (1734–1797) and Richard Henry Lee (1732–1794)—were signers of the Declaration of Independence.

Arthur Lee was educated in England, a common custom for wealthy young men of his day. He returned home to practice medicine in 1764 but soon lost his enthusiasm for that career. He returned to England to study law but delayed his studies to help his brother William set up a trading company. Arthur did not receive his license to practice law until 1775.

While he was in America from 1764 through 1767, Lee read and was impressed by John Dickinson's *Letters from a Farmer in Pennsylvania to the Inhabitants of the British Colonies* (discussed in this chapter), and Lee was moved to add his thoughts to Dickinson's. Like Dickinson, Lee believed that powerful men in Great Britain were trying to make Americans less free than Englishmen. Lee believed these men were trying to turn colony against colony and to divide the colonies from their friends in Great Britain.

Between February 25 and April 28, 1768, Lee wrote weekly essays to the *Virginia Gazette* newspaper. The essays mostly restated Dickinson's ideas but in a more excited style. To rally Americans against people like George Grenville (1712–1770), author of the Stamp Act of 1765, Lee wrote: "Shall we not be grieved to the heart [at this attempt to deprive us of our freedom]? Will not our jurisdictions, liberties, and privileges be totally violated? Shall we not sink into slaves? O liberty! O virtue! O my country."

In his letters, Lee expressed his belief that independence from Great Britain was sure to come in time, but to try to attain it immediately could only be done with violence. Still, he pledged that "I will maintain our liberty at the hazard of my life."

Reactions to Lee's letters were varied. Thomas Jefferson was not impressed with Lee's writing style, but Samuel Adams liked the letters so well that in 1770 he persuaded the Massachusetts legislature to choose Lee as its agent in

Arthur Lee.
Courtesy of the Library of Congress.

London. Lee sent home valuable information about how the British were dealing with American resistance. While in London, he continued to write letters that were passionate pleas on behalf of American rights.

When the Revolutionary War broke out in 1775, Lee became a secret agent of the Second Continental Congress, negotiating with the French and Spanish to secure desperately needed supplies for the American army. In 1776, he was one of three Americans who were chosen to convince the French to come into the war on the American side. The other two men were Silas Deane (1737–1789) and Benjamin Franklin. While in France, Lee became convinced that Deane and Franklin were secretly plotting with the French to profit at the cost of American soldiers' blood. Lee complained furiously to Congress. He succeeded in having Deane recalled home, but Franklin stayed, and became Lee's enemy. Back in America, Samuel Adams and John Adams (1735–1826), and others who did not like Franklin, supported Lee, and there was much quarreling among members of Congress over the issue.

In 1780, Lee returned to America and two years later was elected to the Continental Congress. There, he became increasingly bitter, seeing enemies everywhere, and believing that no one was listening to his ideas. He never married, and died on his Virginia estate in 1792. Some saw him as a hero, while others saw him otherwise; Franklin called him "insane."

In an 1819 letter to Arthur Lee's nephew, Richard Bland Lee, John Adams described Arthur as "a man of whom I cannot think without emotion; a man too early in the service of his country to avoid making [many] enemies; too honest, upright, faithful, and intrepid [brave] to be popular. . . . This man never had justice done him by his country in his lifetime, and I fear he never will have by posterity [all of his descendants]. His reward cannot be in this world."

out British soldiers to patrol the streets of Boston. Bernard's council was elected by the Massachusetts Assembly, and he often complained that instead of advising him, his council worked with the assembly and against him. In 1769, Bernard traveled to England to try and convince Parliament to change the Massachusetts government to give more power to the governor and less power to the elected assembly. This move did not make Bernard popular with the Massachusetts Assembly, and it asked King George III to appoint a new governor. In 1771, Thomas Hutchinson (1711–1780), who had been acting governor in Bernard's absence, was officially appointed governor of Massachusetts.

- Hutchinson proved to be no more popular than Bernard (see entries on Hutchinson letters in chapter 3), because the colonists believed Hutchinson favored British attempts to deny Americans' rights. In June 1773, six months before the Boston Tea Party took place, and one year before the Intolerable Acts went into effect, the Massachusetts Assembly asked King George to remove Hutchinson from office. Hutchinson (who was born in Massachusetts and whose ancestors were early settlers in the New World) sailed to England in June 1774, the very same month the Intolerable Acts went into effect. He never returned to his beloved homeland. General Thomas Gage was appointed in Hutchinson's place, assuming the dual role of governor of Massachusetts and commander in chief of British forces. His orders were to "quiet the people [of Boston] by gentle means. . . . Troops are not to be called out unless it is absolutely necessary." Charged with the task of enforcing the Intolerable Acts, Gage would find it impossible to do so "by gentle means."

Excerpt from the Boston Port Act

*WHEREAS dangerous **commotions and insurrections** have been **fomented** and raised in the town of Boston, in the province of Mass-*

Commotions and insurrections: Disorder and revolts against government.

Fomented: Stirred up.

achuset's Bay, in New England, by **divers** ill-affected persons, to the **subversion** of his Majesty's government, and to the utter destruction of the public peace, and good order of the said town; in which commotions and insurrections certain valuable cargoes of teas, being the property of the East India Company, and on board certain vessels lying within the bay or harbour of Boston, were seized and destroyed: And whereas, in the present condition of the said town and harbour, the **commerce** of his Majesty's subjects cannot be safely carried on there, nor the **customs** payable to his Majesty **duly** collected; and it is therefore **expedient** that the officers of his Majesty's customs should be **forthwith** removed from the said town: . . . be it enacted . . ., That from and after June 1, 1774, it shall not be lawful for any person or persons whatsoever to **lade**, put, . . . off or from any **quay, wharf,** or other place, within the said town of Boston, or in or upon any part of the bay, commonly called The Harbour of Boston, between a certain headland or point called Nahant Point, . . . and a certain other headland or point called Alderton Point, . . . or in or upon any island, creek, landing-place, bank, or other place, within the said bay or headlands, into any ship, vessel, **lighter**, boat, or **bottom**, any goods, wares, or merchandise whatsoever, to be transported or carried into any other country, province, or place whatsoever, or into any other part of the said province of the Massachuset's Bay, in New England; or to take up, . . . within the said town, or in or upon any of the other places **aforesaid,** out of any boat, . . . any goods, . . . to be brought from any other country, province, or place, or any other part of the said province, of the Massachuset's Bay in New England, upon pain of the forfeiture of the said goods, . . . and of the said boat, . . . and of the guns, ammunition, **tackle**, furniture, and **stores**, in or belonging to the same. . . . (Commager, p. 71)

Excerpt from the Quartering Act

[1.] Whereas doubts have been entertained whether troops can be quartered **otherwise** than in **barracks**, in case barracks have been provided sufficient for the quartering of all the officers and soldiers within any town, township, city, district, or place within His Majesty's **dominions** in North America; and whereas it may frequently happen from the situation of such barracks that, if troops should be quartered therein they would not be stationed where their presence may be necessary and required: be it therefore enacted by the King's Most Excellent Majesty, by and with the advice and consent of the **Lords . . . and Commons**, in this present Parliament assembled . . . that, in such

Divers: Diverse; various or several.

Subversion: Attempted destruction.

Commerce: Trade.

Customs: Taxes.

Duly: In a proper manner.

Expedient: Proper.

Forthwith: Immediately.

Lade: To load with cargo.

Quay, wharf: Places for ships to tie up and load or unload.

Lighter: A large flat-bottomed boat used to deliver or unload goods to or from a cargo ship.

Bottom: The part of a ship's hull (main body) below the water line.

Aforesaid: Previously mentioned.

Tackle: A rope and pulley.

Stores: Supplies.

Otherwise: In places other.

Barracks: Buildings used to house soldiers.

Dominions: Nations within the British Empire.

Lords . . . and Commons: Members of Parliament's House of Lords and House of Commons.

*cases, it shall and may be lawful for the persons who now are, or may be hereafter, authorized by law, in any of the provinces within His Majesty's dominions in North America, and they are hereby respectively authorized, empowered, and directed, on the **requisition** of the officer who, for the time being, has the command of His Majesty's forces in North America, to cause any officers or soldiers in His Majesty's service to be quartered and **billeted** in such manner as is now directed by law where no barracks are provided by the colonies.*

*2. And be it further enacted by the authority **aforesaid** that, if it shall happen at any time that any officers or soldiers in His Majesty's service shall remain within any of the said colonies without quarters for the space of twenty-four hours after such quarters shall have been demanded, it shall and may be lawful for the governor of the province to order and direct such and so many uninhabited houses, outhouses, barns, or other buildings as he shall think necessary to be taken (making a reasonable allowance for the same) and make fit for the reception of such officers and soldiers, and to put and quarter such officers and soldiers therein for such time as he shall think proper.*

3. And be it further enacted by the authority aforesaid that this act, and everything herein contained, shall continue and be in force in all His Majesty's dominions in North America, until March 24, 1776. (American Journey [CD-ROM])

What happened next . . .

On the day the Boston Port Bill went into effect, June 1, 1774, the citizens of Boston fasted and prayed. Church bells rang mournfully from morning until night, and public buildings were draped in black, the sign of mourning. British soldiers, conspicuous in their red coats, filled the city. Soon, as Bostonians had hoped, food, supplies, and messages of sympathy poured in from supporters throughout the colonies.

British general Gage tried to carry on with his task of enforcing the Intolerable Acts. In accordance with the terms of the Massachusetts Government Act, he dissolved the elected Massachusetts Council and put his own council in its place. When his councilmen tried to leave home to meet, they were

Requisition: Formal request.

Billeted: (Pronounced BIL-littid) Housed in a nonmilitary building.

Aforesaid: Previously mentioned.

followed by jeering crowds, and some were fired upon. Most of them promptly resigned. On September 2, 1774, Gage wrote to Parliament that he did not have enough troops to enforce the Intolerable Acts. Gage was supposed to keep Boston in line, but he was close to being its prisoner.

Inspired by the sufferings of Boston, a new spirit of unity arose in the colonies. By July, twelve of the thirteen colonies agreed to send representatives to the First Continental Congress in Philadelphia to discuss breaking off all trade with Great Britain. Delegates to that Congress met on September 5, 1774. (The accomplishments of that body and of the Second Continental Congress are discussed in chapter 2.)

Founding Father John Adams opposed mob violence but approved of the Boston Tea Party. *Painting by C. W. Peale. Courtesy of the National Archives and Records Administration.*

Did you know . . .

- Sir Frederick North, who fought in Parliament to punish Boston with the Boston Port Act, was commonly known as Lord North. He served as a member of Parliament for forty years, but the most important event of his career was the American Revolutionary War. Although he did not cause it, he certainly contributed to it with his support of the Tea Tax and the Boston Port Act. Once the war broke out, he favored peace but King George would not relent in his desire to show the colonies who was boss. Several times North tried to resign, but at the urging of his king, he loyally remained in office and defended a war he knew was hopeless and wrong. When the war ended in March 1782 with the surrender of the British at Yorktown, Virginia, a weary and disgusted North insisted that this time he was resigning for sure. King George was furious and would have denied North his pension, but his advisers pointed out that to deny his loyal servant would damage George's public image. North died in 1792 at the age of sixty.

- Founding Father and Boston citizen John Adams was a man of contradictions. As a lawyer and defender of law and order, he opposed mob violence but he approved of the Boston Tea Party. He opposed Great Britain's tax measures, but he did not favor a complete break with the mother country. Although he had not yet decided that independence was the answer to the conflicts between Boston and England, he seemed oddly cheered by the news of the June 1774 closing of the Port of Boston. When he heard about it in May 1774, he wrote to his wife, Abigail Adams (1744–1818): "We live, my dear soul, in an age of trial. What will be the consequence, I know not. The town of Boston . . . must suffer martyrdom. It must expire. And our principal consolation is that it dies in a noble cause— the cause of truth, of virtue, of liberty, and of humanity— and that it will probably have a glorious resurrection to greater wealth, splendor, and power, than ever. . . . Don't imagine from all this that I am in the dumps. Far otherwise. I can truly say that I have felt more spirits and activity since the arrival of this news [of the port closing] than I had done before for years. I look upon this as the last effort of Lord North's despair, and he will as surely be defeated in it as he was in the project of the tea."

Where to Learn More

American Journey (CD-ROM). Woodbridge, CT: Primary Source Media, 1995.

Commager, Henry Steele. *Documents of American History.* New York: Appleton-Century-Crofts, 1958.

Farley, Karin Clafford. *Samuel Adams: Grandfather of His Country.* Austin, TX: Raintree/Steck Vaughn, 1994.

Ferling, John E. *John Adams: A Life.* New York: Henry Holt, 1996.

Fradin, Dennis Brindell. *Samuel Adams: The Father of American Independence.* New York: Clarion Books, 1998.

Hull, Mary E. *The Boston Tea Party in American History.* Springfield, NJ: Enslow Publishers, 1999.

Olesky, Walter. *The Boston Tea Party.* New York: Franklin Watts, 1993.

Potts, Louis W. *Arthur Lee, a Virtuous Revolutionary.* Baton Rouge: Louisiana State University Press, 1981.

Young, Alfred F. *The Shoemaker and the Tea Party: Memory and the American Revolution.* Boston: Beacon Press, 1999.

Edmund Burke

"On Conciliation"

**First published on March 22, 1775;
excerpted from *The Spirit of Seventy-Six*, 1995**

Although King George III (1738–1820) seemed to have surrounded himself with advisers who went along with his vengeful feelings toward the colonies, one member of Parliament stood apart as a champion of colonial rights. He was Edmund Burke (1729–1797), born in Dublin, Ireland. From 1765 to 1782, Burke was private secretary to Charles Watson-Wentworth, the marquis of Rockingham (1730–1782), author of the Declaratory Act of 1766. The Declaratory Act affirmed the right of Parliament to make laws (including tax laws) that would bind the colonists "in all cases whatsoever."

Burke was elected to Parliament in 1766, so he observed firsthand all the talk about the troubles with the American colonies. In early 1775, he gave a famous speech on the topic in Parliament. Afterwards called "On Conciliation," the speech described Burke's views on what ought to be the relationship between England and America. At the time, the Revolutionary War had not yet broken out, but tensions were high. British troops were stationed in Boston, Massachusetts, trying to enforce what Bostonians angrily called the Intolerable Acts. The Intolerable Acts were passed in 1774 to punish Boston for its resistance to paying British-imposed taxes.

"An Englishman is the unfittest person on earth to argue another Englishman into slavery. . . ."

Edmund Burke, from "On Conciliation"

"On Conciliation"
author Edmund Burke.
*Courtesy of the Library
of Congress.*

Burke believed that Parliament *did* have a legal right to tax the colonies. But Burke also believed that sometimes it was necessary to consider other issues in addition to what was legal. His argument is sometimes described as an argument in favor of obeying the spirit of the law, not the letter of the law. Past efforts by the British to tax the colonies—from the Stamp Act of 1765 (which taxed various types of printed material, legal documents, and dice and playing cards) through the tea taxes of 1767 and 1773—had all led to violence and discontent. Concerning the quarrel with the colonies, Burke said that what was legal (the right to tax) did not matter as much as human nature. He thought Parliament should exercise its authority while respecting the people who were subject to that authority.

In the following excerpt, Burke described to Parliament the nature of the colonists: free people with the rights of Englishmen. He also pointed out the practical difficulties of waging a war in a country so far away, with an entire ocean separating the warring nations: "You cannot pump this [ocean] dry," he said. The excerpt includes some of Burke's thoughts on how the British Empire (England and all its colonies) became great, by recognizing the rights of its subjects and gaining peace and loyalty through respect, not by trying to enslave people or take their wealth by force.

Things to remember while reading an excerpt from "On Conciliation":

- Edmund Burke was not a typical politician of his time, or he would have tried to get ahead in politics by pleasing King George instead of arguing against the king's colonial policies. In fact, Burke was more of a philosopher than a politician; he was interested in the pursuit of wisdom rather than achieving wealth or high office.

Edmund Burke, British Supporter of the Colonies

Edmund Burke was a brilliant writer as well as a speaker. He is best remembered for his *Annual Register,* which he proposed in 1758 and edited from 1759 to 1797. His articles in the *Annual Register* described relations between England and America. Because there were no copyright laws in Burke's day, countless American writers wrote about the American Revolution by borrowing freely from Burke's works; Burke was not credited, leaving the impression that other writers' works were original. This deception was exposed in the twentieth century by historian Orin G. Libby, who was doing a study of all the histories of the American Revolution.

Edmund Burke tried repeatedly to get Parliament to see that the British Empire was growing more dependent economically on the colonies. He pointed out that "at the beginning of the century some of these Colonies imported corn from the Mother Country," but for "some time past, the Old World has been fed from the New."

Burke's native country, Ireland, was (and still is) part of the British Empire. His mother was a Roman Catholic; members of that church were persecuted by Protestant Irish and British authorities. Burke felt great sympathy for Catholics, saying they had been reduced to "beasts of burden" by their persecutors.

- Burke had a deep sympathy for oppressed (unjustly treated) people, and he believed England was oppressing the colonies. He lamented that he lived in a time when powerful people in government were not governing wisely. Burke was a man who thought deeply about issues, and he was probably the most knowledgeable man in England about colonial matters. Of the few voices that spoke in Parliament in favor of reconciling with the colonies, his was the most eloquent.

- At the time Burke gave his "On Conciliation" speech in March 1775, the First Continental Congress had already met and sent several documents to King George asking for peace but also making various demands (described in the next chapter). King George was angry; he had not responded to the colonists but wrote to Prime Minister Sir Frederick North (1732–1792) in November 1774: "[T]he

New England governments are in a state of rebellion, blows [fighting] must decide whether they are to be subject to this country or independent."

Excerpt from "On Conciliation"

America, gentlemen say, is a noble object. It is an object well worth fighting for. Certainly it is, if fighting a people be the best way of gaining them. . . .

*In this character of the Americans, a love of freedom is the **predominating** feature which marks and distinguishes the whole: and as an **ardent** [affection] is always a jealous affection, your colonies become suspicious, **restive and unretractable** whenever they see the least attempt to **wrest** from them by force, or shuffle from them by **chicane**, what they think the only advantage worth living for. This fierce spirit of liberty is stronger in the English colonies probably than in any other people of the earth. . . .*

*The temper and character which **prevail** in our colonies are, I am afraid, **unalterable** by any human art. We cannot, I fear, falsify the **pedigree** of this fierce people, and persuade them that they are not sprung from a nation in whose veins the blood of freedom circulates. The language in which they would hear you tell them this tale would detect the **imposition**; your speech would betray you. An Englishman is the unfittest person on earth to argue another Englishman into slavery. . . .*

***Magnanimity** in politics is not seldom the truest wisdom; and a great empire and little minds go ill together. If we are conscious of our situation and glow with **zeal** to fill our place as **becomes our station and ourselves**, we ought to **auspicate** all our public proceedings on America with the old warning of the church, **Sursum corda!** We ought to elevate our minds to the greatness of that trust to which the order of **Providence** has called us. By **adverting to** the dignity of this high calling, our ancestors have turned a savage wilderness into a glorious empire; and have made the most extensive, and the only honourable conquests, not by destroying but by promoting the wealth, the number, the happiness of the human race. Let us get an*

Predominating: Most important.

Ardent: Burning, fiery.

Restive and unretractable: Hard to control and unable to take back their accusations.

Wrest: Pull away.

Chicane: Trickery.

Prevail: Are the strongest force.

Unalterable: Unchangeable.

Pedigree: Family tree.

Imposition: Unfair demand.

Magnanimity: Generosity.

Zeal: Enthusiastic devotion to a cause.

Becomes our station and ourselves: Is suitable to our position in life and our good character.

Auspicate: Begin with a ceremony to bring good luck.

Sursum corda!: "Lift up your hearts!" These are words spoken during Mass (a religious ritual).

Providence: God.

Adverting to: Turning toward.

*American **revenue** as we have got an American empire. English privileges have made it all that it is; English privileges will make it all it can be. (Commager and Morris, pp. 233–34, 236, 238)*

Revenue: A government's income.

What happened next . . .

Edmund Burke's opponents were too powerful, and his proposal that England reconcile with America was voted down, 271 to 78. But among ordinary Englishmen and women there were widespread feelings of sympathy for the American cause. There are many reasons for this. Americans were English, too. They were fighting for freedom. America made the British Empire stronger and to lose the colonies would be a devastating loss. War is expensive. And the king and his advisers were simply being stubborn, in the opinion of many. Over the next several months, the king received many petitions from his subjects pleading the cause of America.

Did you know . . .

- Edmund Burke looked upon the British Empire as a family. The parent (England) was supposed to rule with kindness over its children (the colonies). He believed that in the case of the American colonies, England had been harsh when it should have been lenient. Burke himself was raised in an unhappy family headed by an overly demanding father, and this may have influenced his thinking.

- Burke was not a believer in democracy. He did not think ordinary people should have a say in how they were governed. Rather, he thought that the right to govern belonged to the aristocracy, the privileged class that was born to rule.

- Burke was thoroughly upset over the American Revolution and did not know which side to take. He wrote in August 1776: "I do not know how to wish success to those [the rebellious Americans] whose victory is to separate us from a large and noble part of our empire. Still less do I wish success to injustice, oppression, and absurdity [government policies]. . . . No good can come of any event in this war to any virtuous interest."

Where to Learn More

Burke, Edmund. *The Portable Edmund Burke*. Edited by Isaac Kramnick. New York: Scholastic Paperbacks, 1999.

Commager, Henry Steele, and Richard B. Morris, eds. *The Spirit of 'Seventy-Six: The Story of the American Revolution as Told by Participants*. New York, Da Capo Press, 1995.

"Edmund Burke" in *Encyclopedia of the American Revolution*. Edited by Mark M. Boatner III. Mechanicsburg, PA: Stackpole Books, 1994.

King George III

Proclamation of Rebellion

First published August 23, 1775; excerpted from *Documents of American History*, 1958

In February 1775, King George III (1738–1820) and Parliament declared Massachusetts to be in a state of rebellion. Two months later the first shots of the Revolutionary War rang out in Lexington, Massachusetts. The Americans created the Continental Army, and preparations for war moved forward.

News of continued American resistance infuriated King George. Never before had any British king had to endure disobedience on this scale from his subjects, who were mere commoners. In August 1775, King George issued a Proclamation of Rebellion, which declared *all* the colonies to be in a state of rebellion. This was the same thing as an official declaration of war against America.

King George opened his proclamation by summarizing relations between Great Britain and America as he saw them. He stated that dangerous men had misled his American subjects into forgetting the obedience and loyalty they owed their king. He said that violent protests were preventing his officials in the colonies from carrying out their duties (collecting taxes, for example). George pointed out that matters had reached the point where rebels had taken up arms against British officials.

"All our Officers, civil and military, are obliged to exert their utmost endeavours to suppress [the colonies'] rebellion, and to bring the traitors to justice, [and] all our subjects . . . are bound by law . . . to disclose and make known all traitorous conspiracies and attempts against us, our crown and dignity. . . ."

King George III, from the Proclamation of Rebellion

George III, Britain's king during the American Revolution. *Painting by W. Beechy. Courtesy, Shakespeare Gallery.*

He said that such men were traitors, and he wanted both his loyal subjects and his soldiers in America to be quite clear on what their duty was under the circumstances. His soldiers were to stop any signs of rebellion, and his subjects were supposed to help them, in part by providing British soldiers with information about the traitors in their midst.

Things to remember while reading King George's Proclamation of Rebellion:

- At the time the Proclamation of Rebellion was issued, many Americans still clung to the belief that the king had America's best interests at heart. Loyalty to the British Crown was a deeply ingrained principle, one that was not easily shaken off. The colonists were not aware that King George went along willingly with oppressive measures like the Intolerable Acts of 1774. The Intolerable Acts closed the Port of Boston, gave the British-appointed governor of Massachusetts complete control of town meetings, ordered that British officials who committed major crimes in the colonies would be tried in Great Britain, and required that the colonists house British soldiers in dwellings belonging to private citizens. Americans may have thought King George was their friend, but in reality he was pressuring his advisers to declare his subjects rebels and traitors. On August 23, King George's Proclamation of Rebellion was ready.

- In 1774, the colonies had formed a Continental Congress as a way of voicing their objections to British oppression in a united way (see chapter 2). On July 8, 1775, only six weeks before King George's Proclamation of Rebellion was passed, the Continental Congress passed the Olive Branch Petition (see p. 127) and sent it to London. The petition repeated the colonies' complaints against British oppression, but it also expressed the colonists' loyalty to King George and their desire that harmony be restored. Two pieces of news reached the colonies as Americans waited for an answer to the Olive Branch Petition: (1) King George had issued a Proclamation of Rebellion and (2) King George had refused to even look at the Olive Branch Petition. The king refused because the petition came from the Continental Congress, and he said the Congress was an illegal body.

George III, Benevolent Monarch or "Royal Brute"?

The young George III (1738–1820) was described by British historian J. H. Plumb as "a clod of a boy whom no one could teach. . . . Had he been born in different circumstances it is unlikely that he could have earned a living except as an unskilled laborer." But by an accident of birth, in 1760 he became king of Great Britain and Ireland following the death of his grandfather, George II (1683–1760). (George II's son had died in 1751, leaving the king's first-born grandson, George III, next in line for the throne.) Within twenty-three years, George III lost a large part of the British Empire—the American colonies.

Whether he was bright or not is debatable, but historians agree that George III was a man of good morals, a hard worker, and thrifty. He knew what was expected of him as a king and he performed his duties as best he could. It was expected that he would marry for political reasons, not for love, and he did so in 1761 when he chose a German princess, Charlotte Sophia (1744–1818), to be his wife. George had fallen in love at twenty-one with thirteen-year-old Lady Sarah Lennox, a great granddaughter of King Charles II (1630–1685), but he gave her up out of duty. George and Charlotte Sophia produced fifteen children.

George's handling of the war with America (1775–83) made him unpopular with his subjects. They believed he was letting the war drag on too long with little visible success for the British side. Even before the war ended, George struggled with mental problems that were kept secret from his subjects. He began to suffer from physical ailments and was also

A Proclamation by the King for Suppressing Rebellion and Sedition

*Whereas many of our **subjects** in **divers** parts of our Colonies and **Plantations** in North America, misled by dangerous and ill designing men, and forgetting the **allegiance** which they owe to the power that has protected and supported them; after various disorderly acts committed in disturbance of the publick peace, to the obstruction of lawful commerce, and to the oppression of our loyal subjects carrying on*

Subjects: People under the rule of another.

Divers: Diverse; various or several.

Plantations: Newly established colonies or settlements.

Allegiance: Loyalty.

American Revolution: Primary Sources

troubled by the behavior of his two oldest sons, who carelessly spent great quantities of the thrifty king's money. As George's sufferings increased, so did his popularity with a sympathetic British public. But his popularity fell again when a 1793 war with Holland caused rising prices at home. In 1811, the king's favorite child, Princess Amelia, died. By that time George was totally blind and deaf, and his grief at Amelia's death destroyed him. His son, George IV (1762–1830), began to rule in his place, and when King George III died in 1820, he had been nearly forgotten by his subjects.

King George III's reputation among his English subjects rose and fell, but they did not see him as a tyrant or a brute. If some blamed him for losing the American colonies, the fact that his son proved to be one of England's most hated kings did much to restore the good reputation of the father.

It was King George's American subjects who turned him into a hateful figure. Thomas Paine called him a "royal brute" in *Common Sense*. Thomas Jefferson (1743–1826) listed George's many failures in The Declaration of Independence, referring to George's "history of repeated injuries and usurpations, all having in direct object the establishment of an absolute Tyranny over these States." Today, King George III is generally regarded as a man stubbornly opposed to American independence right up until the end, but not directly responsible for the tax policies that were supported by Parliament and which led to the war.

the same; have at length proceeded to open and **avowed** rebellion, by **arraying** themselves in a hostile manner, to withstand the execution of the law, and **traitorously** preparing, ordering and levying war against us: And whereas there is reason to **apprehend** that such rebellion hath been much promoted and encouraged by the traitorous correspondence, **counsels** and comfort of divers wicked and desperate persons within this realm: To the end therefore, that none of our subjects may neglect or violate their duty through ignorance thereof, or through any doubt of the protection which the law will afford to their loyalty and **zeal**, we have thought **fit**, by and with the advice of our **Privy Council**, to issue our Royal Proclamation, hereby declaring, that not only all our Officers, civil and military, are obliged to **exert their utmost endeavours** to suppress such rebellion, and to

Avowed: Openly declared.

Arraying: Displaying.

Traitorously: Disloyally.

Apprehend: Understand.

Counsels: Advice.

Zeal: Enthusiastic devotion.

Fit: Proper.

Privy Council: King's advisers.

Exert their utmost endeavours: Bear arms.

*bring the traitors to justice, but that all our subjects of this Realm, and the dominions thereunto belonging, are bound by law to be aiding and assisting in the suppression of such rebellion, and to disclose and make known all traitorous **conspiracies** and attempts against us, our crown and dignity; and we do accordingly strictly charge and command all our Officers, as well civil as military, and all others our obedient and loyal subjects, to use their utmost endeavours to withstand and suppress such rebellion, and to disclose and make known all treasons and traitorous conspiracies which they shall know to be against us, our crown and dignity; and for that purpose, that they **transmit** to one of our principal Secretaries of State, or other proper officer, due and full information of all persons who shall be found carrying on correspondence with, or in any manner or degree aiding or **abetting** the persons now in open arms and rebellion against our Government, within any of our Colonies and Plantations in North America, in order to bring to **condign** punishment the authors, perpetrators, and abetters of such traitorous designs.*

Given at our Court at St. James's the twenty-third day of August, one thousand seven hundred and seventy-five, in the fifteenth year of our reign.

God save the King. (Commager, p. 96)

Conspiracies: Agreements to perform illegal acts.

Transmit: Send.

Abetting: Encouraging.

Condign: Deserved or adequate.

What happened next . . .

Still unwilling to cut all ties with King George, on December 6, 1775, the Continental Congress severed relations with Parliament. On December 22, 1775, King George followed up his Proclamation of Rebellion with the American Prohibition Act. It outlawed all trade between Great Britain and the colonies and ordered the seizure of all ships loaded with American goods. The worst part of the Act was its statement that any American sailors captured on the ships could be forced to serve on British warships and fight against their own countrymen. To Americans, this was outrageous and plainly illegal. The American Prohibition Act was a tremendous blow to Americans' belief in English law and the monarchy. Americans began to question their loyalty to King George.

Soon after the king issued the Prohibition Act, British-turned-American writer Thomas Paine (1737–1809) published *Common Sense* (see p. 97). Paine's pamphlet did much to earn King George his reputation—at least in America—as a "royal brute," a reputation he holds to this day.

Did you know . . .

- King George ruled Great Britain from 1760 to 1820, a very long reign extending through very turbulent times. People who are interested in history still argue about him. They wonder: Was he a stupid man who blindly allowed his advisers to talk him into the loss of the American colonies? Was he an evil man, as some Sons of Liberty such as Thomas Paine said? Or was he insane?

- Elizabeth II (1926–), queen of England since 1952, has an official web site that includes a biography of King George III (www.royal.gov.uk/history/george.htm). The biography presents the point of view that while King George opposed American independence, it was his advisers, with the support of Parliament, who created the policies that led to the American Revolution. Therefore, the responsibility was theirs: "George's direct responsibility for the loss of the colonies is not great."

- King George struggled with mental problems that led many to think he was insane. Modern medical experts say he probably suffered from a rare, hereditary blood disorder called porphyria (por-FEAR-ee-uh). It can result in brain injury. A 1994 movie, *The Madness of King George,* explores this subject. Actor Nigel Hawthorne, in the role of George III, received an Academy Award nomination.

Where to Learn More

Commager, Henry Steele. *Documents of American History.* New York: Appleton-Century-Crofts, 1958.

Green, Robert. *King George III.* New York: Franklin Watts, 1997.

Hibbert, Christopher. *George III: A Personal History.* New York: Basic Books, 1999.

"Historic Royal Profiles: George III." *The British Monarchy: The Official Web Site.* [Online] www.royal.gov.uk/history/george.htm (accessed on April 3, 2000).

Lloyd, Alan. *The King Who Lost America: A Portrait of the Life and Times of George III.* Garden City, NY: Doubleday, 1971.

Meyeroff, Stephen. *The Call for Independence: The Story of the American Revolution and Its Causes.* Cherry Hill, NJ: Oak Tree Publishers, 1996.

Plumb, J. H. "George III" in *Encyclopedia of the American Revolution.* Edited by Mark M. Boatner III. Mechanicsburg, PA: Stackpole Books, 1994.

John Dickinson

Letters from a Farmer in Pennsylvania to the Inhabitants of the British Colonies

First published in 1767–68; excerpted from reprint edition, 1903

Mob violence had greeted Parliament's attempts to raise money in the colonies. Apart from the violence, though, many stirring words were written and spoken in response to Parliament's actions. *Letters from a Farmer in Pennsylvania to the Inhabitants of the British Colonies,* written by John Dickinson (1732–1808), were among the most eloquent early objections to British policies. Dickinson was a lawyer and a retired farmer. He studied law in both Philadelphia, Pennsylvania, and London, England. Because of his legal training, he was one of the first to understand that measures like the Townshend Acts posed a danger to colonial liberty. He believed that it was wrong and illegal to impose taxes on people without their consent, given personally or through their representatives.

The Townshend Acts of 1767 appeared just as the colonists were recovering from their joy over the 1766 repeal of the Stamp Act of 1765 (taxes on printed matter, legal documents, dice, and playing cards). The Townshend Acts included (1) a Quartering Act, which ordered the colonies to provide living quarters and supplies such as candles and straw

"Benevolence towards mankind excites wishes for their welfare, and such wishes endear the means of fulfilling them. Those can be found in liberty alone, and therefore her sacred cause ought to be espoused by every man, on every occasion, to the utmost of his power. . . ."

John Dickinson, from Letters from a Farmer . . .

John Dickinson wrote very eloquently about his protests to British policies.
Reproduced by permission of The Granger Collection Ltd.

for mattresses to British troops; (2) an act suspending the New York Assembly (its lawmaking body) for failing to obey earlier Quartering Acts; and (3) a Revenue Act, which called for taxes on lead, glass, paint, tea, and other items. (A revenue is money collected to pay for the expenses of government.)

The Townshend Acts prompted various reactions in the colonies. In the north, the acts were greeted with violence and fierce opposition. In the middle and southern colonies, there was a large group of people who did not like the Townshend Acts but were still loyal to King George III (1738–1820). These were the people whose opinions Dickinson was trying to change in his letters, which he addressed to "My Dear Countrymen."

For twelve weeks beginning on December 2, 1767, the *Pennsylvania Chronicle and Universal Advertiser* printed Dickinson's letters at the rate of one a week. Dickinson's letters explained the meaning and consequences of different aspects of the Townshend Acts. For example, letters five and six explained how to tell the difference between proper laws and improper laws. If Parliament's laws were designed to raise revenue, then the laws were not acceptable. If Parliament meant to regulate trade, such laws were acceptable.

Dickinson's first letter, which follows, began by describing some of his personal qualities. He said he was a retired farmer and an educated gentleman. He said he was interested in promoting the cause of liberty, and he believed that all men had to work to defeat threats to their liberty—threats like the Townshend Acts.

Things to remember while reading an excerpt from the first of the *Letters from a Farmer in Pennsylvania to the Inhabitants of the British Colonies:*

- Dickinson had spent four years studying law in England, and he knew well what the rights of English citizens were. In the following letter and in his eleven other letters, Dickinson pointed out that with the Townshend Acts, Parliament was trampling upon the rights of English citizens in the colonies.

- In his first letter, Dickinson referred several times to the Assembly of New York, the colony's lawmaking body. Dickinson was responding to the Townshend Act that punished New York because that colony had failed to obey the Quartering Acts of 1764 and 1766. The Quartering Acts required colonial authorities to provide living quarters and supplies to British soldiers in America. New Yorkers had complained that the burden of the Quartering Acts fell most heavily on them, because British general Thomas Gage (1721–1787) had his headquarters—and a large number of soldiers—in New York City. When Gage asked the New York Assembly to pay for supplies for his soldiers, the assembly refused. The assembly was punished by having its power to make laws suspended. Dickinson argued that if the other colonies did nothing in response to the suspension of the assembly's power, members of Parliament might pass other awful measures when it suited them.

Excerpt from the first of the Letters from a Farmer in Pennsylvania to the Inhabitants of the British Colonies

*I am a Farmer, settled after a variety of fortunes, near the banks, of the river Delaware, in the province of Pennsylvania. I received a **liberal education**, and have been engaged in the busy scenes of life: But am now convinced, that a man may be as happy without **bustle**, as*

Liberal education: A college education based on arts and sciences.

Bustle: Noisy activity.

with it. My farm is small, my servants are few, and good; I have a little money at [earning] interest; I wish for no more: my employment in my own affairs is easy; and with a contented grateful mind, I am compleating the number of days allotted to me by divine goodness.

Being master of my time, I spend a good deal of it in a library, which I think the most valuable part of my small estate; and being acquainted with two or three gentlemen of abilities and learning, who honour me with their friendship, I believe I have acquired a greater share of knowledge in history, and the laws and constitution of my country, than is generally attained by men of my class, many of them not being so fortunate as I have been in the opportunities of getting information.

*From infancy I was taught to love humanity and liberty. Inquiry and experience have since confirmed my reverence for the lessons then given me, by convincing me more fully of their truth and excellence. **Benevolence** towards mankind excites wishes for their welfare, and such wishes endear the means of fulfilling them. Those can be found in liberty alone, and therefore her sacred cause ought to be **espoused** by every man, on every occasion, to the utmost of his power: as a charitable but poor person does not withhold his **mite**, because he cannot relieve all the distresses of the miserable, so let not any honest man **suppress his sentiments** concerning freedom, however small their influence is likely to be. Perhaps he may "touch some wheel" that may have an effect greater than he expects.*

*These being my sentiments, I am encouraged to offer to you, my countrymen, my thoughts on some late transactions, that in my opinion are of the utmost importance to you. Conscious of my defects, I have waited some time, in expectation of feeling the subject **treated** by persons much better qualified for the task; but being therein disappointed, and **apprehensive** that longer delays will be **injurious**, I venture at length to request the attention of the public, praying only for one thing,—that is that these lines may be read with the same **zeal** for the happiness of British America, with which they were wrote.*

With a good deal of surprise I have observed, that little notice has been taken of an act of parliament, as injurious in its principle to the liberties of these colonies, as the STAMP-ACT was: I mean the act for suspending the legislation of New-York.

The assembly of that government complied with a former act of parliament, requiring certain provisions to be made for the troops in America, in every particular, I think, except the articles of salt, pepper,

Benevolence: Kindly feelings.

Espoused: Given loyalty to.

Mite: A very small amount of money.

Suppress his sentiments: Hold back his views.

Treated: Discussed.

Apprehensive: Fearful.

Injurious: Hurtful.

Zeal: Enthusiastic devotion to a cause.

and vinegar. In my opinion they acted **imprudently**, considering all circumstances, in not complying so far, as would have given satisfaction, as several colonies did: but my dislike of their conduct in that instance, has not blinded me so much, that I cannot plainly perceive, that they have been punished in a manner **pernicious** to American freedom, and justly alarming to all the colonies.

If the BRITISH PARLIAMENT has a legal authority to order, that we shall furnish a single article for the troops here, and to compel obedience to that order; they have the same right to order us to supply those troops with arms, **cloaths**, and every necessary, and to compel obedience to that order also; in short, to lay any burdens they please upon us. What is this but taxing us at a certain sum, and leaving to us only the manner of raising it? How is this mode more tolerable than the STAMP ACT? Would that act have appeared more pleasing to AMERICANS, if being ordered thereby to raise the sum total of the taxes, the mighty privilege had been left to them, of saying how much should be paid for an instrument of writing on paper, and how much for another on **parchment**?

[Next came a complicated paragraph, which stated that an act of Parliament commanding the colonies to house, clothe, and feed British soldiers was really a tax. Some colonies complied with the act simply to show their respect for Great Britain; but by complying, they were not saying it was legal to tax them.]

The matter being thus stated, the assembly of New-York either had, or had not a right to refuse submission to that act. If they had, and I imagine no AMERICAN will say, they had not, then the parliament had no right to compel them to execute it.—If they had not that right, they had no right to punish them for not executing it; and therefore had no right to suspend their legislation, which is a punishment. In fact, if the people of New-York cannot be legally taxed but by their own representatives, they cannot be legally deprived of the privileges of making laws, only for insisting on that exclusive privilege of taxation. If they may be legally deprived in such a case of the privilege of making laws, why may they not, with equal reason, be deprived of every other privilege? Or why may not every colony be treated in the same manner, when any of them shall dare to deny their assent to any **impositions** that shall be directed? Or **what signifies** the repeal of the STAMP-ACT, if these colonies are to lose their other privileges, by not tamely surrendering that of taxation?

There is one **consideration** arising from this suspicion, which is not generally attended to, but **shews** its importance very clearly. It was

Imprudently: Unwisely.

Pernicious: Harmful, destructive.

Cloaths: Clothes.

Parchment: A sheet of paper, often made from sheepskin or goatskin.

Impositions: Unfair taxes.

What signifies: What difference does it make.

Consideration: Factor to be considered.

Shews: Shows.

Prerogative: Exclusive right and power to command.

Regiments to be quartered: Troops to be fed, clothed, and housed.

Compulsion: Forced act.

Is totally indifferent: Makes no difference.

Mutual inattention: Lack of attention to each other.

Maxim: A short way of expressing a truth.

Reposeth: Reposes; rests comfortably.

Ship-money cause, for three shillings and four-pence: A lawsuit involving a very small amount of money.

Agitated: Stirred up.

Ardour: Strong enthusiasm or devotion.

Sat and adjourned: Met formally and broke up.

Inflammatory: Arousing strong emotion.

Sovereign: King.

Wanting: Lacking.

not necessary that this suspension should be caused by an act of parliament. The crown might have refrained from calling the assembly together, by its **prerogative** in the royal governments. This step, I suppose, would have been taken, if the conduct of the assembly of New-York, had been regarded as an act of disobedience to the crown alone: but it is regarded as an act of "disobedience to 'the authority of the BRITISH LEGISLATURE.'" This gives the suspension a consequence vastly more affecting. It is a parliamentary assertion of the supreme authority of the British legislature over these colonies in the part of taxation; and is intended to COMPEL New-York into a submission to that authority. It seems therefore to me as much a violation of the liberty of the people of that province, and consequently of all these colonies, as if the parliament had sent a number of **regiments to be quartered** upon them till they should comply. For it is evident, that the suspension is meant as a **compulsion:** and the method of compelling **is totally indifferent.** It is indeed probable, that the sight of red coats, and the beating of drums would have been most alarming, because people are generally more influenced by their eyes and ears than by their reason: But whoever seriously considers the matter, must perceive, that a dreadful stroke is aimed at the liberty of these colonies: For the cause of one is the cause of all. If the parliament may lawfully deprive New-York of any of its rights, it may deprive any, or all the other colonies of their rights; and nothing can possibly so much encourage such attempts, as a **mutual inattention** to the interest of each other. To divide, and thus to destroy, is the first political **maxim** in attacking those who are powerful by their union. He certainly is not a wise man, who folds his arms and **reposeth** himself at home, seeing with unconcern the flames that have invaded his neighbour's house, without any endeavours to extinguish them. When Mr. Hampden's **ship-money cause, for three shillings and four-pence,** was tried, all the people of England, with anxious expectation, interested themselves in the important decision; and when the slightest point touching the freedom of a single colony is **agitated,** I earnestly wish, that all the rest may with equal **ardour** support their sister. Very much may be said on this subject, but I hope, more at present is unnecessary.

With concern I have observed that two assemblies of this province have **sat and adjourned,** without taking any notice of this act. It may perhaps be asked, what would have been proper for them to do? I am by no means fond of **inflammatory** measures. I detest them.—I should be sorry that any thing should be done which might justly displease our **sovereign** or our mother-country. But a firm, modest exertion of a free spirit, should never be **wanting** on public occasions. It *appears to me, that it would have been sufficient for the assembly, to have ordered our agents to represent to the King's ministers, their sense of the **suspending act**, and to pray for its repeal. Thus we should have borne our testimony against it; and might therefore reasonably expect that on a like occasion, we might receive the same assistance from the other colonies.*

"Concordia res parvae crescunt." Small things grow great by **concord.**—

A FARMER. (Dickinson, Letters, *pp. 5–12)*

What happened next . . .

Dickinson's letters were so popular in Pennsylvania that nearly every other colonial newspaper reprinted them. At town and assembly meetings everywhere, resolutions were passed thanking Dickinson for expressing so well the British threat to liberty. The letters were then printed in book form. American politician Benjamin Franklin (1706–1790) liked them so well that he wrote a preface to the London edition of the book and then arranged to have it translated into French for publication in Europe.

The letters helped unite Americans in resistance, and they had international influence, too. In London, members of Parliament angrily discussed them. Ordinary citizens, who up until then had heard little of the situation in America, now grew alarmed that their own liberties might be taken from them as well. Letters from citizens began to be published in English newspapers, and Dickinson's name became well known throughout the kingdom as the leader of political thought in the American colonies.

Did you know . . .

- John Dickinson was a Quaker, a member of the Society of Friends, who oppose violence. Dickinson strongly objected to British attempts to tax the colonies, but he meant to plead his case like a lawyer, in the hopes that Great Britain and America could reach an understanding.

- Dickinson's letters were published in *London Magazine* in 1768. The magazine expressed the opinion that Dickinson's reasoning was sound and that "nine persons in ten, even in this country, are friends to the Americans, and convinced that they have right on their side." The magazine's editors did not speak for King George or his friends in Parliament, however. The king and Parliament continued to assert Parliament's right to tax the colonies.

- Dickinson had earlier gained some fame when he wrote a pamphlet opposing the Stamp Act of 1765. In it, he pointed out that if the colonists spent all their money paying taxes to Great Britain, there would be none left to buy British goods. He warned that if the British continued to tax the Americans, the colonists would have to manufacture their own goods and would become completely independent from Great Britain. It would not be long before his prediction came true.

- Dickinson believed strongly in education. In 1773, he founded Dickinson College in Carlisle, Pennsylvania, because he thought western Pennsylvania needed a college. He gave the school fifteen hundred books and two farms totaling five hundred acres.

Where to Learn More

Cook, Don. *The Long Fuse: How England Lost the American Colonies, 1760–1785.* New York: Atlantic Monthly Press, 1995.

Dickinson, John. *Empire and Nation: Letters from a Farmer in Pennsylvania.* Edited by Richard Henry Lee. Indianapolis: Liberty Fund, 1998.

Dickinson, John. *Letters from a Farmer in Pennsylvania, to the Inhabitants of the British Colonies.* New York: Outlook Co., 1903.

Benjamin Franklin

"An Edict by the King of Prussia"

First published September 5, 1773; excerpted from Benjamin Franklin's *Writings*, 1987

The years leading up to the start of the Revolutionary War were full of tension and disagreement. But there were some humorous moments, too, thanks in large part to American politician Benjamin Franklin (1706–1790). Along with British citizens, Franklin contributed letters to London newspapers, expressing his views about the demands being made on the colonies. The following excerpt from Franklin's "An Edict by the King of Prussia" appeared in a London newspaper in 1773.

An edict is a formal announcement issued by an authority. In this case, the authority is the king of Prussia, Frederick II (1712–1786), also known as Frederick the Great. Prussia was a state in north central Germany (Prussia was dissolved in 1947 and divided among East and West Germany; Poland; and the former Soviet Union, now fifteen independent republics, the largest of which is Russia).

The "Edict by the King of Prussia" is a joke. Part of the humor comes from Franklin's comparison of the settlement of England in the fifth century by Germans with the settlement of America. In this "Edict," the King of Prussia makes the same

"And whereas the Art and Mystery of making Hats hath arrived at great Perfection in Prussia, and the making of Hats by our remote Subjects ought to be as much as possible restrained."

Benjamin Franklin, from "An Edict by the King of Prussia"

Frederick the Great, the king of Prussia, who was the subject of Benjamin Franklin's "Edict by the King of Prussia" joke.
Reproduced by permission of Corbis-Bettmann.

trade and tax demands on former German colonists in England that England was making on the American colonies in the 1760s and 1770s. Notice the echoes of the Stamp Act and the Townshend Revenue Act in the excerpt. The paragraph about the making of hats pokes fun at Parliament laws that placed tight restrictions on what trade items could go in and out of the colonies.

Things to remember while reading an excerpt from "An Edict by the King of Prussia:"

• Between 1757 and 1774, Benjamin Franklin served at various times as an agent for the colonies of Pennsylvania, Georgia, New Jersey, and Massachusetts. Agents were men who were appointed by the colonies to live in London, England, circulate among important people, and report back on what was happening in Parliament (Great Britain's lawmaking body). The agents made sure Parliament knew what the colonies' needs and wishes were as Parliament prepared to make laws that affected the colonies. During his years as an agent, Franklin lived almost all of the time in London. A charming and witty man, Franklin made friends in high places in government.

• Benjamin Franklin had a sense of humor he could not disguise even during serious moments. Beginning when he was a young man of fifteen, he contributed unsigned humorous articles to his brother's newspaper. (Franklin and his brother did not get along well and his brother would not have published the articles had he known Franklin wrote them.) Franklin's humorous writings were usually done in fun. But by the time he wrote the "Edict," Franklin's words were becoming more biting. He saw that tempers in the colonies were hot over British taxes, that violent protests against the British were a constant threat,

and that Parliament seemed unaware of the dangers. Franklin was growing disenchanted with politicians in Parliament, whom he saw as corrupt. He was also disgusted with the rigid class system of England, in which wealth and privilege were concentrated in a few hands and most people lived in poverty. Franklin expressed his frustration with Parliament through satires like his "Edict." Satire makes fun of foolish or wicked people or ideas.

Benjamin Franklin, Man of Many Talents

Benjamin Franklin (1706–1790) was born in Boston, Massachusetts, one of seventeen children. His father, Josiah, was a devout Puritan candle maker and mechanic and his mother, Abiah, was a highly moral person, a "virtuous Woman," Franklin would later write. Because his family was poor, Franklin received very little formal education and went to work at a young age, first for his father, then for his brother James, a printer of a Boston newspaper. Franklin educated himself by reading every word that came into the print shop and before long he was writing pieces that made fun of upper-class Bostonians. In 1723, when his brother was arrested and imprisoned for these writings, Franklin ran away to Philadelphia, Pennsylvania.

By the age of forty-two, Franklin had become such a successful writer and printer that he was able to retire from business and turn his attention to his many other interests. He entertained himself by pushing for improvements in the city of Philadelphia (establishing a library, a fire company, a college, an insurance company, and a hospital, among other things). He became involved in politics and dabbled in science. His first major invention was the Pennsylvania stove, later renamed the Franklin stove. The Franklin stove improved on an already existing design by adding a flue around which room air could circulate. The flue acted like a radiator, increasing heating efficiency. Franklin said it made a room twice as warm but used only a quarter of the wood. It was for his work with electricity that Franklin became world-famous. In one experiment, Franklin flew a kite in a lightning storm and was able to draw an electric charge out of the sky and store the charge in a Leyden jar, a type of electrical condenser. He also invented the lightning rod to conduct an electric charge safely into the ground, thereby protecting buildings from lightning strikes and fire.

Franklin was nearly seventy years old when the American Revolution began. Loyal at first to Great Britain, whose culture he greatly admired, he soon became a fierce patriot. He was a signer of the Declaration of Independence and contributed to the war effort in many ways, despite his age. He served as an ambassador to France, trying to enlist that country's help in the war. After the war, he helped draft the U.S. Constitution, although he was by then so ill that he could barely speak. He died peacefully on April 17, 1790, shortly after witnessing the inauguration as America's first president of his longtime friend, George Washington (1732–1799).

Excerpt from "An Edict by the King of Prussia"

The SUBJECT of the following Article of FOREIGN **INTELLIGENCE** being exceeding EXTRAORDINARY, is the Reason of its being separated from the usual Articles of Foreign News.

. . . FREDERICK, by the Grace of God, King of Prussia . . . to all present and to come, HEALTH. The Peace now enjoyed throughout our **Dominions,** having afforded us Leisure to apply ourselves to the Regulation of Commerce, the Improvement of our Finances, and at the same Time the **easing our Domestic Subjects** in their Taxes: For these Causes, and other good Considerations us thereunto moving, We hereby make known, that after having **deliberated** these Affairs in our Council, present our dear Brothers, and other great Officers of the state, Members of the same, WE, of our certain Knowledge, full Power and Authority Royal, have made and issued this present Edict,. . .

WHEREAS it is well known to all the World, that the first German Settlements made in the Island of Britain, were by Colonies of People, Subjects to our renowned **Ducal** Ancestors, and drawn from their Dominions . . .; and that the said Colonies have flourished under the Protection of our **august House,** for Ages past, have never been **emancipated** therefrom, and yet have **hitherto** yielded little Profit to the same. And whereas We Ourself have in the last War fought for and defended the said Colonies against the Power of France, and thereby enabled them to make Conquests from the said Power in America, for which we have not yet received adequate Compensation. And whereas it is just and **expedient** that a Revenue should be raised from the said Colonies in Britain **towards our Indemnification;** and that those who are Descendants of our antient Subjects, and thence still owe us due Obedience, should contribute to the **replenishing of our Royal Coffers,** as they must have done had their Ancestors remained in the territories now **to us appertaining;** WE do therefore hereby ordain and command, That from and after the Date of **these Presents,** there shall be levied and paid to our Officers of the Customs, on all Goods, Wares and merchandizes, and on all Grain and other Produce of the Earth exported from the said Island of Britain, and on all Goods of whatever Kind imported into the same, a Duty of Four and an Half per Cent **ad Valorem,** for the Use of us and our Successors.—And that the said Duty may more **effectually** be collected, We

Intelligence: News.

Dominions: Nations within the British Empire.

Easing our Domestic Subjects: Lessening the tax burden on our people at home.

Deliberated: Thought over and discussed.

Ducal: Relating to a dukedom (a royal kingdom).

August House: Majestic family line.

Emancipated: Freed.

Hitherto: Up until now.

Expedient: Urgently needed.

Towards our Indemnification: To make up for our loss.

Replenishing of our Royal Coffers: Refilling our royal treasury.

To us appertaining: Belonging to us.

These Presents: These documents.

Ad Valorem: Latin for "in proportion to the value."

Effectually: Efficiently.

do hereby ordain, that all Ships or Vessels bound from Great Britain to any other Part of the Word, or from any other Part of the World to Great Britain, shall on their respective Voyages touch at our Port of KONINGSBERG, there to be **unladen**, searched, and charged with the said Duties.

. . . AND WHEREAS the Art and Mystery of making Hats hath arrived at great Perfection in Prussia, and the making of Hats by our remote Subjects ought to be as much as possible restrained. And forasmuch as the Islanders before-mentioned, being in Possession of Wool, Beaver, and other Furs, have **presumptuously conceived** they had a Right to make some Advantage thereof, by manufacturing the same into Hats, to the **Prejudice** of our domestic Manufacture, WE do therefore hereby strictly command and ordain, that no Hats or Felts whatsoever, dyed or undyed, finished or unfinished, shall be loaden or put into or upon any Vessel, Cart, Carriage or Horse, to be transported or conveyed out of one Country in the said Island into another Country, or to any other Place whatsoever, by any Person or Persons whatsoever, on Pain of forfeiting the same, with a Penalty of Five Hundred **Pounds Sterling** per Month: We intending hereby that such Hat-makers, being so restrained both in the Production and Sale of their **Commodity,** may find no Advantage in continuing their Business.—But **lest** the said Islanders should suffer Inconveniency by the **Want** of Hats, We are farther graciously pleased to permit them to send their Beaver Furs to Prussia; and We also permit Hats made thereof to be exported from Prussia to Britain, the People thus favoured to pay all Costs and Charges of Manufacturing, Interest, Commission to Our Merchants, Insurance and Freight going and returning, as in the Case of Iron.

And lastly, Being willing farther to favour Our said Colonies in Britain, We do hereby also ordain and command, that all the Thieves, Highway and Street-Robbers, Housebreakers, Forgerers, Murderers, . . . and Villains of every **Denomination**, who have forfeited their Lives to the Law in Prussia, but whom We, in Our great **Clemency**, do not think fit here to hang, shall be emptied out of our **Gaols** into the said Island of Great Britain for the BETTER PEOPLING of that Country.

We flatter Ourselves that these Our Royal Regulations and Commands will be thought just and reasonable by Our much-favoured Colonists in England, the said Regulations being copies from their own Statutes . . . and from other **equitable** Laws made by their Parliaments, or from Instructions given by their Princes, or from Resolutions of both Houses entered into for the GOOD Government of their own Colonies in Ireland and America.

Unladen: Unloaded.

Presumptuously conceived: Improperly assumed.

Prejudice: Injury.

Pounds Sterling: British money, worth twenty shillings.

Commodity: Trade item.

Lest: For fear that.

Want: Lack.

Denomination: Kind.

Clemency: Mercifulness.

Gaols: Jails.

Equitable: Just.

*And all Persons in the said Island are hereby cautioned not to oppose in any **wise** the execution of this Our Edict, or any Part thereof, such Opposition being **HIGH TREASON**, of which all who are suspected shall be transported in **Fetters** from Britain to Prussia, there to be tried and executed according to the Prussian Law. (Franklin, Writings, pp. 698–702)*

Wise: Manner.

High treason: The worst kind of betrayal of one's king and country.

Fetters: Ankle chains.

What happened next . . .

In a letter to his son, William Franklin, dated October 6, 1773, Franklin described how his joke fooled many intelligent people. He told of how he happened to be visiting the home of a friend, Lord Le Despencer, who was prominent in British society. A man in the next room "came running into us, out of breath, with the paper in his hand," Franklin wrote. "'Here!' says he, 'here's news for ye! Here's the king of Prussia, claiming a right to this kingdom!' All stared, and I as much as any body; and he went on to read it. Another man present looked at me and said: 'I'll be hanged if this is not some of your American jokes upon us.' The reading went on, and ended with abundance of laughing, and a general verdict that it [the newspaper article] was a fair hit."

In the same letter to his son, Franklin reported that he sent his clerk to the printer's office the day after his article was published to pick up some copies for his friends and family. All but two copies were sold out, and the rumor was, wrote Franklin, that the article was "spoken of in the highest terms as the keenest and severest piece that has appeared here [in] a long time." It was feared that the article "would do mischief by giving [London] a bad impression of the measures of government" against the colonies. While the public was amused by Franklin's satire, he made no new friends in Parliament with it. The "Hutchinson letters affair" (see chapter 3) followed soon after the publication of the "Edict," and Franklin would find himself embroiled in a scandal and treated with contempt by Parliament.

> Philadᵃ July 5. 1775
>
> Mr. Strahan,
>
> You are a Member of Parliament,
> and one of that Majority which has
> doomed my Country to Destruction.
> ⸺ You have begun to burn our Towns,
> and murder our People. ⸺ Look upon
> your Hands! ⸺ They are stained with the
> Blood of your Relations! ⸺ You and I were
> long Friends: ⸺ You are now my Ene-
> my, ⸺ and
>
> I am,
>
> Yours,
>
> B Franklin

Franklin's Seal

Did you know . . .

- Six days after Benjamin Franklin published the "Edict," he published another piece he liked even better, although the public preferred his "Edict." The other piece was called *Rules by Which a Great Empire May Be Reduced to a Small One*. In it, Franklin addressed himself to all government men who were in charge of running nations within the

British Empire. He listed all the steps the British government had taken to alienate the colonies. The satire came when he wrote as if the government had adopted a conscious policy of alienating America.

- One of Franklin's first and most successful written hoaxes occurred in 1730. He was twenty-four years old and had just become sole owner of his own newspaper, *The Pennsylvania Gazette*. Now he could publish anything he wanted. He once told an acquaintance that whenever he was short of news, he would make up and publish something that amused him. His 1730 story reported a witch trial that historians believe never took place. Nevertheless, Franklin reported: "Saturday last at Mount-Holly . . . near 300 People were gathered together to see an Experiment or two tried on some Persons accused of Witchcraft. It seems the Accused had been charged with making their Neighbours Sheep dance in an uncommon Manner, and with causing Hogs to speak . . . to the great Terror and Amazement of the King's good and peaceable Subjects in this Province. . . . "

- Perhaps Franklin's most famous book was *Poor Richard's Almanack,* first published in 1732. Almanacs are books containing lists, charts, and tables of useful information, but Franklin livened his up with humorous but useful advice. *Poor Richard's* is the source of such still-popular sayings as: "Eat to live, and not live to eat"; "He that lies down with Dogs, shall rise up with fleas"; "Little strokes fell big oaks"; and "Early to bed and early to rise, makes a man healthy, wealthy, and wise."

- One of Franklin's closest friends in England was William Strahan, a self-made man like Franklin himself. Strahan became a member of Parliament in 1775, and in that position he supported the efforts of some members of Parliament to put down the American rebellion. Franklin was angry at Strahan for this and composed a letter to him on July 5, 1775, just before Franklin returned to America: "Mr. Strahan, You are a Member of Parliament, and one of that Majority which has doomed my Country to Destruction. You have begun to burn our Towns, and murder our People. Look upon your Hands! They are stained with the Blood of your Relations! You and I were long Friends: You are now my Enemy." However, Franklin decided the letter was too strong and might destroy an important friendship; it was never sent but was preserved among Franklin's papers.

Where to Learn More

Adler, David A. *Benjamin Franklin—Printer, Inventor, Statesman.* New York: Holiday House, 1992.

Clark, Ronald W. *Benjamin Franklin: A Biography.* New York: Random House, 1983.

Davidson, Margaret. *The Story of Benjamin Franklin: Amazing American.* Milwaukee: Gareth Stevens Publishing, 1997.

Foster, Leila Merrell. *Benjamin Franklin, Founding Father and Inventor.* Springfield, NJ: Enslow, 1997.

Franklin, Benjamin. *Benjamin Franklin's Autobiography.* Edited by J. A. Leo Lemay and P. M. Zall. New York: Norton, 1986.

Franklin, Benjamin. *Writings.* New York: Library of America, 1987.

"Franklin, Benjamin" in *World of Invention.* Edited by Bridget Travers. Detroit: Gale Research, 1994.

Kent, Deborah. *Benjamin Franklin.* New York: Scholastic, 1993.

Thomas Jefferson

A Summary View of the Rights of British America

First published in 1774; excerpted from
***The Portable Thomas Jefferson*, 1975**

In 1774, Benjamin Franklin (1706–1790) was busy in London, England, trying to get his friends in Parliament to see that trouble was brewing in America over British taxes. Opposition to measures such as the Stamp Act, the Declaratory Act, and the Intolerable Acts was reaching crisis proportions. The Stamp Act of 1765 taxed printed matter such as newspapers, legal documents, and even dice and playing cards. The Declaratory Act affirmed the right of Parliament to make laws that would bind the colonists "in all cases whatsoever." The Intolerable Acts closed the Port of Boston, gave the British-appointed governor of Massachusetts complete control of town meetings, ordered that British officials who committed major crimes in the colonies would be tried in Great Britain, and required that the colonists house British soldiers in dwellings belonging to private citizens.

Back in America, Thomas Jefferson (1743–1826), a young member of the Virginia House of Burgesses (the colony's lawmaking body), was making a name for himself as an early and forceful friend of American rights in the face of British oppression. His thoughts came together in a pamphlet

"Single acts of tyranny may be ascribed to the accidental opinion of a day; but a series of oppressions begun at a distinguished period, and pursued unalterably through every change of ministers, too plainly prove a deliberate and systematical plan of reducing us to slavery."

Thomas Jefferson, from A Summary View of the Rights of British America

called *A Summary View of the Rights of British America,* which was published in 1774.

At the time, most Americans believed that King George III (1738–1820) was not responsible for the tense relations between Great Britain and America. They blamed Parliament instead. But Thomas Jefferson disagreed. His pamphlet was a direct attack on the British king, blaming him for the breakdown in relations between England and the colonies.

Jefferson began by complaining that the colonies had repeatedly petitioned King George to do something about their tax complaints, but the king had not had the courtesy to reply. Jefferson then compared the settlement of America to the settlement of England, stating that England had no more rights over America than the countries whose pioneers settled England had over England.

Jefferson emphasized that human rights were derived from the laws of nature, not from a king. This was a theme that would appear in many of his later writings. Jefferson also complained about how King George continued to reject laws abolishing slavery, laws Jefferson said were "the great object of desire" in the colonies. Jefferson declared that "human nature [is] deeply wounded by this infamous practice" of owning slaves. Jefferson also put forth the new argument that Parliament had no right to pass any laws whatsoever for the colonies, whether they were tax laws or any other kind of laws.

Things to remember while reading an excerpt from *A Summary View of the Rights of British America:*

- Parliament insisted that Americans had to pay taxes to help cover British costs left over from the French and Indian War (1754–63). The French and Indian War was fought in America by Great Britain and France to decide who would control North America. In his pamphlet, Jefferson chose to play down the role Great Britain had played in that conflict. He declared that Great Britain had fought that war not to protect the colonies but to protect its own trade interests. Therefore, Jefferson stated, repayment should be in the form of trade privileges, not taxes. An example of a trade privilege would be an agreement to buy tea only from British merchants.

Excerpt from A Summary View of the Rights of British America

Resolved . . . that an humble and dutiful address be presented to his majesty, **begging leave** *to lay before him, as* **chief magistrate** *of the British empire, the united complaints of his majesty's subjects in America; complaints which are* **excited** *by many* **unwarrantable encroachments and usurpations,** *attempted to be made by the legislature of one part of the empire, upon those rights which God and the laws have given equally and independently to all. To represent to his majesty that these his states have often individually made humble application to his imperial throne to obtain, through its intervention, some* **redress** *of their injured rights, to none of which was ever even an answer* **condescended.** *. . . .*

To remind him that our ancestors, before their emigration to America, were the free inhabitants of the British **dominions** *in Europe, and possessed a right which nature has given to all men, of departing from the country in which chance, not choice, has placed them, of going in quest of new* **habitations,** *and of there establishing new societies, under such laws and regulations as to them shall seem most likely to promote public happiness. That their* **Saxon** *ancestors had, under this universal law, in like manner left their native wilds and woods in the north of Europe, had possessed themselves of the island of Britain, then less* **charged** *with inhabitants, and had established there that system of laws which has so long been the glory and protection of that country. Nor was ever any claim of superiority or dependence asserted over them by that mother country from which they had migrated; and were such a claim made, it is believed that his majesty's subjects in Great Britain have too firm a feeling of the rights derived to them from their ancestors, to bow down the* **sovereignty of** *their state before such* **visionary pretensions.** *. . . . America was conquered, and her settlements made, and firmly established, at the expense of individuals, and not of the British public. Their own blood was spilt in acquiring lands for their settlement, their own fortunes expended in making that settlement* **effectual;** *for themselves they fought, for themselves they conquered, and for themselves alone they have right to hold. Not a* **shilling** *was ever issued from the public treasures of his majesty, or his ancestors, for their assistance, till of very late times, after the colonies had*

Begging leave: Humbly asking permission.

Chief magistrate: Top official.

Excited: Prompted.

Unwarrantable encroachments and usurpations: Unjustified, sneaky, and wrongful removal of someone else's rights.

Redress: Resolution.

Condescended: Given in a superior way.

Dominions: Nations within the British Empire.

Habitations: Places to live.

Saxon: Fifth-century European.

Charged: Populated.

Sovereignty of: Right to exercise control over.

Visionary pretensions: Fantasies.

Effectual: Function in the best way.

Shilling: British coin worth one-twentieth of a British pound.

become established on a firm and permanent footing. That then, indeed, having become valuable to Great Britain for her commercial purposes, his parliament was pleased to lend them assistance against an enemy, who would **fain have drawn to herself the benefits of their commerce,** to the great **aggrandizement** of herself, and danger of Great Britain. Such assistance, and in such circumstances, they had often before given to Portugal, and other allied states, with whom they carry on **a commercial intercourse;** yet these states never supposed, that by calling in her aid, they thereby submitted themselves to her sovereignty. Had such terms been proposed, they would have rejected them with disdain. . . . We do not, however, mean to under-rate those aids, which to us were doubtless valuable, on whatever principles granted; but we would **shew** that they cannot give a title to that authority which the British parliament would **arrogate** over us, and that they may amply be repaid by our giving to the inhabitants of Great Britain such exclusive privileges in trade as may be advantageous to them, and at the same time not too restrictive to ourselves.

[Jefferson then went on to describe abuses committed against the colonies by British kings before King George. Jefferson complained that a country settled by "individual adventurers" had been parceled out and distributed among friends and favorites of earlier kings in a way that had never been done in the British Empire before. (For example, in 1632, Maryland was granted to English politician George Calvert [c. 1580–1632], also known as Lord Baltimore.) Jefferson also complained that the American colonists' rights to free trade with all parts of the world was unlawfully taken away by Great Britain. He continued:]

History has informed us that **bodies** of men, as well as individuals, are **susceptible of the spirit of tyranny.** A view of these acts of parliament for regulation . . . of the American trade . . . would undeniably **evince** the truth of this observation.

[Jefferson then described in detail the acts passed by Parliament to restrict the colonies from trading freely and limit what they could manufacture. For example:]

. . . an American subject is forbidden to make a hat for himself of the fur which he has taken perhaps on his own soil; an **instance of despotism** to which no parallel can be produced in the most **arbitrary ages** of British history. By one other act . . . the iron which we make we are forbidden to manufacture. . . . The true ground on which we declare these acts void is, that the British parliament has no right to exercise authority over us.

Fain have drawn to herself the benefits of their commerce: Gladly have taken over their trade to benefit herself.

Aggrandizement: (Pronounced Uh-GRAN-duz-munt) Benefit.

A commercial intercourse: Trade relations.

Shew: Show.

Arrogate: Claim for itself without right.

Bodies: Groups.

Susceptible of the spirit of tyranny: Capable of accepting absolute, unjust power.

Evince: Show clearly.

Instance of despotism: Example of tyranny or absolute, unjust power.

Arbitrary ages: Lawless times.

[Jefferson then complained that while previous kings had from time to time denied the colonists their rights, the current king was doing so at a rapid pace.]

*Scarcely have our minds been able to emerge from the astonishment into which one stroke of parliamentary thunder has involved us, before another more heavy, and more alarming, is fallen on us. Single acts of tyranny may be **ascribed to** the accidental opinion of a day; but a series of oppressions begun at a distinguished period, and pursued **unalterably** through every **change of ministers**, too plainly prove a deliberate and systematical plan of reducing us to slavery.*

[Jefferson then discussed the acts he objected to—the Stamp Act, the Declaratory Act, the Boston Port Act, the Quartering Act, and others. He continued:]

*That these are the acts of power, assumed by a body of men, foreign to our constitutions, and unacknowledged by our laws, against which we do, on behalf of the inhabitants of British America, enter this our solemn and determined protest; and we do earnestly entreat his majesty, as yet the **only mediatory power** between the several states of the British empire, to recommend to his parliament of Great Britain the total revocation of these acts, which, however **nugatory** they be, may yet prove the cause of further discontents and jealousies among us.*

[Jefferson then went on to attack King George personally for neglecting his responsibilities and allowing Parliament to pass laws that injured his subjects. Jefferson concluded:]

*Let not the name of George the third be a **blot** in the page of history. You are surrounded by British counsellors, but remember that they are **parties**. You have no ministers for American affairs, because you have none taken from among us, nor **amenable** to the laws on which they are to give you advice. It **behoves** you, therefore, to think and to act for yourself and your people. The great principles of right and wrong are legible to every reader; to pursue them requires not the aid of many counsellors. The whole art of government consists in the art of being honest. Only aim to do your duty, and mankind will give you credit where you fail. No longer **persevere** in sacrificing the rights of one part of the empire to the **inordinate** desires of another; but deal out to all equal and impartial right. Let no act be passed by any one legislature which may **infringe on** the rights and liberties of another. This is the important post in which fortune has placed you, holding the balance of a great, if a well poised empire. This, sire, is the*

Ascribed to: Said to be caused by.

Unalterably: Unchangeably.

Change of ministers: Election of new government officials.

Only mediatory power: Only authority who can settle disputes.

Nugatory: Unimportant.

Blot: Embarrassment.

Parties: Groups organized to promote their own views.

Amenable: Accountable.

Behoves: Behooves; is proper for.

Persevere: Persist.

Inordinate: Unreasonable.

Infringe on: Violate.

Felicity: Happiness.

Reciprocal: Mutual.

Commodities: Trade items.

Disjoin: Separate.

Interpose: Place [yourself] in a position.

Efficacy: (Pronounced EF-uh-ka-see) Effectiveness.

Apprehensions of future encroachment: Fears of future takeovers of rights.

Fraternal: Brotherly.

*advice of your great American council, on the observance of which may perhaps depend your **felicity** and future fame, and the preservation of that harmony which alone can continue both to Great Britain and America the **reciprocal** advantages of their connection. It is neither our wish, nor our interest, to separate from her. We are willing, on our part, to sacrifice every thing which reason can ask to the restoration of that tranquillity for which all must wish. On their part, let them be ready to establish union and a generous plan. Let them name their terms, but let them be just. Accept of every commercial preference it is in our power to give for such things as we can raise for their use, or they make for ours. But let them not think to exclude us from going to other markets to dispose of those **commodities** which they cannot use, or to supply those wants which they cannot supply. Still less let it be proposed that our properties within our own territories shall be taxed or regulated by any power on earth but our own. The God who gave us life gave us liberty at the same time; the hand of force may destroy, but cannot **disjoin** them. This, sire, is our last, our determined resolution; and that you will be pleased to **interpose** with that **efficacy** which your earnest endeavours may ensure to procure redress of these our great grievances, to quiet the minds of your subjects in British America, against any **apprehensions of future encroachment**, to establish **fraternal** love and harmony through the whole empire, and that these may continue to the latest ages of time, is the fervent prayer of all British America! (Peterson, pp. 3–5, 7–9, 13–14, 20–21)*

What happened next . . .

Jefferson's pamphlet was widely read, both in the colonies and in Great Britain. In America, where most people were still loyal to Great Britain, the pamphlet was seen as too extreme. The pamphlet earned Jefferson a reputation as a skilled writer and an early leader of the revolutionary movement. In Great Britain, the pamphlet was revised a little to tone it down. The revising was probably done by Edmund Burke (1729–1797; author of "On Conciliation," discussed earlier in this chapter, and a friend to American colonists). The revised version was then circulated among Burke's followers, who marveled at the clarity and elegance of the sentiments expressed in it. Other members of Parliament were not so thrilled. Such thoughts as Jefferson expressed had never before been heard either in England or America. Jefferson's name was added to a list of Americans believed to be guilty of treason (betraying king and country).

King George and Parliament continued on the course that would result in the loss of the colonies. They heard and ignored Burke's "On Conciliation" speech and refused to read the numerous petitions sent from America (see chapter 2). In August 1775, King George and Parliament would declare the colonies in a state of rebellion—the same thing as declaring war.

Did you know . . .

- It is ironic that Jefferson complained about King George's position on slavery in *A Summary View of the Rights of British America*. Like other wealthy leaders of the American Revolution, Jefferson himself was a slave owner until the end of his life. It was his optimistic hope that the generation that came after him would end the practice.

- The views Jefferson expressed in *A Summary View of the Rights of British America* first appeared in a paper he read to Virginia lawmakers in 1774. The lawmakers were meeting in secret because the British-appointed governor of Virginia, John Murray (1732–1809), known as Lord Dunmore, dissolved the legislature. He was punishing the legislature for declaring June 1, 1774, a day of mourning to show its sympathy for the citizens of Boston. That was the day the Boston Port Act, one of the Intolerable Acts, went into effect; the port of Boston was closed by the act. At that time, most of Jefferson's fellow lawmakers thought that his words, though eloquent, were too extreme. Later, they would come to believe that what Jefferson said was true.

- After Jefferson's pamphlet was read in England, his name was put on a list of colonists who may have committed treason. Others on the list included Massachusetts politicians John Hancock (1737–1793), John Adams (1735–1826), and Samuel Adams (1722–1803). Nothing ever came of the charge against Jefferson, but in April 1775, British soldiers were on their way to capture Hancock and Samuel Adams in Lexington, Massachusetts, when the first shots of the American Revolution rang out in nearby Concord.

Where to Learn More

Bruns, Roger, ed. *Thomas Jefferson*. New York: Chelsea House, 1987.

Green, Robert. *King George III*. New York: Franklin Watts, 1997.

Hibbert, Christopher. *George III: A Personal History*. New York: Basic Books, 1999.

Lloyd, Alan. *The King Who Lost America: A Portrait of the Life and Times of George III*. Garden City, NY: Doubleday, 1971.

"Monticello: The Home of Thomas Jefferson." Offers "A Day in the Life" tour through the daily activities of Jefferson at home. [Online] www.monticello.org (accessed on March 13, 2000).

Nardo, Don. *The Importance of Thomas Jefferson*. San Diego: Lucent Books, 1993.

Peterson, Merrill D. *The Portable Thomas Jefferson*. New York, Viking Press, 1975.

Rayner, B. L. *Life of Thomas Jefferson*. Revised and edited by Eyler Robert Coates, Sr. [Online] http://www.geocities.com/Athens/Forum/1683/ljindex.htm (accessed on March 13, 2000).

"Thomas Jefferson Memorial." [Online] www.nps.gov/thje/index2.htm (accessed on March 13, 2000)..

Patrick Henry

"Give me liberty, or give me death!"

Speech given March 23, 1775; excerpted from *Patrick Henry*, 1966

O n December 16, 1773, a group of patriots from Boston, Massachusetts, disguised as Indians, dumped 342 chests of tea into Boston Harbor to show their disgust over British taxes. The act became known as the Boston Tea Party. In early 1774, Great Britain passed the Intolerable Acts to punish Boston and Massachusetts for the Tea Party. One of the Intolerable Acts closed the port of Boston. To show their sympathy for the citizens of Boston, who were suffering from having the port closed, members of the Virginia House of Burgesses (the colony's lawmaking body) declared a day of mourning. In response, the British-appointed governor of Virginia, John Murray (1732–1809), known as Lord Dunmore, dissolved the House of Burgesses. The House of Burgesses was still dissolved in early 1775, but its members continued to meet in secret.

Six months earlier, on September 5, 1774, delegates from twelve of the thirteen colonies met at the First Continental Congress to decide what to do about colonial relations with Great Britain. Congress asked that the delegates go home and meet with their fellow lawmakers to discuss the issue. Members of the Virginia House of Burgesses were assembled on March 20, 1775,

"Is life so dear, or peace so sweet, as to be purchased at the price of chains and slavery? Forbid it, Almighty God! I know not what course others may take, but as for me, give me liberty, or give me death!"

Patrick Henry

when Representative Patrick Henry (1736–1799) gave his famous "Give me liberty, or give me death" speech.

By March 1775, American colonists were very angry over British taxation policies, but outright war with Great Britain was not a certainty. There was much discussion, in fact, about how war could be avoided. Henry, who had long been in favor of a break with Great Britain, disagreed with those who wished to avoid a war. Instead, he rose and made a motion regarding military matters. Some delegates objected, saying he was being premature and that his motion closed the door on any chances for peace. Henry then proceeded to give his speech in support of his motion, insisting that war was coming, and it was time to get ready for it.

Henry began by pointing out that every effort toward a peaceful resolution had been met with insults and violence in the form of punishments (like the closing of the port of Boston). As a result, he believed there was no longer any hope of peace. He answered the fears of those who said America was too weak to prevail against Great Britain by saying they would never be any stronger than now. Furthermore, Americans would gain strength from the knowledge that their cause was "holy" and God was on their side. He concluded by saying that not to fight now meant slavery.

Things to remember while reading an excerpt from Patrick Henry's "Give me liberty, or give me death" speech:

- Patrick Henry's biographer, educator Moses Coit Tyler (1835–1900), questioned the motives of the delegates who objected to Henry's military proposals and caused him to make this famous speech. Tyler pointed out that the Virginia convention was *not* a legal meeting of the Virginia legislature; it was a gathering of revolutionaries. "Not a man, probably, was sent to that convention, not a man surely would have gone to it, who was not in substantial sympathy with the prevailing revolutionary spirit," wrote Tyler. Henry's proposals were not unusual; similar measures had been passed in other colonies.

- Tyler suggested that Virginia lawmakers objected "to Patrick Henry himself, and as far as possible to any measure of which he should be the leading champion."

- Henry was thought by many to be too extreme. He was proposing a headlong rush into the unknown, possibly a bloody war. Many of Virginia's lawmakers were wealthy planters who feared that a war with Great Britain would have devastating consequences to their way of life. As Tyler put it:

Patrick Henry, Orator and Statesman

Patrick Henry (1736–1799) was born in Hanover County, Virginia, which at that time was considered frontier territory. It was some distance away from the stately mansions of other notable Virginia families, such as the Washingtons and the Lees. Henry's father, John, was an educated and intelligent man, who was born and raised in Aberdeen, Scotland. He worked at various times as county surveyor, soldier, and judge. Henry's mother was a cheerful and charming woman named Sarah Syme, whose Welsh (from Wales) relatives were famous for their musical and speechmaking abilities. About the young Patrick Henry, biographer Moses Coit Taylor wrote: "He and education never took kindly to each other." Henry was mostly taught at home by his father; his favorite subject was mathematics. In spite of John Henry's lack of money, the lively Henry home was a magnet for visitors, as the senior Henrys entertained often.

At age fifteen, Patrick Henry began his work training at a country store; a year later, he and his brother William opened their own store. William was lazier and more undisciplined than Patrick, and the store lasted only a year. At age eighteen, Henry fell in love with a young lady named Sarah Shelton, who was as poor as he was, and soon they married. Their parents set them up on a small farm, from which they managed to earn a meager living for two years. After a fire destroyed his home, Henry tried storekeeping again, but was no more successful than he had been before. By age twenty-three, with three children to feed and hopelessly in debt, Henry turned to the study of law and began practicing law in 1760. As a lawyer, he finally found an outlet for his speechmaking abilities, and over the next three years he won most of his cases.

Henry's reputation spread throughout Virginia. In 1765, he became a member of the colonial legislature. By age thirty-five, he had six children and was earning barely enough to support them.

As the American Revolution came closer, Henry made outspoken speeches against King George III and called for armed

"Down to that day, no public body in America, and no public man, had openly spoken of a war with Great Britain in any more decisive way than as a thing highly probable, indeed, but still not inevitable." Patrick Henry's famous speech stepped over the line dividing private grumbling about Great Britain from public declarations of war. "The war is coming," he boldly declared; "it has come already."

American statesman Patrick Henry.
Reproduced by permission of the National Portrait Gallery, Smithsonian Institution.

resistance against the British. Henry was very popular with the general public, but his calls for military action were seen as too extreme among his more cautious fellow lawmakers, and he made political enemies. When Virginia lawmakers finally decided to take military action against the British, they gave the military post Henry wanted to

another man. Henry was so angry that he quit his unit in 1776 and went home. He spent most of the remaining years of the war involved in Virginia politics, serving five times as governor.

In 1775, Henry's wife Sarah died. Two years later, he married Dorothea Dandridge, who was half his age and the daughter of a prominent Virginia family (she was the granddaughter of a former governor of Virginia, Alexander Spotswood [1676–1740]; her brother held an important position on the staff of General George Washington [1732–1799]). Henry and his second wife had eleven children together.

By 1786, when he ended his last term as governor, Henry was in poor health, although he was only fifty years old. He stayed active in politics and law for another thirteen years. He finally began to earn large fees from winning lawsuits in front of juries who were impressed by his powerful speaking skills. In his last days, he turned to religion and immersed himself in reading the Bible. He died of cancer in 1799.

Excerpt from "Give me liberty, or give me death!"

*Let us not, I **beseech** you, sir, deceive ourselves longer. Sir, we have done everything that could be done to **avert** the storm which is*

Beseech: Beg.

Avert: Turn away.

Remonstrated: Pleaded in protest.

Supplicated: Asked for in a humble way.

Prostrated: Lain face down.

Implored its interposition: Urgently sought its involvement.

Arrest: Stop.

Ministry: A government department.

Slighted: Overlooked in a discourteous way.

Spurned: Rejected in a rude way.

Inviolate: Intact.

Inestimable: Of a value so great it cannot be calculated.

Contending: Fighting.

Basely: In a shabby way.

God of hosts: God of many.

Formidable an adversary: Awe-inspiring opponent.

Irresolution: Indecision.

Effectual: Effective.

Supinely: Face-up.

Delusive phantom: False or misleading ghost or spirit.

Invincible: Incapable of being defeated.

Vigilant: Watchful

Election: Choice.

Forged: Formed or made.

*now coming on. We have petitioned; we have **remonstrated;** we have **supplicated;** we have **prostrated** ourselves before the throne, and have **implored its interposition** to **arrest** the tyrannical hands of the **ministry** and Parliament. Our petitions have been **slighted;** our remonstrances have produced additional violence and insult; our supplications have been disregarded; and we have been **spurned** with contempt from the foot of the throne.*

*In vain, after these things, may we indulge the fond hope of peace and reconciliation. There is no longer any room for hope. If we wish to be free; if we mean to preserve **inviolate** those **inestimable** privileges for which we have been so long **contending;** if we mean not **basely** to abandon the noble struggle in which we have been so long engaged, and which we have pledged ourselves never to abandon until the glorious object of our contest shall be obtained,—we must fight! I repeat it sir,—we must fight! An appeal to arms, and to the **God of hosts,** is all that is left us.*

[Those who observed Henry's speech say that up to this point he was fairly calm. In the next part of the speech, according to Tyler, "his manner gradually deepened into an intensity of passion and a dramatic power which were overwhelming."]

*They tell us, sir, that we are weak,—unable to cope with so **formidable an adversary.** But when shall we be stronger? Will it be the next week, or the next year? Will it be when we are totally disarmed, and when a British guard shall be stationed in every house? Shall we gather strength by **irresolution** and inaction? Shall we acquire the means of **effectual** resistance by lying **supinely** on our backs, and hugging the **delusive phantom** of Hope, until our enemies shall have bound us hand and foot?*

*Sir, we are not weak, if we make a proper use of those means which the God of nature hath placed in our power. Three millions of people armed in the holy cause of liberty, and in such a country as that which we possess, are **invincible** by any force which our enemy can send against us.*

*Besides, sir, we shall not fight our battles alone. There is a just God who presides over the destinies of nations, and who will raise up friends to fight our battles for us. The battle, sir, is not to the strong alone: it is to the **vigilant,** the active, the brave. Besides, sir, we have no **election.** If we were base enough to desire it, it is now too late to retire from the contest. There is no retreat but in submission and slavery. Our chains are **forged.** Their clanking may be heard on the* *plains of Boston. The war is **inevitable**. And let it come! I repeat it, sir, let it come!*

*It is vain, sir, to **extenuate** the matter. Gentlemen may cry peace, peace, but there is no peace. The war is actually begun. The next **gale** that sweeps from the north will bring to our ears the clash of **resounding arms**. Our **brethren** are already in the **field**. Why stand we here idle? What is it that gentlemen wish? What would they have? Is life so dear, or peace so sweet, as to be purchased at the price of chains and slavery? Forbid it, Almighty God! I know not what course others may take, but as for me, give me liberty, or give me death! (Tyler, pp. 142–45)*

Inevitable: Unavoidable.

Extenuate: Offer excuses in order to lessen the seriousness of something.

Gale: Strong wind.

Resounding arms: Very loud weapons.

Brethren: People who share a common purpose with one another.

Field: Battlefield.

What happened next . . .

Following Henry's speech, his fellow delegates sat in stunned silence for several minutes. They had expected a speech about military preparations, and what they had gotten instead was fiery talk about God, Heaven, slavery, and death. To hold back from war, Henry had grandly said, would be "an act of disloyalty to the majesty of Heaven." Finally, his fellow delegates pulled themselves together and passed Henry's motion, which proposed that Virginia "be immediately put into a posture of defense." Henry was put in charge of the committee to draw up a plan for arming and training Virginia's army of citizen-soldiers.

When Governor Dunmore heard what had taken place at the Virginia Convention, he sent a small group of British soldiers to seize the gunpowder that the revolutionaries had already stored in Williamsburg, Virginia. When hundreds of armed and angry Virginians threatened to take back the powder, Dunmore agreed to pay for the gunpowder but to show who was boss, he declared Patrick Henry an outlaw just as Henry was about to set off for the Second Continental Congress. Unfortunately for Dunmore, he had too few soldiers to pose any real threat to Henry, who appeared and served as a delegate at the Congress in May 1775.

Did you know . . .

- Patrick Henry's reputation as a forceful speaker on behalf of liberty was made on the day he gave this speech. To this day, Henry's "Give me liberty, or give me death" speech continues to be memorized and recited by American schoolchildren. But the speech was never written down by Henry. Different versions were reported by spectators. Historians have debated whether the preceding excerpt contains Henry's actual words, or are only more or less his actual words.

- In his speech, Henry made his own declaration of war against Great Britain. He went on to serve briefly as a soldier in the American Revolutionary War. During the war and after, he served five terms as governor of Virginia. After the war, he argued for the return of property and rights to Americans who had remained loyal to King George III (1738–1820), saying they would make good citizens of the new country.

Where to Learn More

Crompton, Samuel Willard. *100 Colonial Leaders Who Shaped North America*. San Mateo, CA: Bluewood Books, 1999.

Grote, Joann A. *Patrick Henry: American Statesman and Speaker*. New York: Chelsea House, 1999.

Mayer, Henry. *A Son of Thunder: Patrick Henry and the American Republic*. New York: Franklin Watts, 1986.

Sabin, Louis. *Patrick Henry, Voice of American Revolution*. New York: Troll Communications, 1990.

Tyler, Moses Coit. *Patrick Henry*. New York: Ungar, 1966.

Thomas Paine

Common Sense

**First published January 9, 1776; excerpted
from *The Spirit of Seventy-Six*, 1995**

Thomas Paine (1737–1809) first arrived in the American colonies from England in November 1774. This was the same year the Intolerable Acts were passed by Parliament to punish Boston and all of Massachusetts for dumping British tea into Boston Harbor (the Boston Tea Party, December 1773). The Intolerable Acts closed the Port of Boston, gave the British-appointed governor of Massachusetts complete control of town meetings, ordered that British officials who committed major crimes in the colonies would be tried in Great Britain, and required that the colonists house British soldiers in dwellings belonging to private citizens. Boston was suffering from the closure of its port, and the colonies were in an uproar. Colonists wondered who would be next to feel the wrath of Parliament. To show their support and sympathy for Massachusetts, in September 1774, twelve of the thirteen colonies had sent delegates to the First Continental Congress to discuss what to do about deteriorating relations with Great Britain.

In 1774–75, Americans were more or less divided into three groups on the issue of America's relationship with Great

> "Everything that is right or reasonable pleads for separation. The blood of the slain, the weeping voice of nature cries, ''Tis time to part.'"
>
> *Thomas Paine*

Thomas Paine, a Lover of Mankind

Thomas Paine (1737–1809) was born in Thetford, England, on January 29, 1737, the son of a poor farmer and corset maker (a corset is a tight-fitting undergarment). He only attended school until age thirteen, then quit to work with his father. Not finding farming to his liking, Paine quit sometime between the ages of sixteen and nineteen and went to work aboard a privateer. A privateer is a privately owned ship authorized by a government during wartime to attack and capture enemy vessels. At that time England was at war with France. Paine had been brought up to believe in pacifism (the belief that disputes between nations should and can be settled peacefully). His service on the privateer marked a permanent break with that tradition of his youth. In those days, the officers of a ship exercised absolute power over crewmen. The cruelty Paine endured during his eighteen months at sea confirmed his early opinion that power corrupted the people who wielded it.

After leaving the privateer job, for the next twenty-four years, Paine worked a variety of jobs and was unhappy with them all. During these years, he lived in terrible poverty. His first wife died in 1760 and his second wife, whom he married in 1771, left him three years later because he could not support her. All the while, he was educating himself by reading books about politics and the natural sciences.

At some point, he met American statesman Benjamin Franklin in London, England, who suggested he go to Philadelphia, Pennsylvania, and look for work. In 1774, Paine took his advice and sailed for America. Using Franklin's name as a reference, Paine landed a job as a writer. A magazine published his essays attacking slavery and calling for the end of the slave trade. He received widespread recognition for this seventy-nine-page pamphlet *Common Sense,* published in 1776.

Paine spent the rest of the Revolution serving with George Washington's army and writing *The Crisis Papers,* thirteen pamphlets describing the progress of the war. The first was published in December 1776, during one of the darkest moments of the Revolution. It was the dead of winter, and Washington's troops were starving, freezing, and without adequate clothing.

Paine's words were stirring and seemed to have a miraculous effect on Washington's troops. They rallied and won surprise victories at Trenton and Princeton, New Jersey. Over the next seven years Paine continued to write and publish. His last *Crisis Paper* was published on April 19, 1783.

Paine seldom took money for his writings because he said it would cheapen their value. After the war was over, he held a number of political jobs and wrote on

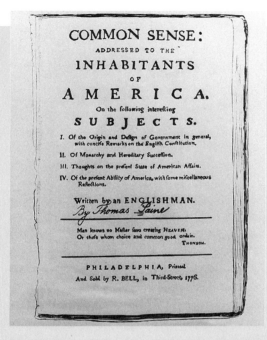

The title page of Thomas Paine's *Common Sense*.
Reproduced by permission of Corbis-Bettmann.

political matters. The issues he embraced included the injustice of slavery, the inferior status of women in society, and the adoption of a strong central government. He also devoted some time to science and his inventions, including the smokeless candle and an iron bridge.

In the 1790s, Paine found himself caught up in quarrels over the French Revolution (1789–99), when the people of France revolted against their king, Louis XVI (1754–1793). Paine was enraged when British politician Edmund Burke wrote a book criticizing the people of France for their revolution. In response, Paine published *The Rights of Man* on March 13,

1791. The book immediately created a sensation both in England and America.

Paine's book defended the French Revolution. The book offered an explanation of the reasons why Europeans were miserable, living as they did in desperate poverty, with no education. As he had done before the American Revolution, Paine spoke out against monarchy (absolute power of a nation by one person). He offered a plan for popular education, relief of the poor, pensions for aged people, and public work for the unemployed. England's leaders felt threatened by his proposals and feared his words would lead to a revolution. The British government ordered Paine's book banned and the publisher jailed. Paine himself was charged with treason, and an order went out for his arrest. But by then he was on his way to France. Paine was tried anyway, found guilty, and declared an outlaw.

In France, Paine was imprisoned for expressing his opinions but was rescued by James Monroe (1758–1831), the American minister to France.

During his last years, Paine continued to write. In one pamphlet, he criticized George Washington, by then a national idol. Many Americans were disgusted by that and he lost his popularity. He died in New Rochelle, New York, on June 8, 1809.

Britain. There were Loyalists, who wished to remain within the British Empire and be governed by Parliament and King George III (1738–1820). There were moderates, who saw that Parliament and the king were trying to exercise more control over America than ever before but hoped a compromise could be reached. And there were Patriots, who mostly still professed allegiance to King George but insisted that he recognize their rights to control their own government. Even though Paine was a newcomer and could not really call himself an American, he became a Patriot. However, Paine aligned himself with the very small group of Patriots who at that time wanted America to proclaim complete independence from Great Britain.

Born and raised in grinding poverty, Paine was a champion of the poor and downtrodden. One of his first published American essays was entitled "African Slavery in America." It established a reputation for him in a small way. Urged to use his talents in the cause of independence, he wrote perhaps his most famous work, *Common Sense,* and published it on January 9, 1776, a little over two months after America received the news that King George considered the colonies to be in a state of rebellion. By the time Paine's pamphlet was published, America and Great Britain had already been fighting for eight months. They would fight another six months before America was able to make a final break and declare its independence. Paine's *Common Sense* gave the more moderate Americans a strong push toward declaring independence.

Common Sense was a history of the dispute between America and Great Britain. It called for American colonists to rise up in rebellion against the British king who was attempting to enslave them and to proclaim their independence. The following excerpt shows that Paine criticized the very idea of a government of the aristocracy—a government run by people of a privileged class. Some historians say that *Common Sense* is not only the most brilliant pamphlet to come out of the American Revolution, it is one of the most brilliant ever written in English. Where other Revolutionary-era writers addressed the most educated people of the day, Paine spoke to ordinary men and women.

Things to remember while reading an excerpt from *Common Sense:*

- In *Common Sense,* Paine addressed those who still thought King George meant well toward the colonies but was being misled by his advisers into adopting harsh laws. Not true, according to Paine; the king was no better than his advisers and probably worse.

- Six months before Paine published *Common Sense,* in July 1775, the Continental Congress had appointed George Washington (1732–1799) commander in chief of a new Continental Army. Although hoping for peace, the Congress was preparing for war. Washington's army was made up of men whose terms of duty were to expire at the end of December 1775. He hoped for something dramatic that would inspire his men to reenlist. *Common Sense* would prove to be the drama Washington was looking for.

Excerpt from Common Sense

*But there is another and greater distinction for which no truly natural or religious reason can be assigned, and that is the distinction of men into kings and **subjects**. Male and female are the distinctions of nature, good and bad the distinctions of heaven; but how a race of men came into the world so **exalted** above the rest, and distinguished like some new species, is worth inquiring into, and whether they are the means of happiness or of misery to mankind.*

*In the early ages of the world, according to the **Scripture chronology** there were no kings; the consequence of which was there were no wars; it is the pride of kings which throws mankind into confusion. Holland without a king hath enjoyed more peace for this last century than any of the **monarchical** governments in Europe. . . .*

*Government by kings was first introduced into the world by the **heathens**, from whom the **children of Israel** copied the custom. It was the most prosperous invention the Devil ever set on foot for the promotion of **idolatry**. The heathens paid divine honors to their deceased kings, and the Christian world has improved on the plan by doing the*

Subjects: Common citizens.

Exalted: Elevated; raised in status.

Scripture chronology: The Bible's version of the arrangement of past events.

Monarchical: Ruled by a king or queen.

Heathens: Non-religious people.

Children of Israel: Descendants of the Biblical figure Jacob, who considered themselves God's chosen people.

Idolatry: A blind or excessive devotion to something.

*same to the living ones. How **impious** is the title of sacred Majesty applied to a worm, who in the midst of his splendor is crumbling into dust!*

As the exalting one man so greatly above the rest cannot be justified on the equal rights of nature, so neither can it be defended on the authority of Scripture; for the will of the Almighty . . . expressly disapproves of government by kings. . . .

[Paine then continues to speak about the evils of monarchy in general. He proceeds to speak specifically about monarchy in England, saying that while "England . . . hath known some few good monarchs . . . [it has] **groaned beneath** a much larger number of bad ones." He goes on to speak of the noble cause of American revolution, saying: "The sun never shined on a cause of greater worth." Paine then has much to say to those who favored patching things up with Britain. He ends his argument by asking and answering the question, Why is reconciliation good for America?]

*I have heard it asserted by some, that as America has flourished under her former connection with Great Britain, the same connection is necessary towards her future happiness, and will always have the same effect. Nothing can be more **fallacious** than this kind of argument. We may as well assert that because a child has thrived upon milk, it is never to have meat, or that the first twenty years of our lives is to become a **precedent** for the next twenty. But even this is admitting more than is true; for I answer **roundly** that America would have flourished as much, and probably much more, had no European power taken any notice of her. The **commerce** by which she hath enriched herself are the necessaries of life, and will always have a market while eating is the custom of Europe. . . .*

*But Britain is the parent country, some say. Then the more shame upon her conduct. Even brutes do not devour their young, nor savages make war upon their families; **wherefore**, the assertion, if true, turns to her **reproach**; but it happens not to be true, or only partly so, and the phrase* parent *or* mother country *hath been **jesuitically** adopted by the king and his **parasites**, with a low . . . design of gaining an unfair bias on the **credulous** weakness of our minds. Europe, and not England, is the parent country of America. This new world hath been the **asylum** for the persecuted lovers of civil and religious liberty from every part of Europe. **Hither** hath they fled, not from the tender embraces of the mother, but from the cruelty of the monster; and it is so far true of England, that the same **tyranny** which drove the first emigrants from home pursues their descendants still. . . .*

Impious: (Pronounced IM-pee-us) Lacking respect.

Groaned beneath: Suffered through.

Fallacious: Misleading.

Precedent: Something to be used as an example in dealing with later actions.

Roundly: With full force.

Commerce: Trade.

Wherefore: Why.

Reproach: Criticism.

Jesuitically: In a way that tries to mislead.

Parasites: Those who take advantage of others' generosity without making any useful return.

Credulous: Believing too readily.

Asylum: Shelter.

Hither: To this place.

Tyranny: A government in which a single ruler holds absolute power.

*I challenge the warmest **advocate** for reconciliation to show a single advantage that this continent can reap by being connected with Great Britain. I repeat the challenge, not a single advantage is derived. Our corn will fetch its price in any market in Europe, and our imported goods must be paid for, buy them where we will.*

*But the injuries and disadvantages which we sustain by that connection are without number; and our duty to mankind at large, as well as to ourselves, instruct us to **renounce** the alliance: because any submission to, or dependence on, Great Britain, tends directly to involve this continent in European wars and quarrels, and set us **at variance** with nations who would otherwise seek our friendship, and against whom we have neither anger nor complaint. As Europe is our market for trade, we ought to form no partial connection with any part of it. 'Tis the true interest of America to steer clear of European **contentions**, which she can never do while by her dependence on Britain she is made the **makeweight** on the scale of British politics.*

*Europe is too thickly planted with kingdoms to be long at peace, and whenever a war breaks out between England and any foreign power, the trade of America goes to ruin, because of her connection with Britain. The next war may not turn out like the last, and should it not, the advocates for reconciliation now will be wishing for a separation then, because **neutrality** in that case would be a **safer convoy than a man of war**. Everything that is right or reasonable pleads for separation. The blood of the slain, the weeping voice of nature cries, "'Tis time to part." Even the distance at which the Almighty hath placed England and America is a strong and natural proof that the authority of the one over the other was never the design of heaven. . . . (Commager and Morris, pp. 286, 288–89)*

Advocate: One who argues for a cause.

Renounce: Give up with a formal announcement.

At variance: In conflict.

Contentions: Rivalries.

Makeweight: Something added on a scale in order to meet a required weight.

Neutrality: Non-involvement.

Safer convoy than a man of war: A safer escort in battle than a combat ship.

What happened next . . .

According to Paine, *Common Sense* sold more than one hundred thousand copies in a few weeks (the total population of the colonies was about three million). Eventually, five hundred thousand copies were sold. In no time, nearly everyone had either read Paine's pamphlet or heard of it, and it was the topic of discussion everywhere. Public opinion in favor of a rebellion against Great Britain was given a huge boost by the publication of *Common Sense.*

Many men joined General Washington's army or reenlisted after hearing what Paine had to say. Washington noted: "I find *Common Sense* is working a powerful change in the minds of men." On January 14, 1776, Washington had 8,212 soldiers in his army. In June 1776, the British prepared to capture New York City and General Washington moved to block them. By that time, Washington had nineteen thousand soldiers, and by the end of August, he had twenty-seven thousand soldiers. (Writer Paul Johnson estimated that "at no point did [Washington's] total forces number more than sixty thousand soldiers.")

In England, reactions to *Common Sense* were favorable among those who already sympathized with the colonists. One such sympathizer was Edmund Burke (1729–1797; author of "On Conciliation," described earlier). Burke called *Common Sense* "that celebrated pamphlet, which prepared the minds of the people for independence." A London newspaper reported that even some Englishmen who had been violently opposed to the idea of American independence were converted by Paine's pamphlet. However, it did not deter King George and Parliament from their goal of putting down the rebellion in America.

Paine had concluded *Common Sense* with the bold suggestion that if America were an independent nation, it could seek help from foreign countries (who would be unwilling to help a country that was a dependent of Great Britain). In February 1776, even before American independence was declared, the Continental Congress sent Congressman Silas Deane (1737–1789) of Connecticut to ask France for help. Thus, Deane became America's first diplomat abroad.

Did you know . . .

- Paine's *Common Sense* was first published anonymously (without his name on it). Immediately a guessing game began. Could it have been written by Benjamin Franklin (1706–1790) or Thomas Jefferson (1743–1826)? John Adams (1735–1826) was another guess. Adams, a Boston lawyer and early leader of the Revolutionary movement, never liked Thomas Paine; he thought Paine was a troublemaker. About *Common Sense,* Adams wrote: "The Arguments in favour of Independence I liked very well." But Adams thought some of Paine's comments were "ridiculous," especially his arguments, based on the Old Testament of the Bible, that a monarchy was unlawful.

- Paine never accepted any payment for his published works because he said it would cheapen their value. But it hurt his vanity that no one knew who had written *Common Sense,* so when the second edition was published in January 1776, Paine signed it "by an Englishman."

- Thomas Paine was a self-educated Englishman, a rebel, and an inventor (a smokeless candle, an iron bridge). Historians say his sympathy for the poor and oppressed sprang from his Quaker upbringing. Quakers are members of the Society of Friends. The Society had a great deal of influence in colonial America. Members believed in peace, justice, charity, spiritual equality, and liberty for all.

- Thomas Paine was a great admirer of most Quaker beliefs, but he objected to their pacifism (pronounced PASS-uh-fiz-um), the belief that disputes between nations should and can be settled peacefully. In fact, he served as a soldier in George Washington's army for a short time before being appointed to a government post by a Continental Congress grateful for his writings on America's behalf.

- Thomas Paine was hugely successful in using the media to change people's minds. Today, the Thomas Paine National Historical Association (TPNHA) annually presents the Thomas Paine Award to a journalist whose work reflects Paine's ideals and commitment to free expression. As Paine said: "When opinions are free . . . truth will prevail." Past winners of the award include Mike Wallace (1918–), of the CBS News television program *60 Minutes*; "Doonesbury" comic strip cartoonist/satirist Garry Trudeau (1948–); CNN correspondent Charlayne Hunter Gault (1942–); and *New York Times* columnist Anthony Lewis (1927–).

Where to Learn More

Commager, Henry Steele, and Richard B. Morris, eds. *The Spirit of 'Seventy-Six: The Story of the American Revolution as Told by Participants.* New York: Da Capo Press, 1995.

Fruchtman, Jack, Jr. *Thomas Paine: Apostle of Freedom*. New York: Four Walls Eight Windows, 1994.

Meltzer, Milton. *Tom Paine: Voice of Revolution*. New York: Franklin Watts, 1996.

Paine, Thomas. *Paine: Collected Writings*. Edited by Eric Foner. New York: Library of America, 1995.

Thomas Paine National Historical Association. [Online] http://www.thomas-paine.com/tpnha (accessed on March 14, 2000).

Great Congressional Documents

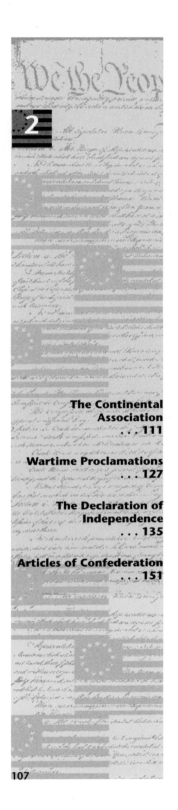

The Continental Association ...111

Wartime Proclamations ...127

The Declaration of Independence ...135

Articles of Confederation ...151

Beginning in 1765, the British government, which was heavily in debt, had tried to tax the American colonies to help pay the bills. The taxes met with increasing resistance until finally, in December 1773, Bostonians dumped 342 chests of British tea into Boston Harbor. This episode became known as the Boston Tea Party. In 1774, the British government passed the Intolerable Acts to punish Boston for the tea party. The Intolerable Acts closed the Port of Boston, gave the British-appointed governor of Massachusetts complete control of town meetings, ordered that British officials who committed major crimes in the colonies would be tried in Great Britain, and required that the colonists house British soldiers in dwellings belonging to private citizens.

Before the passage of the Intolerable Acts, the colonies had gone their separate ways and there had been little sense of unity among them. But as they watched Boston suffer from the closing of its port, the other colonies wondered if they might be the next to suffer from the British forcing taxes and punishments on them. It became clear that something must be done to address these threats from the British in a united way.

First Continental Congress president Peyton Randolph. *Courtesy of the Library of Congress.*

The colonial answer was to send representatives to the First Continental Congress in 1774. The Congress was supposed to make the colonists' feelings known to King George III (1738–1820) and ask him for a remedy. When he failed to respond in a satisfactory way, the Second Continental Congress was formed and met in 1775.

The First Continental Congress met on September 5, 1774, at Carpenter's Hall in Philadelphia, Pennsylvania. Twelve of the thirteen colonies sent delegates to the Congress. Georgia, a small colony with a forceful and popular British-appointed governor, James Wright (1716–1785), chose not to participate this time. Virginia House of Burgesses member Peyton Randolph (c. 1721–1775) (see sidebar entry on Virginia Delegates on p. 114) was named president of the Congress.

Most of the delegates had never met before, and they spent a great deal of time sizing each other up. The participants came with conflicting views about what exactly they were protesting and what they hoped to accomplish at the meeting. But most agreed that matters had reached a point where the colonies no longer needed a "parent"—a "mother country"—and they resented being dominated by Great Britain. The name they chose for themselves, "Continental Congress," suggests that the delegates realized they were on the brink of something huge, something that would finally embrace the entire American continent.

Members of the First Continental Congress could basically be divided into two groups: conservatives, who hoped to patch up the quarrel with England, and radicals—especially the Massachusetts and Virginia delegates—who were determined to resist.

Many issues were discussed, and at considerable length. Delegate John Adams (1735–1826) described the process as "very tedious." But a truly remarkable harmony emerged from the discussions. Resolutions were passed, and "addresses" prepared, which stated the colonies' case to King George and to the people of Great Britain and America. Included in the addresses was a warning to the people of Great Britain: "Take care that you do not fall into the pit that is preparing for us"—a pit in which British citizens would lose their rights and liberty.

The most important document produced by the First Continental Congress was the Continental Association (also called "The Association"). The Continental Association was important because it marked the first time that all the colonies were joined in a common goal—to punish Great Britain in ways that would hurt. The document stated the colonists' complaints and described a boycott of British imports and exports that would remain in effect until their complaints were addressed. (A boycott is a refusal to buy goods from or sell them to another.) The colonies were one of Britain's major trading partners. The delegates believed that the measures adopted by the Association would bring England to the verge of financial ruin in a very short period of time. The Congress adjourned on October 26, 1774, after agreeing to meet on May 10, 1775, if King George did not respond to its complaints in a satisfactory way.

King George did not respond satisfactorily, and the Second Continental Congress came together in May 1775. Many delegates were still not ready for an open break with Great Britain. Congress did take action to put the colonies in a state of readiness for war, however, and it seemed a good idea to make a statement to justify these actions. Two documents were adopted by the Congress soon after it reassembled: the Declaration of the Causes and Necessity of Taking Up Arms and, to please the more conservative, the Olive Branch Petition. The Declaration of the Causes and Necessity of Taking Up Arms justified the actions Congress had already taken to get ready for a possible war. The Olive Branch Petition repeated colonial grievances but declared colonial attachment to King George and expressed a desire for harmony. Following the adoption of these documents, the Second Continental Congress then adjourned on August 2, 1775.

A little more than a month later, the Second Continental Congress came together once again. Delegates learned that King George had rejected the Olive Branch Petition and had proclaimed that the colonies were in a state of rebellion. The Revolutionary Congress continued its discussions, and the following year voted on its second great document, the Declaration of Independence, adopted on July 4, 1776. Its third great document, the Articles of Confederation and Perpetual Union, was adopted on November 15, 1777.

The purpose of the Declaration of Independence was to formally announce to the world that America was withdrawing from the British Empire and to explain the reasons why. But as Congress found itself fully engaged in a war for independence, it became clear that it was impossible to run a war and make quick decisions when each newly created state was operating independently. The need for a government powerful enough to defeat the British led to the adoption of the Articles of Confederation. The Articles served as the basis of government for the new country until the Federal Constitution was adopted in 1788.

The Continental Association

Adopted by the First Continental Congress

**Enacted October 20, 1774; excerpted
from *Documents of American History***

Ever since 1765, the British had been trying to tax the colonies to pay British bills, and discontent gradually spread throughout America. Matters came to a head in December 1773 when Bostonians dumped 342 chests of British tea into Boston Harbor. To punish them, the British Parliament passed the Intolerable Acts in 1774. The Intolerable Acts closed the Port of Boston, gave the British-appointed governor of Massachusetts complete control of town meetings, ordered that British officials who committed major crimes in the colonies would be tried in Great Britain, and required that the colonists house British soldiers in dwellings belonging to private citizens.

The colonies had been established by British merchants as trade ventures and at first the colonies could not have survived without the merchants. But America had grown and prospered, and by 1775, the colonies felt able to survive on their own. They feared that new acts and taxes passed by the British were going to destroy the prosperity the colonies had carefully built up and nurtured for more than a century. Their fears deepened with the punishment of Boston, and so

"To obtain redress of [our] grievances, which threaten destruction to the lives, liberty, and property of his majesty's subjects, in North-America, we are of the opinion, that a non-importation, non-consumption, and non-exportation agreement, faithfully adhered to, will prove the most speedy, effectual, and peaceable measure. . . . "

From the Continental Association

111

King George III, riding his horse. *Reproduced by permission of The Granger Collection Ltd.*

the colonies came together in a Continental Congress to decide how best to express their displeasure to King George III (1738–1820) and Parliament.

It was Virginia delegate Richard Henry Lee (1732–1794; see sidebar on p. 114) who formally proposed the boycott of British goods that is outlined in the Continental Association. A boycott is a refusal to buy, sell, or use certain products from a particular company or country, usually for a political reason. On September 27, 1774, after twenty-two days of discussion and debate over the proposal, the First Continental Congress voted to cut off all trade relations with Great Britain. A committee was appointed to decide how to achieve this goal. The committee prepared the document called the Continental Association, which was signed by congressional representatives on October 20, 1774. Their signatures on this document marked the real beginning of American unity.

The Continental Association begins with an expression of loyalty to King George. It is followed by several grievances (complaints) and then by the specific details of what the colonies planned to do to ensure that their grievances were addressed. They planned to discontinue imports, exports, and the slave trade; they also planned to develop American agriculture and industry to lessen dependence on imported goods.

An important provision of the Continental Association had to do with committees of correspondence. Committees of correspondence already existed in the colonies. Their purpose was the exchange of information at a time in the country's history when producing newspapers was a time-consuming process—newspapers were published weekly. The Continental Association gave the committees of correspondence the power to enforce the measures agreed upon in that document.

Things to remember while reading the Continental Association:

- Even though all the members of Congress signed the Continental Association, they were still deeply divided over the issue of separation or independence from Great Britain. At this point, some were merely hoping for a

Virginia Delegates to the First Continental Congress

Of the fifty-six delegates to the First Continental Congress, the group from Virginia was the most distinguished. The group included Patrick Henry (1736–1799), Richard Henry Lee (1732–1794), Peyton Randolph (c. 1721–1775), and George Washington (1732–1799).

The occasion of the First Continental Congress gave Patrick Henry his first opportunity to show off his speaking skills before a large group of the best-educated and most influential men in the colonies. Some people (who favored a break with England) found Henry's words stirring, while others (who feared a break) found them chilling when he boldly stated, "The distinctions between Virginians, Pennsylvanians, New Yorkers and New Englanders are no more. I am not a Virginian, but an American." With these words, Henry encouraged the delegates to work toward a large and noble purpose and not try to seek advantages for their individual colonies. For example, some larger colonies were seeking to have the number of votes in the Congress be determined by the size of the colony.

Congressman Richard Henry Lee was born into a famous Virginia family and was a close friend of Patrick Henry. In 1752, at the age of twenty, Lee formed his own military group of volunteers. He offered their services to the British during the French and Indian War (1754–63; fought in America by Great Britain and France to decide who would control North America). Lee was insulted when his soldiers were rudely rejected for being amateurs. The experience contributed to his dislike of the British, and he become an outspoken voice in favor of taking strong measures against Great Britain. He suggested the boycott of British goods that is outlined in the Continental Association. Lee became a member of the Virginia Committee of Correspondence, whose duty was to see that Virginians observed the boycott.

Peyton Randolph, who was the first president of the Continental Congress, was descended from an old and distinguished Virginia family. Among the famous American Revolutionary War figures who were connected to the Randolph family was Thomas Jefferson

repeal of the Intolerable Acts, although others, such as John Adams (1735–1826) and Samuel Adams (1722–1803), long had independence in mind.

• An interesting provision of the Continental Association was the agreement to "neither import nor purchase, any

Richard Henry Lee was among the group of distinguished Virginia delegates at the First Continental Congress.

Randolph was a lawyer and a charitable man who helped support the widows and orphans left behind by the French and Indian War. He was a large and imposing figure who commanded the respect and admiration of his peers and was the first choice of delegates to the First Continental Congress to lead them. At the time he was in poor health, and in late 1775 he died suddenly. He was only fifty-four years of age and left no children. His sizable land holdings in Virginia passed to his wife, Betty.

George Washington also came from an old Virginia family. Like Richard Henry Lee, Washington had reason to dislike the British dating back to the French and Indian War. Washington helped the British during that war by leading two companies of Virginia militia (citizen soldiers) into battle. He gained valuable military experience and might have stayed in the militia, but he learned that his rank of lieutenant colonel was going to be reduced so that British officers could always have a higher rank than the colonial officers. He resigned in disgust and held a grudge against the British for this unfair treatment.

(whose mother was born a Randolph). According to his biography in the 21-volume *Dictionary of American Biography*, Randolph was "the most popular leader in Virginia in the decade before the Revolution," and when talk of revolution grew louder, "he was made the presiding officer of every important revolutionary assemblage in Virginia."

slave." At the time, there was heated debate both in Britain and in America over slavery, with people questioning whether it was moral or even whether it was a good business practice. The use of forced labor evolved in the colonies because of labor shortages. This was especially

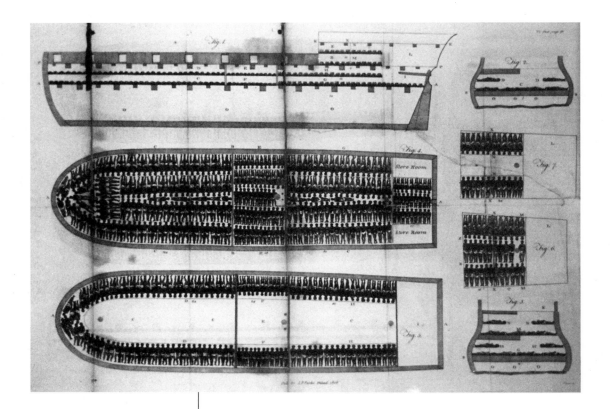

A diagram of a British slave ship, showing the layout for stowing nearly three hundred slaves lying down. British merchants often shipped slaves to the American colonies. *Courtesy of the Library of Congress.*

true in the agricultural southern colonies, but about one-half million slaves were working in all thirteen colonies in 1775. At the time the Continental Association was adopted, greedy London merchants reaped the profit from importing African slaves into the colonies, and they would suffer the most if no slaves were imported. The British also liked to send prisoners to the colonies to work out their punishment as servants. They too fell under the heading of slaves. But for the next several years, the Continental Congress would be far too busy with other matters to deal with the issue of slavery. In fact, it would take nearly a hundred years—and a bloody Civil War (1861–65)—before slavery actually ended in America.

• The provision about rice in the Continental Association came at the urging of South Carolina. That colony's delegates claimed the local economy would be ruined if exports from South Carolina stopped completely. So rice was exempt from the ban on exports.

The Continental Association

*We, his majesty's most loyal subjects, the **delegates** of the several colonies of New-Hampshire, Massachusetts-Bay, Rhode-Island, Connecticut, New-York, New-Jersey, Pennsylvania, the three lower counties of Newcastle, Kent and Sussex on Delaware, Maryland, Virginia, North-Carolina, and South-Carolina, **deputed** to represent them in a continental Congress, held in the city of Philadelphia, on the 5th day of September, 1774, **avowing our allegiance** to his majesty, our affection and regard for our fellow-subjects in Great-Britain and elsewhere, affected with the deepest anxiety, and most alarming **apprehensions,** at those grievances and distresses, with which his Majesty's American subjects are oppressed; and **having taken under our most serious deliberation**, the state of the whole continent, find, that the present unhappy situation of our affairs is **occasioned by a ruinous system of colony administration**, adopted by the British **ministry** about the year 1763, evidently calculated for enslaving these colonies, and, with them, the British Empire. **In prosecution of which system,** various acts of parliament have been passed, for raising a **revenue** in America, for depriving the American subjects, in many instances, of the constitutional trial by jury, exposing their lives to danger, by directing a new and illegal trial beyond the seas, for crimes alleged to have been committed in America: And in prosecution of the same system, several **late,** cruel, and oppressive acts have been passed, **respecting** the town of Boston and the Massachusetts-Bay, and also an act for extending the [boundaries of the] province of Quebec, so as to border on the western frontiers of these colonies, establishing an **arbitrary** government therein, and discouraging the settlement of British subjects in that wide extended country; thus, by the influence of civil principles and ancient prejudices, to dispose the inhabitants to act with hostility against the free Protestant colonies, whenever a wicked ministry shall **chuse** so to direct them.*

*To **obtain redress of** these grievances, which threaten destruction to the lives, liberty, and property of his majesty's subjects, in North-America, we are of the opinion, that a non-importation, **non-consumption**, and non-exportation agreement, **faithfully adhered to,** will prove the most speedy, **effectual**, and peaceable measure: And, therefore, we do, for ourselves, and the inhabitants of the several*

Delegates: Representatives.

Deputed: Appointed.

Avowing our allegiance: Declaring our loyalty.

Apprehensions: Fears.

Having taken under our most serious deliberation: After careful consideration.

Occasioned by a ruinous system of colony administration: Brought on by a destructive way of governing.

Ministry: Government department.

In prosecution of which system: In carrying out this form [of government].

Revenue: A government's income.

Late: Recent.

Respecting: Concerning.

Arbitrary: Not limited by laws.

Chuse: Choose.

Obtain redress of: Make right.

Non-consumption: Not eating, drinking, or using British goods.

Faithfully adhered to: Carried out without change.

Effectual: Effective.

colonies, whom we represent, firmly agree and **associate**, under the sacred ties of virtue, honour and love of our country, as follows:

1. That from and after the first day of December next, we will not import, into British America, from Great-Britain or Ireland, any **goods, wares, or merchandise** whatsoever, or from any other place, any such goods, wares, or merchandise, as shall have been exported from Great-Britain or Ireland; nor will we, after that day, import any East-India tea from any part of the world; nor any molasses, syrups, **paneles**, coffee, or pimento, from the British plantations or from Dominica; nor wines from **Madeira**, or the **Western Islands**; nor foreign **indigo**.

2. We will neither import nor purchase, any slave imported after the first day of December next; after which time, we will wholly discontinue the slave trade, and will neither be concerned in it ourselves, nor will we hire our vessels, nor sell our **commodities** or **manufactures** to those who are concerned in it.

3. As a non-consumption agreement, strictly adhered to, will be an **effectual security for the observation** of the non-importation, we, as above, solemnly agree and associate, that from this day, we will not purchase or use any tea, imported on account of the East-India company, or any on which a **duty hath** been or shall be paid; and from and after the first day of March next, we will not purchase or use any East-India tea whatever; nor will we, nor shall any person for or under us, purchase or use any of those goods, wares, or merchandize, we have agreed not to import, which we shall know, or have cause to suspect, were imported after the first day of December, except such as come under the rules and directions of the tenth article **hereafter mentioned**.

4. The earnest desire we have not to injure our fellow-subjects in Great-Britain, Ireland, or the West-Indies, **induces us to suspend** a non-exportation, until the tenth day of September, 1775; at which time, if the said acts and parts of acts of the British parliament herein after mentioned, are not **repealed**, we will not directly or indirectly, export any merchandize or commodity whatsoever, to Great-Britain, Ireland, or the West-Indies, except rice to Europe.

5. **Such as are merchants**, and use the British and Irish trade, will give orders, as soon as possible, to their **factors, agents and correspondents**, in Great-Britain and Ireland, not to

Associate: Join as partners.

Goods, wares, or merchandise: Items bought and sold in business.

Paneles: Pieces of cloth.

Madeira: (Pronounced ma-DEER-uh) Islands of Portugal.

Western Islands: West Indies.

Indigo: A blue dye obtained from plants.

Commodities: Trade articles.

Manufactures: Finished products made from raw materials.

Effectual security for the observation: Adequate guarantee for the success.

Duty: Tax.

Hath: Has.

Hereafter mentioned: Spoken of later in this document.

Induces us to suspend: Leads us to put off.

Repealed: Done away with.

Such as are merchants: Those who earn a living buying goods and then selling them at a profit.

Factors, agents and correspondents: Those who act for, represent, and communicate with (merchants).

ship any goods to them, on any pretence whatsoever, as they cannot be received in America; and if any merchant, residing in Great-Britain or Ireland, shall directly or indirectly ship any goods, wares or merchandize, for America, in order to break the said non-importation agreement, or in any manner **contravene** the same, **on such unworthy conduct being well attested**, it ought to be made public; and **on the same being so done, we will not, from thenceforth, have any commercial connexion** with such merchant.

6. That such as are owners of vessels will give positive orders to their captains, or masters, not to receive on board their vessels any goods prohibited by the said non-importation agreement, on pain of immediate **dismission** from their service.

7. We will use our **utmost endeavours** to improve the breed of sheep, and increase their number to the greatest extent; and to that end, we will kill them as seldom as may be, especially those of the most profitable kind; nor will we export any to the West-Indies or elsewhere; and those of us, who are or may become overstocked with, or can conveniently spare any sheep, will dispose of them to our neighbours, especially to the poorer sort, on **moderate** terms.

8. We will, in our **several stations**, encourage **frugality, economy, and industry**, and promote agriculture, arts and the manufactures of this country, especially that of wool; and will **discountenance** and discourage every **species** of **extravagance and dissipation**, especially all horse-racing, and all kinds of gaming, **cock fighting**, exhibitions of **shews**, plays, and other expensive diversions and entertainments; and on the death of any relation or friend, none of us, or any of our families will go into any further mourning dress, than a black **crape** or ribbon, on the arm or hat, for gentlemen, and a black ribbon and necklace for ladies, and we will discontinue the giving of gloves and scarves at funerals.

9. Such as are **venders** of goods or merchandize will not take advantage of the scarcity of goods, that may be **occasioned by this association**, but will sell the same at the rates we have been **respectively** accustomed to do, for twelve months last past.—And if any vender of goods or merchandize shall sell such goods on higher terms, or shall, in any manner, or by any device whatsoever, violate or depart from this agreement, no person ought, nor will any of us deal with any such

Contravene: Violate.

On such unworthy conduct being well attested: When these bad acts are found to be true.

On the same being so done, we will not, from thenceforth, have any commercial connexion: When that happens, we will not engage in any further business.

Dismission: Dismissal; firing.

Utmost endeavors: Greatest efforts.

Moderate: Reasonable.

Several stations: Various positions in society.

Frugality, economy, and industry: Spending money and using resources wisely, and working hard.

Discountenance: Disapprove of.

Species: Kind.

Extravagance and dissipation: Flashy luxury and wasteful spending.

Cock fighting: Fighting between two game birds; people gathered to watch and bet on the birds.

Shews: Shows.

Crape: A band of fabric.

Venders: Merchants; sellers.

Occasioned by this association: Brought about by this union of colonies.

Respectively: Individually.

person, or his or her factor or agent, at any time thereafter, for any commodity whatever.

10. In case any merchant, trader, or other person, shall import any goods or merchandize, after the first day of December, and before the first day of February next, the same ought *forthwith*, at the *election* of the owner, to be either re-shipped or delivered up to the committee of the country or town, wherein they shall be imported, to be stored at the *risque* of the importer, until the non-importation agreement shall cease, or be sold under the direction of the committee *aforesaid*; and in the last-mentioned case, the owner or owners of such goods shall be *reimbursed* out of the sales, the first cost and charges, the profit, if any, to be applied towards relieving and employing such poor inhabitants of the town of Boston, as are immediate sufferers by the Boston port-bill; and a particular account of all goods so returned, stored, or sold, to be inserted in the public papers; and if any goods or merchandizes shall be imported after the said first day of February, the same ought forthwith to be sent back again, without breaking any of the packages thereof.

11. That a committee be chosen in every county, city, and town, by those who are qualified to vote for representatives in the legis-lature, whose business it shall be attentively to observe the conduct of all persons *touching* this association; and when it shall be made to appear, to the satisfaction of a majority of any such committee, that any person within the limits of their appointment has violated this association, that such majority do forthwith cause the truth of the case to be published in the *gazette*; to the end, that all such foes to the rights of British-America may be publicly known, and universally *contemned* as the enemies of American liberty; and *thenceforth* we respectively will break off all dealings with him or her.

12. That the committee of correspondence, in the respective colonies, do frequently inspect the *entries of their custom-houses,* and inform each other, from time to time, of the *true state thereof,* and of every other *material circumstance* that may occur relative to this association.

13. That all manufactures of this country be sold at reasonable prices, so that no *undue* advantage be taken of a future scarcity of goods.

Forthwith: At once.

Election: Choice.

Risque: Risk.

Aforesaid: Spoken of earlier.

Reimbursed: Repaid.

Touching: Connected to.

Gazette: Newspaper.

Contemned: Looked upon with contempt; despised.

Thenceforth: From that time forward.

Entries of their customhouses: Items that have been brought in by ships to special buildings, have passed government inspection there, and have been allowed to enter the country.

True state thereof: The real condition of the inspected items.

Material circumstance: Notable situation.

Undue: Unjust or improper.

14. *And we do further agree and resolve, that we will have no trade, commerce, dealings or intercourse whatsoever, with any colony or province, in North-America, which shall not* **accede** *to, or which shall hereafter violate this association, but will hold them as unworthy of the rights of freemen, and as* **inimical** *to the liberties of their country.*

And we do solemnly bind ourselves and our **constituents**, *under the ties* **aforesaid**, *to adhere to this association, until such parts of the several acts of parliament passed since the loss of the last war [French and Indian War], as impose or continue duties on tea, wine, molasses, syrups, paneles, coffee, sugar, pimento, indigo, foreign paper, brass, and painters' colours, imported into America, and extend the powers of the admiralty courts beyond their ancient limits, deprive the American subject of trial by jury, authorize the judge's certificate to indemnify the prosecutor from damages, that he might otherwise be liable to from a trial by his peers, require oppressive security from a claimant of ships or goods seized, before he shall be allowed to defend his property, are repealed.—And until that part of the act of the 12 G. 3. ch. 24, entitled "An act for the better securing his majesty's dock-yards, magazines, ships, ammunition, and stores," by which any persons charged with committing any of the offences therein described, in America, may be tried in any* **shire** *or county within the* **realm**, *is repealed—and until the four acts, passed the last session of parliament,* **viz.** *that for stopping the port and blocking up the harbour of Boston—that for altering the charter and government of the Massachusetts-Bay—and that which is entitled "An act for the better administration of justice,* **&c.**"—*and that "for extending the limits of Quebec,* **&c.**" *are repealed. And we recommend it to the provincial conventions, and to the committees in the respective colonies, to establish such farther regulations as they may think proper, for* **carrying into execution** *this association.*

The foregoing association being determined upon by the Congress, was ordered to be **subscribed** *by the several members thereof; and thereupon, we have hereunto set our respective names accordingly.*

IN CONGRESS, PHILADELPHIA, October 20, 1774.
Signed, PEYTON RANDOLPH, President. (Commager, pp. 84–87)

Accede: (Pronounced ak-SEED) Agree.

Inimical: Harmful or unfriendly.

Constituents: (Pronounced con-STIT-yew-ents) People represented by elected officials.

Aforesaid: Mentioned before.

Shire: British county.

Realm: Kingdom or system of government.

Viz.: From the Latin word *videlicet,* meaning "namely."

&c.: Et cetera.

Carrying into execution: Making (the association) a legal body with complete rules and regulations.

Subscribed: Signed (at the end of a legal document).

The First Continental Congress met from September 5 to October 26, 1774. Its first important document was the Continental Association.
Reproduced by permission of Archive Photos.

What happened next . . .

Members of Congress adjourned the meeting on October 26, 1774, and agreed to meet again on May 10, 1775, if King George did not address their complaints satisfactorily by that date. Their actions had fallen short of an open break with the mother country, but at the same time many people began to realize that the colonies were on the brink of war.

It remained to be seen whether the people of the colonies would agree to live without their usual entertainments and luxuries such as rum, molasses, and sugar. Many citizens everywhere objected to the terms outlined in the document, and the colony of Georgia did not agree to them at all. One colonist complained that the restrictions were so burdensome that he might just as well be a slave. He declared, "If I must be enslaved, let it be by a king at least, and not by a parcel of upstart lawless Committee-men. If I must be devoured, let me be devoured by the jaws of a lion, and not gnawed to [death] by rats and vermin."

John Adams, Founding Father

John Adams (1735–1826) was born in Quincy (then called Braintree), Massachusetts, the first of the three sons of his farmer father, also named John, and the hot-tempered Susanna Boylston Adams. The boy's parents encouraged their independent son to take part in town meetings, teaching him that his conscience must serve as his guide to life. The young Adams was educated at Harvard College (now Harvard University) in Cambridge, Massachusetts, and he began to practice law in 1758. In 1764, he married bright, strong-willed Abigail Smith, who became his lifelong soul mate and intellectual partner.

Adams was an early and eloquent foe of British oppression and one of the foremost agitators for American independence from Britain. A man with a splendid mind, he wrote vivid diaries, letters, and essays and gave patriotic speeches. When war was unavoidable, it was Adams who proposed George Washington to head America's Continental Army, and it was Adams who persuaded Thomas Jefferson to be the chief writer of the Declaration of Independence. Adams helped organize the American army and visited foreign countries to enlist their aid in the battle against Britain. When the war finally ended in 1783, Adams, Benjamin Franklin, and John Jay negotiated the Treaty of Paris (France) that officially ended the Revolutionary War. In 1785, Adams went to England to serve as the first official representative of the newly independent United States. In 1789, Adams was elected vice president under George Washington. He served for eight years before being elected the second president of the United States.

In 1824, Adams had the pleasure of seeing his son, John Quincy Adams, take the oath of office as the sixth president of the United States. On July 4, 1826, the fiftieth anniversary of the Declaration of Independence, ninety-year-old John Adams died at his home.

The committees responsible for enforcing the boycott eagerly went to work to make sure people were complying. Their enforcement methods were often rough—a favorite was tarring and feathering, a rather painful procedure involving covering a person's body with hot tar, then feathers. Before long there were riots in the streets against such tactics. But for the most part, people cooperated by having nothing to do with Great Britain or its goods. Between 1774 and 1775, the value of imports from England decreased by an astonishing 90

John Adams was a key member of the Continental Congress. *Painting by Gilbert Stuart. Courtesy of the Library of Congress.*

percent! The First Continental Congress drew the colonies together in a common cause, in a way colonies had never come together before. This was the most important accomplishment of the First Continental Congress.

As far as Great Britain was concerned, the Continental Congress was an illegal body with no right to meet at all, or to pass laws. The fact that Congress *did* meet showed that Britain was losing its power over the colonies. Charles Lee (1731–1782), who would later become a general on the American side when the war broke out, had friends in Parliament, Great Britain's lawmaking body. In December 1774, he wrote to one of them, Edmund Burke (1729–1797), saying that he had traveled throughout the colonies "and cannot express my astonishment at the unanimous, ardent spirit reigning through the whole. They are determined to sacrifice everything, their property, their wives, children, and blood, rather than cede [give up] a tittle [the tiniest bit] of what they conceive to be their rights. The tyranny exercised over Boston, indeed, seems to be resented by the other colonies in a greater degree than by the Bostonians themselves."

British merchants soon felt the pinch of the boycott. They petitioned Parliament, imploring it to give in to the colonies' demands, repeal the Intolerable Acts, and relieve the merchants' "grievous distress."

Did you know . . .

- Congressman John Adams was an important part of the First Continental Congress. He had long been in the forefront of resistance to British authority. As a delegate from Massachusetts, the colony suffering the most from the Intolerable Acts, Adams had much to gain from steering

John Adams's Writings

John Adams wrote many letters and diary entries describing his journeys to Philadelphia and his attendance at the First and Second Continental Congresses. These writings are considered the liveliest and most enjoyable version of what went on both in and out of Congress. Adams and his fellow Massachusetts delegates left Boston for the first session of the first Congress on August 10, 1774. On their way to Philadelphia, the delegates met people in carriages and on horseback who had come to show their sympathy for Boston and their support for the Congress (Boston was suffering from Great Britain closing Boston's port to all business). Adams stopped in New York City and met some New York delegates for the first time. In his diary, he commented on their homes, their appearance, and their personalities. He also found time to do some sightseeing; he came to the conclusion that New York could not compare to the splendor of Boston, although he did admire its architecture. Here from his diary is his impression of New Yorkers:

> With all the opulence and splendor of this city, there is very little good breeding to be found. We have been treated with [great] respect; but I have not seen one real gentleman, one well-bred man, since I came to town. At their entertainments there is no conversation that is agreeable; there is no modesty, no attention to one another. They talk very loud, very fast, and all together. If they ask you a question, before you can utter three words of your answer they will break out upon you again, and talk away.

Adams threw himself into the work of Congress with his customary dedication. He often grew exasperated at the slow pace of the decision making. His letters to his wife, Abigail Adams (1744–1818), were his main respite from the cares of Congress. The letters mixed political talk with gossip, and expressed his desire to have her with him. (She remained at home in Braintree, Massachusetts, near Boston, with the couple's young children.) In this excerpt from one of his letters to Abigail, Adams expressed his disgust with Congress:

> I wish I had given you a complete history . . . of the behavior of my compatriots. No mortal tale can equal it. [I witness] the fidgets, the whims, the caprice, the vanity, the superstition. . . .

As he confided to his diary, Adams believed that one reason for the slow pace of Congress was that it was made up of men of "wit, sense, learning, acuteness, subtlety, eloquence . . . each of whom has been [accustomed] to lead and guide in his own Province. . . . Every man [was] an orator, a critic, a statesman; and therefore every man upon every question must show his oratory, his criticism, and his political abilities." If "it was moved and seconded that we should come to a resolution that three and two make five," Adams complained, "we should be entertained with logic and rhetoric, law, history, politics, and mathematics, and then—we should pass the resolution, unanimously, in the affirmative."

the delegates in the direction they finally chose—toward opposing royal tyranny and joining in a common cause with Massachusetts. Adams put in many hours helping to compose the documents prepared by the Congress (see sidebar entry on Adams's writings on p. 125).

- Like Adams, Congressman John Hancock (1737–1793) of Massachusetts was an early patriot, and a strong supporter of the boycott of British goods. He was a wealthy merchant who looked upon British customs officials with contempt; they in turn despised him. One of Hancock's first open acts of resistance against British oppression took place in 1768, when customs officials boarded one of his ships and he forcibly removed them. Later, his ship *Liberty* was ordered seized by customs officials, who were attacked by a Boston mob when they docked. Hancock was charged with failing to pay duty on his cargo. His name became a legend among Boston's agitators.

Where to Learn More

Bliven, Bruce. *The American Revolution, 1760–1783.* New York: Random House, 1981.

Burnett, Edmund Cody. *The Continental Congress.* New York: Norton, 1964.

Commager, Henry Steele. *Documents of American History.* New York: Appleton-Century-Crofts, 1958.

Dictionary of American Biography. 21 volumes. New York: Scribner's, 1957.

Draper, Theodore. *A Struggle for Power: The American Revolution.* New York: Times Books, 1996.

"Journals of the Continental Congress—In Thirty-Four Volumes." [Online] http://memory.loc.gov/ammem/amlaw/lwjclink.html (accessed on March 19, 2000).

Marrin, Albert. *The War for Independence: The Story of the American Revolution.* New York: Atheneum, 1988.

Meltzer, Milton, ed. *The American Revolutionaries: A History in Their Own Words, 1750–1800.* New York: HarperTrophy, reprint edition, 1993.

Montross, Lynn. *The Reluctant Rebels: The Story of the Continental Congress, 1774–1789.* New York: Harper & Brothers, 1950.

Wartime Proclamations

Declaration of the Causes and Necessity of Taking Up Arms

The Olive Branch Petition

Adopted by the Second Continental Congress July 1775; excerpted from *Documents of American History*

In London, when King George III (1738–1820) heard of the goings-on in the colonies, he wrote to Lord Frederick North (1732–1792), his prime minister: "The New England governments are in a state of rebellion, blows [war] must decide whether they are to be subject to this country or independent."

George's declaration that "blows must decide" the issue of the colonies' relationship with England ensured that a Second Continental Congress would meet. Since the king would not listen to the colonists' grievances, members of Congress assembled for the second time on May 10, 1775. Massachusetts politician John Hancock (1737–1793) was elected president of the Congress.

The first shots of the American Revolution had been fired at the Battle of Lexington and Concord less than a month earlier, and the Battle of Bunker Hill (in Boston) took place in June 1775, while Congress was meeting. As far as many people were concerned, the war had started. But matters were moving too fast for some members of Congress, who were still deeply divided over the question of separation from England. Two early documents adopted by the Second Continental Congress

"We are reduced to the alternative of chusing an unconditional submission to the tyranny of irritated ministers, or resistance by force.—The latter is our choice."

From the Declaration of the Causes and Necessity of Taking Up Arms

127

Colonists fight with mounted British soldiers at the Battle of Lexington in 1775.
Reproduced by permission of The Granger Collection Ltd.

were the Declaration of the Causes and Necessity of Taking Up Arms and the Olive Branch Petition. The first document justified actions Congress had already taken to get ready for a possible war. The second document offered a way out short of war; it asked King George to put an end to hostile actions until a reconciliation could be worked out. Both documents were written by Continental congressman John Dickinson (1732–1808; see sidebar on p. 131), although fellow congressman Thomas Jefferson (1743–1826) assisted him with the first document.

Things to remember while reading excerpts from the Declaration of the Causes and Necessity of Taking Up Arms and the Olive Branch Petition:

- George Washington (1732–1799) was one of the Virginia delegates to the Continental Congress. He attended sessions wearing his old Virginia militia uniform from the

French and Indian War (1754–63) to show that he was ready to take military action against the British. A militia is a citizen army; its members are not professional soldiers.

- On June 15, 1775, about three weeks before it adopted the Declaration of the Causes and Necessity of Taking Up Arms, Congress named George Washington the commander in chief of a yet-to-be formed Continental Army (its first members were colonial militia men, then fighting at Bunker Hill). Washington made his way to Bunker Hill to assume command of his army. The Declaration of the Causes and Necessity of Taking Up Arms was adopted on July 6 as an address for Washington to deliver to his men.

Excerpt from the Declaration of the Causes and Necessity of Taking Up Arms

*We are reduced to the alternative of **chusing** an **unconditional submission** to the tyranny of **irritated ministers**, or resistance by force.—The latter is our choice.—We have counted the cost of this contest, and find nothing so dreadful as voluntary slavery. . . . Our cause is just. Our union is perfect. Our internal resources are great, and, if necessary, foreign assistance is undoubtedly attainable. . . . With hearts fortified with these **animating reflections**, we most solemnly, before God and the world, declare, that, exerting the utmost energy of those powers, which our **beneficent** Creator hath graciously bestowed upon us, the arms we have been compelled by our enemies to assume, we will, in defiance of every hazard, with unabating firmness and perseverance, employ them for the preservation of our liberties; being with one mind resolved to die freemen rather than to live slaves. (Commager, p. 95)*

Chusing: Choosing.

Unconditional submission: Giving in.

Irritated ministers: Upset members of government.

Animating reflections: Thoughts that keep one's spirits up.

Beneficent: (Pronounced ben-uh-FIH-sunt) Kindly.

Excerpt from the Olive Branch Petition

*Attached to your Majesty's person, family, and government, with all devotion that principle and affection can inspire; connected with Great Britain by the strongest ties that can unite societies, and **deploring** every event that tends in any degree to weaken them, we solemnly assure your Majesty, that we not only most ardently desire the former harmony between her and these Colonies may be restored, but that a **concord** may be established between them upon so firm a basis as to **perpetuate** its blessings, uninterrupted by any future **dissensions** to succeeding generations in both countries, and to transmit your Majesty's name to posterity, adorned with that **signal** and lasting glory that has attended the memory of those **illustrious personages**, whose virtues and abilities have **extricated** states from dangerous **convulsions**, and by securing happiness to others have erected the most noble and durable monuments to their own fame.*

*We therefore beseech your Majesty, that . . . measures may be taken for preventing the further destruction of the lives of your Majesty's subjects; and that such **statutes** as more immediately distress any of your Majesty's Colonies may be repealed. . . . (Commager and Morris, pp. 279–80)*

Deploring: Regretting.

Concord: Agreement.

Perpetuate: Make [its blessings] last forever.

Dissensions: Differences of opinion.

Signal: Extraordinary.

Illustrious personages: Well known and very distinguished persons.

Extricated: Freed.

Convulsions: Violent disturbances or turmoil.

Statutes: Laws.

What happened next . . .

The Olive Branch Petition was adopted and carried to England by Richard Penn, reaching London on August 14, 1775. Penn was a descendant of famous Quaker William Penn (1644–1718), who had founded Pennsylvania, and he was known to be loyal to King George. The king stubbornly refused to look at the document Penn brought. King George considered Congress an illegal body, and any documents Congress produced were illegal documents. On November 9, Congress learned of King George's refusal to look at the Olive Branch Petition (the text of his refusal, called the Proclamation of Rebellion, appears on p. 58). Many Americans who had been uncertain about the wisdom of declaring independence now saw that separation from England was a certainty. King George had left them no choice. Congress met again, as members had

John Dickinson, Man of Contradictions

John Dickinson (1732–1808) was the son of a small-town Maryland judge, and he too studied law, first in Philadelphia, Pennsylvania, and later in London, England. While in England, he grew disenchanted with Parliament, believing its members were corrupt and without talent, and he returned to practice law in Philadelphia. By 1760, he was well known as a talented lawyer, one who could see both sides of controversial issues. In 1760, he was elected to the Delaware legislature, but in 1762 he began to serve in the Pennsylvania legislature.

Dickinson was one of the first people to see the hidden dangers in the Stamp Act of 1765, a prime example of taxation without representation. He wrote several pamphlets suggesting that Britain was trying to "bleed" the colonies into obedience. In 1767, he argued in his *Letters from a Pennsylvania Farmer* that British taxes on the colonies were contrary to natural law and unconstitutional. Yet he continued to work for a reconciliation with England and was seen as a man who, in John Adams's words, held "the Sword in one Hand [and] the Olive Branch [a symbol of peace] in the other."

Continuing to oppose taking up arms against the mother country, Dickinson voted against the Declaration of Independence, yet when war finally came, he was one of only two congressmen who

John Dickinson, one of the earliest opponents of the Stamp Act. *Etching by Albert Roisenthal from painting by Charles Willson Peale. Reproduced by permission of Archive Photos.*

immediately enlisted to fight (Thomas McKean was the other one). He never had to fight, but he was ready to give up his life if necessary.

During and after the war he served in various elective positions, and in 1787, in ill health, he became Delaware's delegate to the convention that drew up the Federal Constitution. He wrote several letters urging the states to adopt the Constitution; these and his many other political writings earned him the title "Penman of the Revolution." After 1787, he took a less active role in politics. He died in Wilmington, Delaware, on Valentine's Day, 1808.

agreed, in the spring of 1776. This meeting soon led to the adoption of the Declaration of Independence.

Did you know . . .

- John Dickinson, author of the Declaration of the Causes and Necessity of Taking Up Arms and the Olive Branch Petition, strongly opposed all the taxes placed by the British on Americans, and was famous and popular for his *Letters from a Farmer in Pennsylvania to the Inhabitants of the British Colonies* in 1767 (see p. 63). However, as a Quaker, he objected to using force against the mother country, and he lost popularity because of this position.

- Massachusetts politician John Adams (1735–1826) made fun of Dickinson and his Olive Branch Petition in his *Autobiography*. He accused Dickinson and others like him in Congress of trying "to oppose . . . the Independence of the Country." Adams wrote that other Quakers had gone to Dickinson's wife and mother and urged them to influence Dickinson to oppose war with England. According to Adams, Dickinson's mother warned her son that if he offended England, "Johnny you will be hanged, your Estate will be forfeited and [taken away], you will leave your Excellent Wife a Widow and your charming Children Orphans, Beggars and infamous." Adams wrote his *Autobiography* long after these events took place. It was intended for the enjoyment of his family, not for publication, so he had no qualms about making comments like this. Adams's grandson, Charles Francis Adams (1807–1886), published his grandfather's writings in the 1850s, nearly forty years after his grandfather died.

- The olive branch appears in the biblical story of Noah and his ark. The olive branch was brought by a dove to Noah to let him know that the forty-day flood he had endured was about to end. The olive branch—and the dove—later came to be regarded as symbols of peace.

Where to Learn More

Bliven, Bruce. *The American Revolution, 1760–1783*. New York: Random House, 1981.

Burnett, Edmund Cody. *The Continental Congress.* New York: Norton, 1964.

Commager, Henry Steele, and Richard B. Morris, eds. *The Spirit of 'Seventy-Six: The Story of the American Revolution as Told by Participants.* New York: Da Capo Press, 1995.

Dictionary of American Biography. 21 volumes. New York: Scribner's, 1957.

Draper, Theodore. *A Struggle for Power: the American Revolution.* New York: Times Books, 1996.

"Journals of the Continental Congress—In Thirty-Four Volumes." [Online] http://memory.loc.gov/ammem/amlaw/lwjclink.html (accessed on March 19, 2000).

Marrin, Albert. *The War for Independence: The Story of the American Revolution.* New York: Atheneum, 1988.

Meltzer, Milton, ed. *The American Revolutionaries: A History in Their Own Words, 1750–1800.* New York: HarperTrophy, reprint edition, October 1993.

Montross, Lynn. *The Reluctant Rebels: The Story of the Continental Congress, 1774–1789.* New York: Harper & Brothers, 1950.

The Declaration of Independence

Adopted by the Second Continental Congress

Enacted July 3, 1776; excerpted from the National Archives and Records Administration

By the spring of 1776, the Second Continental Congress was still debating over the next step to take in light of the decision of King George III (1738–1820) that "blows [war] must decide" the disagreement with the colonies. Independence from Great Britain was still considered an extreme step by many delegates. Congressmen wondered how they would explain the disagreement to the public, who were still loyal to King George, if not to Parliament. But finally, on June 7, 1776, Virginia statesman Richard Henry Lee (1732–1794) urged Congress to declare independence, presenting a motion that had been adopted by his home state. The motion said:

> *Resolved, that these United Colonies are, and of right ought to be, free and independent States, that they are absolved from all allegiance to the British Crown, and that all political connection between them and the state of Great Britain is, and ought to be totally dissolved.*

Congress then elected five men—Thomas Jefferson (1743–1826) of Virginia, John Adams (1735–1826) of Massachusetts, Benjamin Franklin (1706–1790) of Pennsylvania, Roger Sherman (1721–1793) of Connecticut, and Robert Livingston (1746–1813) of New York—to draw up a declaration of

"We hold these truths to be self-evident, that all men are created equal, that they are endowed by their Creator with certain unalienable Rights, that among these are Life, Liberty and the Pursuit of Happiness."

From the Declaration of Independence

Robert Livingston, congressman from New York and one of five men elected to create a declaration of independence. *Courtesy of the Library of Congress.*

independence. The Committee of Five, as they were called, went to work to produce one of the greatest documents to come out of the Congress, the Declaration of Independence (1776). Historians generally agree that while it is considered a landmark document today, the Declaration of Independence was regarded as nothing special at the time it was written, and it was more or less forgotten until years after the Revolution ended.

Thomas Jefferson, Foremost Spokesman for Freedom

Thomas Jefferson (1743–1826) was the son of Peter Jefferson, a surveyor (he made the first accurate map of Virginia) and a landowner, and Jane Randolph, of the famous Virginia Randolph family. The family was not wealthy, but through his mother Thomas was connected to some of the most distinguished people in the colonies. He studied at Virginia's College of William and Mary, and in 1767 began to practice law. His courtroom career was hampered by his weak voice and lack of speaking skills, but he made a name for himself as a writer and revolutionary when his *Summary View of the Rights of British America* was published in 1774.

In 1770, Jefferson began designing and building Monticello, an estate near his family home. In 1772 he brought his new wife, Martha Wyles Skelton, to Monticello. The couple had six children; only two lived to maturity, and Martha died in 1782. Jefferson attended the First (1774) and Second Continental Congresses (1775–77), was the chief writer of the Declaration of Independence, and returned to Virginia to serve in the legislature (1776–79) and then as governor (1779–81). He never fought in the war; he did not have a taste for a soldier's duties.

From 1783 to 1789, Jefferson carried out various functions for the newly formed United States before being appointed George Washington's secretary of state. Jefferson resigned in 1793 and returned to Monticello. Three years later,

Thomas Jefferson, one of America's greatest early leaders. *Courtesy of the Library of Congress.*

he became vice president under John Adams, then beat Adams to serve two terms as America's third president (1801–9). As president, he more than doubled the size of the United States with the Louisiana Purchase, then sponsored the Lewis and Clark Expedition, a journey to explore the American Northwest, newly purchased from France. He retired to Monticello for the last time in 1809, where he devoted himself to his many different interests, including science, architecture, and education. He died on July 4, 1826, the fiftieth anniversary of the adoption of the Declaration of Independence, and the same day that John Adams died. Jefferson is remembered today as one of the greatest of all Americans.

John Adams had such a strong personality that he dominated the Committee of Five. He wrote in his *Autobiography* that he chose Jefferson to write the Declaration of Independence because Jefferson "had the Reputation of a masterly Pen." Up until that time, according to Adams, the thirty-three-year-old Jefferson had not spoken "three Sentences together" in Congress. He disliked public speaking—apparently his voice was weak—but he was well read and an eloquent writer.

The Declaration was a formal announcement by thirteen formerly separate colonies (Georgia had joined the group) that they now considered themselves an independent and united nation. The Declaration offered the reasons why a separation from Great Britain was necessary, and it laid out the truths for which the Revolutionary War was fought.

The text of the Declaration of Independence can be divided into five sections. First is the introduction (the first paragraph). It states that the quarrel between the two unnamed nations is not a small squabble but is a major event in world history. Next comes the preamble. Still without mentioning Great Britain and America by name, the preamble outlines a way of thinking about government that makes a revolution right and good. The third and fourth sections accuse King George and the British people of specific wrongs against America. The fifth section, the conclusion, ends with the powerful phrase "we mutually pledge to each other our Lives, our Fortunes, and our sacred Honor." Honor—which can mean esteem, respect, reverence, reputation, or good name—was considered an important virtue in the eighteenth century.

Things to remember while reading the Declaration of Independence:

- Jefferson refers in his opening paragraph to "a decent respect to the opinions of mankind," which required the colonies to "declare the causes which impel them to the separation." He was explaining that the purpose of the Declaration of Independence was to formally announce to the whole world that there was no possibility of reconciling with Great Britain, that America was withdrawing from the British Empire, and to explain the reasons why.

- America's first diplomat abroad, Silas Deane (1737–1789) of Connecticut, had sailed for France in April 1776 to explore the possibilities of an alliance in the event of war. In the early stages of the conflict between America and Britain, France was not very receptive to the idea of giving help to the colonists. France wanted to be sure the colonies were really seeking independence, and that the colonies were capable of putting up a long, effective fight to attain it. The French were not anxious to get into a fight with Great Britain and then find that the colonies were no longer involved. The Declaration of Independence was a way of showing the French that America was serious about independence. The French did send some secret aid, but they did not get openly involved until General George Washington (1732–1799) won decisive victories at Trenton and Princeton, New Jersey, in the winter of 1776–77.

The Declaration of Independence

The unanimous Declaration of the thirteen united States of America,

*When in the Course of human events, it becomes necessary for one people to dissolve the political bands which have connected them with another, and to assume among the powers of the earth, the separate and equal station to which the Laws of Nature and of Nature's God entitle them, a decent respect to the opinions of mankind requires that they should declare the causes which **impel** them to the separation.*

We hold these truths to be self-evident,** that all men are created equal, that they are **endowed** by their Creator with certain **unalienable Rights**, that among these are Life, Liberty and the Pursuit of Happiness.—That to **secure** these rights. **Governments are instituted among Men, deriving their just powers from the consent of the governed,

*—That whenever any Form of Government becomes destructive of these **ends**, it is the Right of the People to alter or to **abolish** it, and to*

Impel: Force.

We hold these truths to be self-evident: We assert that the truths stated here require no proof or explanation.

Endowed: Provided.

Unalienable Rights: Rights that cannot be given away or taken away.

Secure: Guard from the risk of loss.

Governments are instituted among Men, deriving their just powers from the consent of the governed: The authority of a government depends on the approval of the people.

Ends: Goals or obligations.

Abolish: Do away with.

Effect: Bring about.

Prudence: Careful management.

Transient: Passing quickly.

Mankind are more disposed to suffer, while evils are sufferable, than to right themselves by abolishing the forms to which they are accustomed: People will put up with bad things as long as they can, before they will try to make matters better by doing away with the form of government they are used to.

Usurpations: Illegal possession of something that belongs to another.

Pursuing invariably the same Object evinces a design to reduce them under absolute Despotism: The purpose of the acts committed against them is to force the people to accept the rule of a governing body against their will.

Sufferance: Toleration of pain or distress.

Constrains: Forces.

Tyranny: Unjust power.

Candid: Fair, impartial.

Inestimable: Of a value that is so great it cannot be calculated.

Formidable: Arousing fear.

Fatiguing them into compliance: Getting them to go along by tiring them.

Annihilation: Abolishment.

Convulsions: Violent disturbances.

*institute new Government, laying its foundation on such principles, and organizing its powers in such form, as to them shall seem most likely to **effect** their Safety and Happiness. **Prudence,** indeed will dictate that Governments long established should not be changed for light and **transient** causes; and accordingly all experience hath shewn, that **mankind are more disposed to suffer, while evils are sufferable, than to right themselves by abolishing the forms to which they are accustomed.** But when a long train of abuses and **usurpations,** pursuing invariably the same Object evinces a design to reduce them under absolute Despotism, it is their right, it is their duty, to throw off such Government, and to provide new Guards for their future Security.—Such has been the patient **sufferance** of these Colonies; and such is now the necessity which **constrains** them to alter their former Systems of Government. The history of the present King of Great Britain is a history of repeated injuries and usurpations, all having in direct object the establishment of an absolute **Tyranny** over these States. To prove this, let Facts be submitted to a **candid** world.*

> *He has refused his Assent to Laws, the most wholesome and necessary for the public good.*

> *He has forbidden his Governors to pass Laws of immediate and pressing importance, unless suspended in their operation till his Assent should be obtained; and when so suspended, he has utterly neglected to attend to them.*

> *He has refused to pass other Laws for the accommodation of large districts of people, unless those people would relinquish the Right of Representation in the Legislature, a right **inestimable** to them and **formidable** to tyrants only.*

> *He has called together legislative bodies at places unusual, uncomfortable, and distant from the depository of their public Records, for the sole purpose of **fatiguing them into compliance** with his measures.*

> *He has dissolved Representative Houses repeatedly, for opposing with manly firmness his invasions on the rights of the people.*

> *He has refused for a long time, after such dissolutions, to cause others to be elected; whereby the Legislative powers, incapable of **Annihilation,** have returned to the People at large for their exercise; the State remaining in the mean time exposed to all the dangers of invasion from without, and **convulsions** within.*

Rough draft of the original Declaration of Independence. *Courtesy of the Library of Congress.*

*He has endeavoured to prevent the population of these States; for that purpose obstructing the **Laws for Naturalization of Foreigners**; refusing to pass others to encourage their migrations hither, and raising the conditions of new Appropriations of Lands.*

He has obstructed the Administration of Justice, by refusing his Assent to Laws for establishing Judiciary powers.

Laws for Naturalization of Foreigners: Laws granting citizenship to the foreign-born.

*He has made Judges dependent on his Will alone, for the **tenure of their offices**, and the amount and payment of their salaries.*

*He has erected a multitude of New Offices, and sent hither swarms of Officers to **harrass** our people, and **eat out their substance.***

He has kept among us, in times of peace, Standing Armies without the Consent of our legislatures.

He has affected to render the Military independent of and superior to the Civil power.

He has combined with others to subject us to a jurisdiction foreign to our constitution, and unacknowledged by our laws; giving his Assent to their Acts of pretended Legislation:

For Quartering large bodies of armed troops among us:

For protecting them, by a mock Trial, from punishment for any Murders which they should commit on the Inhabitants of these States:

For cutting off our Trade with all parts of the world:

For imposing Taxes on us without our Consent:

For depriving us in many cases, of the benefits of Trial by Jury:

For transporting us beyond Seas to be tried for pretended offences:

For abolishing the free System of English Laws in a neighbouring Province, establishing therein an Arbitrary government, and enlarging its Boundaries so as to render it at once an example and fit instrument for introducing the same absolute rule into these Colonies:

For taking away our Charters, abolishing our most valuable Laws, and altering fundamentally the Forms of our Governments:

For suspending our own Legislatures, and declaring themselves invested with power to legislate for us in all cases whatsoever.

He has abdicated Government here, by declaring us out of his Protection and waging War against us.

He has plundered our seas, ravaged our Coasts, burnt our towns, and destroyed the lives of our people.

Tenure of their offices: The terms under which they hold their positions.

Harrass: Harass; to disturb or irritate in a persistent way.

Eat out their substance: Use up all their supplies (by the terms of the Quartering Act).

He is at this time transporting large Armies of foreign **Mercenaries** to compleat the works of death, desolation and tyranny, already begun with circumstances of Cruelty & **perfidy** scarcely paralleled in the most barbarous ages, and totally unworthy of the Head of a civilized nation.

He has constrained our fellow Citizens taken Captive on the **high Seas** to bear Arms against their Country, to become the executioners of their friends and Brethren, or to fall themselves by their Hands.

He has excited **domestic insurrections** amongst us, and has endeavoured to bring on the inhabitants of our frontiers, the merciless Indian Savages, whose known rule of warfare, is an **undistinguished destruction,** of all ages, sexes and conditions.

In every stage of these Oppressions We have Petitioned **for Redress** in the most humble terms: Our repeated Petitions have been answered only by repeated injury. A Prince whose character is thus marked by every act which may define a Tyrant, is unfit to be the ruler of a free people.

Nor have We been **wanting** in attentions to our British brethren. We have warned them from time to time of attempts by their legislature to extend an **unwarrantable** jurisdiction over us. We have reminded them of the circumstances of our emigration and settlement here. We have appealed to their native justice and **magnanimity,** and we have **conjured** them by the ties of our common kindred to **disavow these usurpations,** which, would inevitably interrupt our connections and correspondence. They too have been deaf to the voice of justice and of **consanguinity.** We must, therefore, **acquiesce** in the necessity, which **denounces** our Separation, and hold them, as we hold the rest of mankind, Enemies in War, in Peace Friends.

We, therefore, the Representatives of the united States of America, in General Congress Assembled, appealing to the Supreme Judge of the world for the **rectitude** of our intentions, do, in the Name, and by the Authority of the good People of these Colonies, solemnly publish and declare, That these United Colonies are, and of Right ought to be Free and Independent States; that they are Absolved from all Allegiance to the British Crown, and that all political connection between them and the State of Great Britain, is and ought to be totally dissolved; and that as Free and Independent States, they have full Power to levy War, conclude Peace, contract Alliances, establish Commerce, and to do all other Acts and Things which Independent

Mercenaries: Hired soldiers.

Perfidy: Treachery, betrayal.

High Seas: Open waters that no nation controls.

Domestic insurrections: Revolts at home.

Undistinguished destruction: Destruction without regard to (age, sex, and conditions).

For Redress: That it be made right.

Wanting: Lacking.

Unwarrantable: Unjustified; inexcusable.

Magnanimity: (Pronounced mag-nuh-NIH-muh-tee) Generosity.

Conjured: Called upon.

Disavow these usurpations: End the illegal attacks on privileges belonging to another.

Consanguinity: (Pronounced kon-sang-GWIN-uh-tee) Blood relationship.

Acquiesce: (Pronounced ak-wee-ESS) Agree to without protest.

Denounces: Formally announces.

Rectitude: Rightness.

**The signing of the
Declaration of
Independence.**
*Painting by John Trumbull.
Courtesy of the National
Archives and Records
Administration.*

States may of right do. And for the support of this Declaration, with a firm reliance on the protection of divine Providence, we mutually pledge to each other our Lives, our Fortunes and our sacred Honor.

[The Declaration of Independence was signed by fifty-six representatives of the thirteen colonies. In alphabetical order by state, they were:

Connecticut: Samuel Huntington, Roger Sherman, William Williams, and Oliver Wolcott; Delaware: Thomas McKean, George Read, and Caesar Rodney; Georgia: Button Gwinnett, Lyman Hall, and George Walton; Maryland: Charles Carroll, Samuel Chase, William Paca, and Thomas Stone; Massachusetts: John Adams, Samuel Adams, Elbridge Gerry, John Hancock, and Robert Treat Paine; New Hampshire: Josiah Bartlett, Matthew Thornton, and William Whipple; New Jersey: Abraham Clark, John Hart, Francis Hopkinson, Richard Stockton, and John Witherspoon; New York: William Floyd, Francis Lewis, Philip Livingston, and Lewis Morris; North Carolina: Joseph Hewes, William Hooper, and John Penn; Pennsylvania:

"Remember the Ladies"

Even before the American colonies formally declared independence, members of the Continental Congresses had been discussing what form a new government should take. While Congressman John Adams was in Philadelphia, Pennsylvania, in 1775 considering this and other questions, he received a letter from his wife, Abigail, offering her opinion:

> In the new code of laws which I suppose it will be necessary for you to make, I desire you would remember the ladies and be more generous and favorable to them than your ancestors. Do not put such unlimited power into the hands of the husbands. Remember, all men would be tyrants if they could. If particular care and attention is not paid to the ladies, we are determined to foment [stir up] a rebellion, and will not hold ourselves bound by any laws in which we have no voice or representation.

Abigail Adams, who urged her husband, John, to "remember the ladies" when deciding how the new government should look.
Reproduced by permission of the National Portrait Gallery, Smithsonian Institution.

These were bold words coming from a woman of the eighteenth century! John Adams responded that her words made him laugh. "Depend upon it," he replied, "we know better than to repeal our masculine systems." To this Abigail Adams responded: "I can not say I think you very generous to the Ladies, for whilst you are proclaiming peace and good will to Men, Emancipating [setting free] all Nations, you insist upon retaining an absolute power over Wives. But you must remember that Arbitrary power [based on whims] is like most things which are very hard, very liable to be broken. . . . "

George Clymer, Benjamin Franklin, Robert Morris, John Morton, George Ross, Benjamin Rush, James Smith, George Taylor, and James Wilson; Rhode Island: William Ellery and Stephen Hopkins; South Carolina: Thomas Heyward, Jr., Thomas Lynch, Jr., Arthur Middleton, and Edward Rutledge; and Virginia: Carter Braxton, Benjamin Harrison,

Thomas Jefferson, Francis Lightfoot Lee, Richard Henry Lee, Thomas Nelson, Jr., and George Wythe.] (National Archives and Records Administration web site)

What happened next . . .

Members of the Continental Congress approved the Declaration of Independence on July 4, 1776. Church bells rang out over Philadelphia to announce the historic event. John Adams wrote to his wife, Abigail Adams (1744–1818), "Yesterday the greatest question was decided which ever was debated in America, and a greater, perhaps, never was nor will be decided among men. . . . Britain has been filled with folly, and America with wisdom."

On July 5, the Committee of Five took Jefferson's rough draft to a printer, who made several copies to be sent to various groups for examination. On July 19, Congress ordered that parchment copies be drawn up and signed by every member of Congress. (Parchment is a surface for writing, often made from sheepskin or goatskin.) The actual signing by most members of the Continental Congress took place on August 2, 1776 (some members were not present on that day and signed later).

Congress president John Hancock (1737–1793) was the first to sign the Declaration of Independence, and he did so in a big, bold hand (remarking, some say, that he wrote large "so the king doesn't have to put on his glasses.") The secretary of Congress, Charles Thomson, signed as a witness to Hancock's signature. The other delegates signed the document beginning at the right, below the text, in order according to the geographic location of the states (as they would now be called) they represented. New Hampshire, the northernmost state, went first. Georgia, the southernmost state, went last. John Dickinson (1732–1808) of Pennsylvania, and Robert R. Livingston (1746–1813) of New York, refused to sign. Dickinson still hoped for a peace with Britain, and Livingston, who was one of the Committee of Five, thought it was too soon for such a document to be adopted.

Copies of this first printing were sent around to the former colonies, now states, but the names of the signers were kept secret. These men were sure to lose their lives at the hands of the British if the new country failed to win independence. But then, on January 18, 1777, after the Continental (American) Army won major victories at Trenton and Princeton, New Jersey, members of Congress ordered a second printing of the Declaration. This copy, complete with the names of all the signers, was printed by Baltimore newspaper publisher Mary Katherine Goddard (1736–1816).

Did you know . . .

- The Continental Congress rejected two parts of Thomas Jefferson's original draft of the Declaration of Independence. One of the passages referred to the English people in words the Congress thought were too strong. The other passage denounced the slave trade. Ironically, Thomas Jefferson was himself a slave owner.

- When the document was read in New York on July 9, patriots became so enthusiastic that they tore down a statue of King George (the lead statue was melted down to make bullets—an estimated forty-two thousand of them).

- Throughout history, the term "men" has often been used to refer to people in general. However, when the Declaration of Independence stated that "all men are created equal," it referred only to white men, not women or slaves. It took the Civil War (1861–65) to end slavery, and black men were granted the right to vote in 1870. Women were not granted the right to vote until 1920.

- In the early days of the new United States of America, there were no official government buildings in which to store the Declaration of Independence. Instead, it traveled with the Continental Congress as that body, threatened by the British, moved from place to place during the Revolutionary War. The document had many homes before it moved

John Hancock, the first person to sign the Declaration of Independence.
Reproduced by permission of The Granger Collection Ltd.

John Hancock, Patriot

John Hancock (1737–1793) was born in Quincy (then called Braintree), Massachusetts, two years after John Adams was born in the same town. Hancock's father was a clergyman who left John an orphan at an early age. He was adopted by his uncle, Thomas Hancock, and inherited his uncle's merchant business in 1764, thereby becoming one of the richest men in Boston. Like John Adams, he had graduated from Massachusetts's Harvard College in 1754. He joined with Samuel Adams and John Adams in opposing the Stamp Act in 1765, and then took to smuggling to show his opposition to the Townshend Acts.

Hancock was a member of both the First and Second Continental Congresses and was the first member to sign the Declaration of Independence. He led six thousand Massachusetts troops in fighting the British in Rhode Island in 1778, but he was not considered a very good soldier. In 1780, he became the first governor of Massachusetts. He held that position off and on (he once resigned for health reasons) until his death in 1793. At the same time, he played an important role in getting the U.S. Constitution ratified

to its permanent site in Washington, D.C., in 1952. During World War II (1939–45), it was placed at Fort Knox in northern Kentucky, the heavily guarded storehouse for the country's supply of gold.

• The original Declaration of Independence is now housed in the National Archives Building in Washington, D.C. The document is badly faded because of the poor care it received throughout the nineteenth century. Today it is showcased during the daytime with other important records chronicling the growth of the United States. At night, it moves into an underground vault for safekeeping.

Where to Learn More

Adams, Charles Francis, ed. *The Works of John Adams, Second President of the United States: With a Life of the Author, Notes and Illustrations.* 10 vols. Boston: Little, Brown and Company, 1850–1856. Excerpted in *The Spirit of Seventy-Six: The Story of the American Revolution as Told by Participants.* Bicentennial edition. Edited by Henry Steele Commager and Richard B. Morris. New York: Harper-Row, 1975.

Adams, John. *The John Adams Papers.* Selected, edited, and interpreted by Frank Donovan. New York: Dodd, 1965.

Bober, Natalie. *Abigail Adams: Witness to a Revolution.* New York: Atheneum Books for Young Readers, 1995.

Bober, Natalie. *Thomas Jefferson: Man on a Mountain.* Aladdin Paperbacks, 1997.

Bruns, Roger, ed. *Thomas Jefferson.* New York: Chelsea House, 1987.

"Declaration of Independence." Surfing the Net with Kids. [Online] http://surfnetkids.com/declaration.htm (accessed on April 4, 2000).

"The Declaration of Independence: A History" and "The Writing and Publicizing of the Declaration of Independence, the Articles of Confederation, and the Constitution of the United States." National Archives and Records Administration, Exhibit Hall. [Online] http://www.nara.gov/exhall/exhibits.html (accessed on April 4, 2000).

Ferling, John E. *John Adams: A Life*. New York: Henry Holt, 1996.

Meltzer, Milton. *Thomas Jefferson: The Revolutionary Aristocrat*. New York: Franklin Watts, 1991.

Monticello: The Home of Thomas Jefferson. Offers "A Day in the Life" tour through the daily activities of Jefferson at home. [Online] www.monticello.org (accessed on March 13, 2000).

Morse, John T., Jr. *Thomas Jefferson* (American Statesmen Series, Vol. 11). New York: Chelsea House, 1997.

Nardo, Don. *The Importance of Thomas Jefferson*. San Diego: Lucent Books, 1993.

Rayner, B. L. *Life of Thomas Jefferson*. Revised and edited by Eyler Robert Coates, Sr. [Online] http://www.geocities.com/Athens/Forum/1683/ljindex.htm (accessed on March 13, 2000).

"Thomas Jefferson Memorial." [Online] www.nps.gov/thje/index2.htm (accessed on March 13, 2000).

Articles of Confederation

Issued by the Second Continental Congress

*Agreed to November 15, 1777; ratified
and in effect March 1, 1781*

Excerpted from *American Memory* (CD-ROM)

Before the United States declared its independence in July 1776, each colony ran its own affairs. The closest thing the colonies had to a national government was the British Parliament. After their bad experiences with Parliament, which led to the outbreak of revolution, the colonies were not inclined to trust a strong national government; they preferred to keep power for themselves. But after declaring independence from England and its laws, Congress knew itself to be just a group of men without clearly defined authority or a constitution that would make Congress a legal body. This was going to make it very difficult to run a war.

Clearly, some kind of document was needed to help guide the new states through a war and the formation of a new country. Richard Henry Lee (1732–1794) proposed the Articles of Confederation and Perpetual Union (usually referred to simply as the Articles of Confederation) at the same time he offered the resolution for independence (June 1776) quoted earlier. A month later, John Dickinson (1732–1808) was appointed to a committee to study the idea of confederation (the union of a group of states for a common purpose). After a

"The said States hereby severally enter into a firm league of friendship with each other, for their common defense, the security of their liberties, and their mutual and general welfare, binding themselves to assist each other, against all force offered to, or attacks made upon them, or any of them, on account of religion, sovereignty, trade, or any other pretense whatever."

From the Articles of Confederation

month of study, the first draft of the Articles was presented to Congress for consideration and adoption.

The first draft provided for a strong central government. Congress adopted a revised draft on November 15, 1777, that seemed to give the federal government many powers but actually made it secondary to the states.

Under the proposed Articles of Confederation, the states agreed to defend one another against outside threats. Citizens of each state would enjoy the same rights and privileges in every state, including the freedom to come and go from one state to another. There would be free trade among states, with no one paying higher taxes on trade than anyone else. The Articles also proposed a common treasury to pay for the expenses of government—expenses for "the common defense, or general welfare." Each state would pay into the treasury in proportion to the state's land area. That proposal would cause considerable controversy in the debate over adopting the Articles.

Things to remember while reading the Articles of Confederation:

- While Congress was considering the document, word came that British general Sir William Howe (1729–1814) wished to discuss a compromise of the dispute between Great Britain and America. Massachusetts congressman John Adams (1735–1826), who was opposed to any such compromise, was appointed, along with fellow Continental congressmen Benjamin Franklin (1706–1790) and Edward Rutledge (1749–1800), to represent "the free, independent States of America" in a conference with Howe. Upon meeting with Howe, the congressmen were informed, according to Adams, that Howe "could not confer with Us as Members of Congress, or public Characters, but only as private Persons and British subjects." Howe proposed only that "the Colonies should return to their Allegiance and Obedience to the Government of Great Britain." Adams responded that this "was not now to be expected." The conference ended with no resolution. As a result, everyone's attention turned to conducting a war and away from the Articles of Confederation.

- As expected, the difficulties of running a war without a central government soon became obvious. Whenever Congress requested the states to send money or supplies for soldiers, for example, many people in the states complained that the congressmen were reckless power seekers. On top of this, members of Congress fought constantly among themselves throughout the entire war. They grew irritable at the long hours they had to work—without pay. Their surroundings were uncomfortable and they were far from home and family. Wartime shortages made living difficult. As was true with the soldiers who fought the war, from time to time members of Congress would return home, to be replaced with amateurs. Under the circumstances, it was truly remarkable that they got anything done.

- Debate over the Articles lasted for more than a year. Congress was repeatedly interrupted by more immediate concerns having to do with the war. Many congressmen

Revolutionary War Documents on the World Wide Web

One of the most interesting ways to start learning about the American Revolution is by looking at the historical documents produced during the Revolutionary period. But this information is housed in libraries, museums, and other places that are available only to the few who can afford the time and money to go and view the documents in person. But in an exciting development, the Internet is making these documents available to all. One of the leaders in the movement to share this knowledge with the world is the Library of Congress in Washington, D.C.

The Library of Congress, the inspiration of Thomas Jefferson, is the largest library in the United States. It is supported mainly by federal money, and it serves both Congress and the public. The Library of Congress owns 117 million items of all kinds relating to American history, including photographs of famous people and old baseball cards. Approximately four million of these items are available to users of the World Wide Web through the National Digital Library Program.

The American Memory Historical Collections (http://memory.loc.gov/ammem/amhome.html) is a major part of the National Digital Library Program. In the collection entitled "Documents from the Continental Congress and the Constitutional Convention, 1774–1789" (http://memory.loc.gov/ammem/bdsds/bdsdhome.html), all sorts of historical documents, including early printed versions of the Declaration of Independence and the Constitution, are available for viewing. Text versions of these documents are also available at this site.

Another Web site that features documents that range from newspaper articles to political documents is called Archiving Early America (http://earlyamerica.com/). At http://odur.let.rug.nl/~welling/usa/, users can find biographies, essays, and links to Revolutionary War–era documents. Finally, Yale Law School's Avalon Project features documents relating to law, history, government, and other topics (http://www.yale.edu/lawweb/avalon/avalon.htm).

feared their colonies would suffer if a republican, or central, government was established. Others believed the nation was simply too large to be adequately governed by the republican form of government that was being proposed. In such a form of government, power rests with the people, who exercise their power through elected repre-

Library of Congress, Washington, D. C.

sentatives. Many citizens feared that legislators (law makers) of a large republic would lose touch with the people they represented, and soon those legislators would become tyrants.

- The reality of the war finally won out over the fears of a central government. Wartime required instant decision-making as well as foreign aid. The country had to have people who would be recognized by foreign countries as lawful representatives of an American government and therefore eligible to ask for assistance. Otherwise, foreign leaders might consider Americans to be British subjects. Furthermore, a feeling of nationalism was growing—the sense that America was and should be a united nation, not thirteen separate colonies.

- Six versions of the Articles were prepared, and Congress settled on the final version, which follows, in 1777.

An old etching of the Library of Congress building. The idea for the library came from early American patriot Thomas Jefferson.
Courtesy of the Library of Congress.

Presents: Documents.

Delegates: Representatives.

Affixed: Attached (at the end of the document).

Confederation: A group of states united for a common purpose.

Perpetual: Lasting for an unlimited length of time.

Stile: Name.

Confederacy: Union of states.

Sovereignty: Complete independence and self-government.

Jurisdiction: Authority.

Delegated: Given over to representatives.

In Congress assembled: When this body of representatives meets formally.

Severally: Separately.

Sovereignty: Another government claiming authority.

Secure and perpetuate: Guard from danger and prolong the existence of.

Intercourse: Communication.

Paupers, vagabonds, and fugitives from justice excepted: Very poor people, homeless wanderers, and those running from the law are not included.

Immunities: Freedoms from certain duties or obligations.

Articles of Confederation

*To all to whom these **Presents** shall come, we the undersigned **Delegates** of the States **affixed** to our Names send greeting. Articles of **Confederation** and **perpetual** Union between the states of New Hampshire, Massachusetts-bay, Rhode Island and Providence Plantations, Connecticut, New York, New Jersey, Pennsylvania, Delaware, Maryland, Virginia, North Carolina, South Carolina and Georgia.*

*I. The **Stile** of this **Confederacy** shall be "The United States of America."*

*II. Each state retains its **sovereignty**, freedom, and independence, and every power, **jurisdiction,** and right, which is not by this Confederation expressly **delegated** to the United States, **in Congress assembled.***

*III. The said States hereby **severally** enter into a firm league of friendship with each other, for their common defense, the security of their liberties, and their mutual and general welfare, binding themselves to assist each other, against all force offered to, or attacks made upon them, or any of them, on account of religion, **sovereignty**, trade, or any other pretense whatever.*

*IV. The better to **secure and perpetuate** mutual friendship and **intercourse** among the people of the different States in this Union, the free inhabitants of each of these States, **paupers, vagabonds, and fugitives from justice excepted,** shall be entitled to all privileges and **immunities** of free citizens in the several States; and the people of each State shall have **free ingress and regress** to and from any other State, and shall enjoy therein all the privileges of trade and **commerce,** subject to the same **duties, impositions, and restrictions** as the **inhabitants thereof respectively,** provided that such restrictions shall not extend so far as to prevent the removal of property imported into any State, to any other State, of which the owner is an inhabitant; provided also that no imposition, duties or restriction shall be laid by any State, on the property of the United States, or either of them.*

*If any person guilty of, or charged with, **treason, felony, or other high misdemeanor** in any State, shall flee from justice, and be found in any of the United States, he shall, upon demand of the Governor or executive power of the State from which he fled, be delivered up and removed to the State having jurisdiction of his offense.*

Full faith and credit shall be given in each of these States to the records, acts, and **judicial proceedings** of the courts and **magistrates** of every other State.

V. For the most convenient management of the general interests of the United States, delegates shall be annually appointed in such manner as the legislatures of each State shall direct, to meet in Congress on the first Monday in November, in every year, with a power reserved to each State to recall its delegates, or any of them, at any time within the year, and to send others in their **stead** for the remainder of the year.

No State shall be represented in Congress by less than two, nor more than seven members; and no person shall be capable of being a delegate for more than three years in any term of six years; nor shall any person, being a delegate, be capable of holding any office under the United States, for which he, or another one for his benefit, receives any salary, fees or **emolument** of any kind.

Each State shall maintain its own delegates in a meeting of the States, and while they act as members of the committee of the States.

In determining questions in the United States in Congress assembled, each State shall have one vote.

Freedom of speech and debate in Congress shall not be **impeached** or questioned in any court or place out of Congress, and the members of Congress shall be protected in their persons from arrests or imprisonments, during the time of their going to and from, and attendance on Congress, except for treason, felony, or **breach of the peace.**

VI. No State, without the consent of the United States in Congress assembled, shall send any **embassy** to, or receive any embassy from, or enter into any conference, agreement, alliance or treaty with any King, Prince or State; nor shall any person holding any office of profit or trust under the United States, or any of them, accept any present, emolument, office or title of any kind whatever from any King, Prince or foreign State; nor shall the United States in Congress assembled, or any of them, grant any **title of nobility.**

No two or more States shall enter into any treaty, confederation or alliance whatever between them, without the consent of the United States in Congress assembled, **specifying** accurately the purposes for which the same is to be entered into, and how long it shall continue.

No State shall lay any **imposts** or duties, which may interfere with any **stipulations** in treaties, entered into by the United States in

Free ingress and regress: The right to come and go freely.

Commerce: Buying or selling of goods on a large scale.

Duties, impositions, and restrictions: Taxes, other similar types of payments, and limitations.

Inhabitants thereof respectively: Those who live in the different states.

Treason, felony, or other high misdemeanor: Betrayal of his or her country, very serious crimes, or lesser crimes.

Judicial proceedings: Legal matters.

Magistrates: People who enforce laws.

Stead: Place.

Emolument: (Pronounced im-MOL-ya-ment) Payment.

Impeached: Challenged.

Breach of the peace: Violation of law and order.

Embassy: An official representative (ambassador) and his or her staff.

Title of nobility: Title such as king or prince.

Specifying: Clearly stating.

Imposts: Payments similar to taxes.

Stipulations: Terms or conditions.

Pursuance of: Carrying out.

Deemed: Thought.

Body of forces: A group of people organized for military or hostile purposes.

Requisite to garrison: Sufficient to provide workers for.

Militia: An army made up of citizens, not professional soldiers.

Accoutered: Equipped.

Stores: Warehouses.

A due number: Enough.

Equipage: Furnishings.

Resolution: Firm decision.

Imminent: About to occur.

Admit of: Allow for.

Grant commissions: Give authority to carry out a task.

Letters of marque or reprisal: Documents issued by a nation or state allowing private citizens to seize goods or citizens of another nation or state or to equip a ship with arms to attack enemy ships.

Raised: Assembled.

Incurred: Met with.

Defrayed: Paid.

Common treasury: A place that holds funds contributed by all the states.

Surveyed: Boundaries determined.

Congress assembled, with any King, Prince or State, in **pursuance of** any treaties already proposed by Congress, to the courts of France and Spain.

No vessel of war shall be kept up in time of peace by any State, except such number only, as shall be **deemed** necessary by the United States in Congress assembled, for the defense of such State, or its trade; nor shall any **body of forces** be kept up by any State in time of peace, except such number only, as in the judgement of the United States in Congress assembled, shall be deemed **requisite to garrison** the forts necessary for the defense of such State; but every State shall always keep up a well-regulated and disciplined **militia**, sufficiently armed and **accoutered**, and shall provide and constantly have ready for use, in public **stores, a due number** of field pieces and tents, and a proper quantity of arms, ammunition and camp **equipage.**

No State shall engage in any war without the consent of the United States in Congress assembled, unless such State be actually invaded by enemies, or shall have received certain advice of a **resolution** being formed by some nation of Indians to invade such State, and the danger is so **imminent** as not to **admit of** a delay till the United States in Congress assembled can be consulted; nor shall any State **grant commissions** to any ships or vessels of war, nor **letters of marque or reprisal,** except it be after a declaration of war by the United States in Congress assembled, and then only against the Kingdom or State and the subjects thereof, against which war has been so declared, and under such regulations as shall be established by the United States in Congress assembled, unless such State be infested by pirates, in which case vessels of war may be fitted out for that occasion, and kept so long as the danger shall continue, or until the United States in Congress assembled shall determine otherwise.

VII. When land forces are **raised** by any State for the common defense, all officers of or under the rank of colonel, shall be appointed by the legislature of each State respectively, by whom such forces shall be raised, or in such manner as such State shall direct, and all vacancies shall be filled up by the State which first made the appointment.

VIII. All charges of war, and all other expenses that shall be **incurred** for the common defense or general welfare, and allowed by the United States in Congress assembled, shall be **defrayed** out of a **common treasury,** which shall be supplied by the several States in proportion to the value of all land within each State, granted or **surveyed** for any person, as such land and the buildings and improvements thereon shall be estimated according to such mode as the

United States in Congress assembled, shall from time to time direct and appoint.

The taxes for paying that proportion shall be **laid and levied** by the authority and direction of the legislatures of the several States within the time agreed upon by the United States in Congress assembled.

IX. The United States in Congress assembled, shall have the **sole and exclusive** right and power of determining on peace and war, except in the cases mentioned in the sixth article—of sending and receiving ambassadors—entering into treaties and alliances, provided that no treaty of commerce shall be made whereby the legislative power of the respective States shall be **restrained from imposing such imposts and duties on foreigners, as their own people are subjected to,** or from prohibiting the exportation or importation of any **species** of goods or **commodities** whatsoever—of establishing rules for deciding in all cases, what captures on land or water shall be legal, and in what manner prizes taken by land or naval forces in the service of the United States shall be divided or **appropriated**—of granting letters of marque and reprisal in times of peace—appointing courts for the trial of **piracies** and felonies committed on the **high seas** and establishing courts for receiving and determining finally appeals in all cases of captures, provided that no member of Congress shall be appointed a judge of any of the said courts.

The United States in Congress assembled shall also be **the last resort on appeal** in all disputes and differences now **subsisting** or that hereafter may arise between two or more States concerning boundary, jurisdiction or any other causes whatever; which authority shall always be exercised in the manner following. Whenever the legislative or executive authority or lawful agent of any State in **controversy** with another shall present a **petition** to Congress stating the matter in question and **praying for** a hearing, notice thereof shall be given by order of Congress to the legislative or executive authority of the other State in controversy, and a day assigned for the appearance of the parties by their lawful agents, who shall then be directed to appoint by **joint consent**, commissioners or judges to **constitute** a hearing and determining the matter in question: but if they cannot agree, Congress shall name three persons out of each of the United States, and from the list of such persons each party shall **alternately strike out one**, the **petitioners** beginning, until the number shall be reduced to thirteen; and from that number not less than seven, nor more than nine names as Congress shall direct, shall in the Congress

Laid and levied: Imposed and collected.

Sole and exclusive: Only and unshared.

Restrained from imposing such imposts and duties on foreigners, as their own people are subjected to: Not allowed to make trade agreements that keep them from charging foreigners the same taxes the states' residents must pay.

Species: Kind.

Commodities: Trade articles.

Appropriated: Set apart.

Piracies: Robberies.

High seas: Open waters that no nation controls.

The last resort on appeal: A legal case cannot go to any higher government body.

Subsisting: Existing.

Controversy: Dispute.

Petition: Formal document.

Praying for: Requesting.

Joint consent: Agreement by all parties.

Constitute: Set up.

Alternately strike out one: Cross off names, taking turns.

Petitioners: Persons making or presenting a formal document.

be **drawn out by lot,** and the persons whose names shall be so drawn or any five of them, shall be commissioners or judges, to hear and finally **determine** the controversy, so always as a major part of the judges who shall hear the **cause** shall agree in the determination; and if either party shall neglect to attend at the day appointed, without showing reasons, which Congress shall judge sufficient, or being present shall refuse to **strike,** the Congress shall proceed to nominate three persons out of each State, and the secretary of Congress shall strike in behalf of such party absent or refusing; and the judgement and sentence of the court to be appointed, in the manner **before prescribed,** shall be final and conclusive; and if any of the parties shall refuse to submit to the authority of such court, or to appear or defend their claim or cause, the court shall nevertheless proceed to pronounce **sentence, or judgement,** which shall in like manner be final and decisive, the judgement or sentence and other proceedings being in either case **transmitted** to Congress **lodged** among the acts of Congress for the security of the parties concerned; provided that every commissioner, before he sits in judgement, shall take an oath, to be administered by one of the judges of the supreme or superior court of the State, where the cause shall be tried, "well and truly to hear and determine the matter in question, according to the best of his judgement, without favor, affection, or hope of reward,": provided also that no State shall be deprived of territory for the benefit of the United States.

All controversies concerning the **private right of soil** claimed under different grants of two or more States, whose jurisdictions as they may respect such lands, and the States which have passed such grants are adjusted, the said grants or either of them being at the same time claimed to have originated **antecedent to** such settlement of jurisdiction, shall on the petition of either party to the Congress of the United States, be finally determined as near as may be in the same manner as is before prescribed for deciding disputes respecting territorial jurisdiction between different States.

The United States in Congress assembled shall also have the sole and exclusive right and power of regulating the **alloy and value of coin struck** by their own authority, or by that of the respective States—**fixing the standards of weights and measures** throughout the United States—regulating the trade and managing all affairs with the Indians, [who are] not members of any of the States, provided that the legislative right of any State within its own limits be not **infringed or violated**—establishing or regulating post offices from

Drawn out by lot: Chosen at random.

Determine: Make a decision about.

Cause: The subject under discussion.

Strike: Make and confirm the terms of the decision.

Before prescribed: Set down earlier (in this document) as a rule or guide.

Sentence, or judgement: The penalty, or decision.

Transmitted: Sent.

Lodged: Contained.

Private right of soil: Land ownership.

Antecedent to: (Pronounced ann-ta-SEED-int) Before.

Alloy and value of coin struck: The combination of metals used in, and the value of, the money produced.

Fixing the standards of weights and measures: Establishing how much gold or silver will be used in coins in combination with other metals.

Infringed or violated: Stepped on or disregarded.

one State to another, throughout all the United States, and **exacting such postage** on the papers passing through the same as may be **requisite to defray the expenses of the said office**—appointing all officers of the land forces, in the service of the United States, excepting **regimental officers**—appointing all the officers of the naval forces, and **commissioning** all officers whatever in the service of the United States—making rules for the government and regulation of the said land and naval forces, and directing their operations.

The United States in Congress assembled shall have authority to appoint a committee, to sit in the recess of Congress, to be **denominated** 'A Committee of the States,' and to consist of one delegate from each State; and to appoint such other committees and civil officers as may be necessary for managing the general affairs of the United States under their direction—to appoint one of their members to **preside**, provided that no person be allowed to serve in the office of president more than one year in any term of three years; to **ascertain** the necessary sums of money to be raised for the service of the United States, and to **appropriate and apply** the same for defraying the public expenses—to borrow money, or **emit bills** on the credit of the United States, transmitting every half-year to the respective States an **account** of the sums of money so borrowed or emitted—to build and equip a navy—to agree upon the number of land forces, and to make **requisitions** from each State for its **quota**, in proportion to the number of white inhabitants in such State; which requisition shall be **binding**, and **thereupon** the legislature of each State shall appoint the regimental officers, raise the men and **cloath**, arm and equip them in a **solid-like** manner, at the expense of the United States; and the officers and men so cloathed, armed and equipped shall march to the place appointed, and within the time agreed on by the United States in Congress assembled. But if the United States in Congress assembled shall, **on consideration of circumstances** judge proper that any State should not raise men, or should raise a smaller number of men than the quota thereof, such extra number shall be raised, **officered,** cloathed, armed and equipped in the same manner as the quota of each State, unless the legislature of such State shall judge that such extra number cannot be safely spread out in the same, in which case they shall raise, officer, cloath, arm and equip as many of such extra number as they judge can be safely spared. And the officers and men so cloathed, armed, and equipped, shall march to the place appointed, and within the time agreed on by the United States in Congress assembled.

Exacting such postage: Ordering the payment of postage.

Requisite to defray the expenses of the said office: Enough to pay the costs of running the post office.

Regimental officers: Colonels.

Commissioning: Appointing.

Denominated: Called.

Preside: Be in charge.

Ascertain: (Pronounced ASS-ser-TANE) Find out.

Appropriate and apply: Order and spend.

Emit bills: Put money in circulation.

Account: List.

Requisitions: Written requests.

Quota: Share.

Binding: An obligation.

Thereupon: Immediately following that.

Cloath: Clothe; supply with clothing.

Solid-like: Quality.

On consideration of circumstances: After thinking it over carefully.

Officered: Made officers.

The United States in Congress assembled shall never engage in a war, nor grant letters of marque or reprisal in time of peace, nor enter into any treaties or alliances, nor coin money, nor regulate the value thereof, nor ascertain the sums and expenses necessary for the defense and welfare of the United States, or any of them, nor emit bills, nor borrow money on the credit of the United States, nor appropriate money, nor agree upon the number of vessels of war, to be built or purchased, or the number of land or sea forces to be raised, nor appoint a commander in chief of the army or navy, unless nine States **assent** to the same; nor shall a question on any other point, except for **adjourning** from day to day be determined, unless by the votes of the majority of the United States in Congress assembled.

The Congress of the United States shall have power to adjourn to any time within the year, and to any place within the United States, so that no period of adjournment be for a longer duration than the space of six months, and shall publish the **journal of their proceedings** monthly, except such parts thereof relating to treaties, alliances or military operations, as in their judgement require secrecy; and the **yeas and nays** of the delegates of each State on any question shall be entered on the journal, when it is desired by any delegates of a State, or any of them, at his or their request shall be furnished with a **transcript** of the said journal, except such parts as are above excepted, to lay before the legislatures of the several States.

X. The Committee of the States, or any nine of them, shall be authorized to **execute,** in the recess of Congress, such of the powers of Congress as the United States in Congress assembled, by the consent of the nine States, shall from time to time think **expedient to vest them with;** provided that no power be delegated to the said Committee, for the exercise of which, by the Articles of Confederation, the voice of nine States in the Congress of the United States assembled be **requisite.**

XI. **Canada acceding to** this confederation, and adjoining in the measures of the United States, shall be admitted into, and entitled to all the advantages of this Union; but no other colony shall be admitted into the same, unless such admission be agreed to by nine States.

XII. All bills of credit emitted, monies borrowed, and debts **contracted** by, or under the authority of Congress, **before the assembling of the United States,** in pursuance of the present confederation, shall be deemed and considered as a charge against the United States, for payment and satisfaction whereof the said United States, and the public faith are hereby solemnly pledged.

XIII. Every State shall **abide by the determination** of the United States in Congress assembled, on all questions which by this confed-

Assent: Agree.

Adjourning: Calling a meeting to an end.

Journal of their proceedings: The official record of votes, speeches, and debates; still published today as the *Congressional Record.*

Yeas and nays: Yes and no votes.

Transcript: Printed copy.

Execute: Carry out.

Expedient to vest them with: Proper to place in their control.

Requisite: Required.

Canada acceding to: If Canada agrees to join.

Contracted: Taken on.

Before the assembling of the United States: Before the new nation was formed.

Abide by the determination: Go along with the decision.

American Revolution: Primary Sources

*eration are submitted to them. And the Articles of this Confederation shall be **inviolably observed** by every State, and the Union shall be perpetual; nor shall any alteration at any time hereafter be made in any of them; unless such alteration be agreed to in a Congress of the United States, and be afterwards confirmed by the legislatures of every State.*

*And Whereas it hath pleased the Great Governor of the World to incline the hearts of the legislatures we respectively represent in Congress, to approve of, and to authorize us to **ratify** the said Articles of Confederation and perpetual Union. Know Ye that we the undersigned delegates, by virtue of the power and authority to us given for that purpose, do by these presents, in the name and in behalf of our respective **constituents**, fully and entirely ratify and confirm each and every of the said Articles of Confederation and perpetual Union, and all and singular the matters and things therein contained: And we do further solemnly **plight and engage** the faith of our respective constituents, that they shall abide by the determinations of the United States in Congress assembled, on all questions, which by the said Confederation are submitted to them. And that the Articles thereof shall be inviolably observed by the States we respectively represent, and that the Union shall be perpetual.*

In Witness whereof we have hereunto set our hands in Congress. Done at Philadelphia in the State of Pennsylvania the ninth day of July in the Year of our Lord One Thousand Seven Hundred and Seventy-Eight, and in the Third Year of the independence of America.

Agreed to by Congress 15 November 1777

In force after ratification by Maryland, 1 March 1781

[The Articles of Confederation were signed by forty-eight representatives of the thirteen colonies. In alphabetical order by state, they were:

Connecticut: Andrew Adams, Titus Hosmer, Samuel Huntington, Roger Sherman, and Oliver Wolcott; Delaware: John Dickinson, Thomas McKean, and Nicholas Van Dyke; Georgia: Edward Langworthy, Edward Telfair, and John Walton; Maryland: Daniel Carroll and John Hanson; Massachusetts: Samuel Adams, Francis Dana, Elbridge Gerry, John Hancock, Samuel Holten, and James Lovell; New Hampshire: Josiah Bartlett and John Wentworth, Jr.; New Jersey: Nathaniel Scudder and John Witherspoon; New York: James Duane, William Duer, Francis Lewis, and Gouverneur Morris; North Carolina: Cornelius Harnett, John Penn, and John Williams; Pennsylvania:

Inviolably observed: Carried out without any violation; not disregarded under any circumstances.

Ratify: Approve and make law.

Constituents: (Pronounced con-STIT-you-ents) People represented by elected officials.

Plight and engage: Promise and involve.

Native Americans in the Revolution

When it became clear that a war with Great Britain was likely, members of the Second Continental Congress knew they would have problems with Native Americans. They knew that the Natives had many grievances against the colonists, because American settlers trespassed on their land and American traders cheated them. The Natives were friendlier towards England, who in 1763 had promised to keep American colonists out of lands claimed by the Natives west of the Appalachian Mountains.

The congressmen knew they were not likely to get cooperation from the Native Americans in a war, but they hoped to at least get neutrality (non-involvement) from them. So, Congress appointed commissioners to go out and deliver this speech to the Indians:

Brothers and friends! . . . This is a family quarrel between us and Old England. You Indians are not concerned in it. We don't wish you to take up the hatchet against the king's troops. We desire you to remain at home, and not join on either side, but keep the hatchet buried deep. . . . Brothers, observe well! What is it we have asked of you? Nothing but peace . . . and if application should be made to you by any of the king's unwise and wicked ministers to join on their side, we only advise you to deliberate [think it over and discuss], with great caution, and in your wisdom look forward to the consequences of a compliance. For if the king's troops take away our property, and destroy us who are of the same blood as themselves, what can you, who are Indians, expect from them afterwards?"

The speech brought little if any good results for the Americans. Most of the tribes who joined the fight sided with Great Britain. The result was, when the war ended, the new American nation looked upon the Indians as enemies, no matter which side they had supported, and the Indians' British allies showed little gratitude for their help in the conflict.

William Clingan, Robert Morris, Joseph Reed, Daniel Roberdeau, and John Bayard Smith; Rhode Island: John Collins, William Ellery, and Henry Marchant; South Carolina: William Henry Drayton, Thomas Heyward, Jr., Richard Hutson, Henry Laurens, and John Mathews; and Virginia: Thomas Adams, John Banister, John Harvie, Francis Lightfoot Lee, and Richard Henry Lee.] (American Journey [CD-ROM])

What happened next . . .

The Articles of Confederation had to be submitted to the thirteen states for approval. By 1779, the document had been approved by all the states except Maryland—and Maryland was stubbornly opposed. For two years, it seemed that the Articles of Confederation would fail because of Maryland's opposition. Maryland's point was this: Land west of the thirteen states should belong to the new United States, not to Virginia, the Carolinas, Georgia, Connecticut, and Massachusetts, all of whom claimed to extend to the Mississippi River. Maryland's representatives said they would not sign until the states with western land claims gave up their claims to the United States. One by one they did, and with this issue resolved, Maryland ratified the Articles, and they went into effect on March 1, 1781.

The Articles did not resolve all of the problems that had faced the First and Second Continental Congresses. The new Congress could still not levy taxes. Its operating funds would come from the states; each state would contribute according to the worth of privately owned land within its borders. But Congress now had power over foreign relations and could now make agreements with foreign governments. It could wage war and make peace, raise an army and navy, make money, set up a postal service, and it had many other powers it did not have before. The new country was governed by these Articles until Congress's next great document, the Constitution, was adopted in 1788.

The Continental Congresses were unique bodies in world history. They forged a new nation from thirteen separate colonies. Making up rules as they went along, with little authority or money, the Second Congress managed to direct and win a war against the mighty British Empire, then the most powerful nation in the world. Along the way, the Revolutionary Congresses composed several great documents that were the forerunners of the American Constitution. That document has lasted more than two hundred years as the basic law of the land.

Did you know . . .

- The Articles of Confederation that were eventually adopted were largely the work of John Dickinson, who had been responsible for so many other congressional documents and political writings (see p. 63). John Adams was not on the committee that drafted the document, but as usual, he had much to say on the topic. He wrote his wife Abigail, explaining the major point that had kept the delegates arguing for so long. "If a confederation should take place, one great question is, how we shall vote," he told her. "Whether each colony shall count one; or whether each shall have a weight in proportion to its number, or wealth, or exports and imports, or a compound ratio of all."

- Dickinson had proposed a system of one colony, one vote. Adams held that the delegates to Congress represented all the people, not the states, and that voting should be proportionate to a state's population. In the end, Dickinson's point of view carried the day.

- The Articles contained a provision for the admission of Canada to the confederation. Americans had long fooled themselves that Canada, a British possession but home to mostly French speakers, would wish to become "the fourteenth colony." Surely, they thought, these people would want to throw off British domination, too! In 1775, the Second Continental Congress had prepared an address to the "oppressed Inhabitants of Canada." In it, Canadians were told: "We yet entertain hopes of your uniting with us in the defence of our common liberty." But the Canadians were not interested in Congress's proposal. Undaunted, in 1777, Congress again had invited them to join the confederation.

- The 1781 ratification of the Articles of Confederation ended the Second Continental Congress. On March 2, 1781, it became "The United States in Congress Assembled."

Where to Learn More

American Journey (CD-ROM). Woodbridge, CT: Primary Source Media, 1995.

Boatner, Mark M. "Indians in the Colonial Wars and in the Revolution" in *Encyclopedia of the American Revolution*. Mechanicsburg, PA: Stackpole Books, 1994.

Burnett, Edmund Cody. *The Continental Congress*. New York: Norton, 1964.

Dictionary of American Biography. 21 volumes. New York: Scribner's, 1957.

Draper, Theodore. *A Struggle for Power: The American Revolution.* New York: Times Books, 1996.

"Journals of the Continental Congress—In Thirty-Four Volumes." [Online] http://memory.loc.gov/ammem/amlaw/lwjclink.html (accessed on March 19, 2000).

Marrin, Albert. *The War for Independence: The Story of the American Revolution.* New York: Atheneum, 1988.

Meltzer, Milton, ed. *The American Revolutionaries: A History in Their Own Words, 1750–1800.* New York: HarperTrophy, reprint edition, 1993.

Montross, Lynn. *The Reluctant Rebels: The Story of the Continental Congress, 1774–1789.* New York: Harper & Brothers, 1950.

Scandal and Betrayal

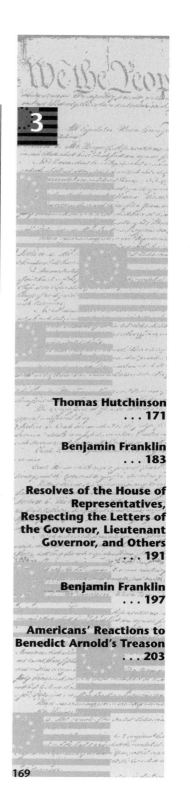

Beginning in 1765, Great Britain tried to collect taxes in America to pay its own bills. Americans grew increasingly angry. They claimed that Parliament, Great Britain's lawmaking body, had no right to tax people who had no representation in Parliament. Men who were supposed to collect the taxes were abused by the colonists and had their property damaged or destroyed. A major center for this kind of activity was Boston, Massachusetts, where mobs rioted in the streets and total disorder resulted. Finally, fearful that they were losing their hold over America, the British sent armed soldiers to keep the peace in Boston. Bostonians resented the presence of the soldiers, and in 1770, the tension led to the event known as the Boston Massacre, in which five Americans were killed by British soldiers. The tension continued to escalate, and relations between Great Britain and America became more hostile.

Thomas Hutchinson (1711–1780; see sidebar entry on Hutchinson on p. 173) was a key figure in the events in Boston that led up to the Revolutionary War. Born and raised in Massachusetts, he had a long and distinguished career in colonial government. He had been appointed by Parliament to several

Thomas Hutchinson
. . . 171

Benjamin Franklin
. . . 183

Resolves of the House of Representatives, Respecting the Letters of the Governor, Lieutenant Governor, and Others
. . . 191

Benjamin Franklin
. . . 197

Americans' Reactions to Benedict Arnold's Treason
. . . 203

high positions and was finally named governor in 1771. Hutchinson's great misfortune was that he was a Loyalist (he was loyal to King George and Parliament) and he was a conservative (a person who wished to preserve society's existing institutions). He loved his home colony, and he was sad to watch the rioting in Boston and hear the angry talk about breaking off from the mother country (Britain). Between 1767 and 1769, Hutchinson, his brother-in-law, Andrew Oliver (1706–1774), and several other Massachusetts citizens wrote of what they were observing in Massachusetts and sent the letters to friends back in England.

In 1772, colonial statesman Benjamin Franklin (1706–1774) got hold of the letters written by Hutchinson and the others. When the content of the letters was leaked to the public, Hutchinson found himself feared and hated as the worst kind of traitor. He remained America's foremost traitor until late in the Revolutionary War. In 1780, the actions of another ambitious and talented man shocked America. That year, General Benedict Arnold (1741–1801) suddenly betrayed his country and went over to the British side.

The first part of this chapter explores the events written about in the scandalous Hutchinson letters, so called because he was the best known of the writers. What happened after their discovery and publication years later is also examined. The Hutchinson letters affair illustrates the tragedy that can result from the decisions of well-meaning people with conflicting loyalties. The second part of this chapter explores America's reaction to the news that one of its greatest war heroes—Benedict Arnold—had betrayed the cause of independence.

Thomas Hutchinson

Letters of Thomas Hutchinson

Published in 1768–69; excerpted from *The Life of Thomas Hutchinson, Royal Governor of the Province of Massachusetts Bay*

At the time he wrote the two letters that follow, Thomas Hutchinson (1711–1780) held two important government offices at the same time: lieutenant governor of Massachusetts (in August 1769, he would become governor) and chief justice of the Massachusetts superior court. He was a scholarly, intelligent, law-abiding person, the man in charge of making sure that British laws were obeyed in Massachusetts. The tax laws had so angered Americans that when British-appointed agents and British soldiers tried to collect taxes, they were threatened and attacked by mobs. As far as Hutchinson was concerned, the taxes might be unpopular, but they *were* the law, and it was his job to uphold the law. Hutchinson was dismayed by the violent mobs who were protesting British taxes. He remarked: "The people seem to me in a state of absolute dementation [madness]."

Hutchinson's letters were written to a Mr. Thomas Whately, private secretary to a Member of Parliament. His first letter to Whately opened with the information that British tax collectors had recently been forced by Boston mobs to flee to Castle William, a fortress in Boston Harbor. He then described

"I never think of the measures necessary for the peace and good order of the colonies without pain. . . . there must be a great restraint of natural liberty."

Thomas Hutchinson

the events leading up to their flight. Mob violence had broken out after a boat, the *Liberty*, was seized by customs officers for smuggling. The boat belonged to John Hancock (1737–1793), a wealthy and very popular Boston merchant. Hutchinson concluded his description with the remarks that even though some ignorant men seemed to be controlling events in Boston, he did not believe that the chaos could last long. He also informed Mr. Whately that Mr. Hallowell, an important British customs agent, would be delivering his letter in person.

The strange, uneasy situation in Boston continued. Patriots like Samuel Adams (1722–1803) spoke passionately about liberty and the rights of man, and urged Bostonians to take up arms against the king's soldiers. Meanwhile, conservatives like Hutchinson made enemies by speaking about authority, law, and the illegal use of force.

Thomas Hutchinson wrote his letter of January 20, 1769, four months after additional British soldiers were sent to Boston to keep the peace. His letter was in response to a letter from Whately, which had been personally delivered by the captain of the ship that carried it, Captain Scott. In his letter, Hutchinson thanked Whately for letting him know what was going on in Parliament—that members were discussing how to deal with colonial unrest. Hutchinson then described the problems he was having with the Sons of Liberty—men he called "enemies of government" and "one half dozen of the most wicked fellows . . . of any upon the globe." Hutchinson complained that the Sons of Liberty were openly and illegally speaking about independence from England. What made it worse, Hutchinson wrote, was that the Sons were getting support and encouragement from certain members of Parliament who supported their cause. Hutchinson informed Whately that the Sons were spreading a rumor that the Townshend Acts were going to be repealed (the Acts placed taxes on lead, glass, paint, tea, and other items).

Hutchinson went on to thank Whately for the information that colonial supporters in Parliament were actually very few. Hutchinson said he was spreading that word around. He wrote of his hope that the Sons of Liberty would be punished by Parliament. He also hoped that the services of people such as himself, who upheld the law despite very difficult circumstances, were properly rewarded by Parliament.

Thomas Hutchinson

Thomas Hutchinson (1711–1780) was the great-grandson of the famous Anne Hutchinson (1591–1643), who came from England to the New World on the *Mayflower* in 1634 and was banished from Massachusetts for her religious beliefs. A brilliant student, Hutchinson entered college when he was thirteen and received a master's degree when he was only nineteen. He then joined his father's overseas trading business, where he demonstrated a superior understanding of money and made a small fortune.

In 1734, he married Margaret (Peggy) Sanford, who bore twelve children; five of them survived infancy to form a very close family. Hutchinson loved Peggy tenderly, once saying that to him she seemed "something more than human." Her death in childbirth in 1754 was the most painful event of his life. Peggy's sister married Andrew Oliver, author of several of the letters that were part of the Hutchinson letters affair.

Biographers describe Hutchinson as moral, intelligent, and humorless, with a low opinion of his fellow citizens. A wealthy and ambitious man, he was also a snob; these qualities did little to endear him to Bostonians. Still, before writing the letters that contributed to the start of the American Revolution, Hutchinson was highly regarded for his good character; today he is remembered for his historical writings, which are regarded as the best of his time.

Thomas Hutchinson. *Reproduced by permission of Archive Photos.*

His career in public service began with his 1734 election to the Massachusetts House of Representatives. By 1760, when he was appointed chief justice of Massachusetts, he held five public offices at the same time, a fact that excited envy and hatred among many Bostonians. In 1771, he was appointed royal governor by King George III, to whom he remained loyal throughout his life.

In 1774, King George named General Thomas Gage as governor in Hutchinson's place. Hutchinson sailed to England, where he had many friends, but he remained homesick until his sudden death in 1780. He was buried in Croydon, England.

Hutchinson then said that the problems in Boston had reached crisis proportions. He said he could hardly wait the three or four weeks it would take to find out what Parliament was going to do about the crisis. He hoped that Parliament's punishment of the rebels was not too severe, but he did hope it was something more meaningful than the Declaratory Act. The Declaratory Act affirmed the right of Parliament to make laws that would bind the colonists "in all cases whatsoever."

Hutchinson's pen then flowed on to the paragraph that would get him into real trouble when his letters were made public three years later. He wrote that it pained him to think what Parliament would have to do to reassert its control over the colonies. Parliament was going to have to take away from the colonies some of their freedoms. He thought that was an unfortunate but necessary undertaking.

Things to remember while reading the letters of Thomas Hutchinson:

- Hutchinson's letter of June 18, 1768, was written after the 1767 Townshend Acts went into effect. The Townshend Acts called for taxes on lead, glass, paint, tea, and other items. They also set up a new system of customs commissioners to make sure the taxes were collected. The customs commissioners had recently arrived in Boston and opened for business. One of their first accomplishments was to seize John Hancock's boat for violating a provision of the Townshend Acts. Hutchinson referred to this incident in his letter as a violation of "the acts of trade."

- Hutchinson's first letter referred to the customs officers' appeal to the governor for help after they were chased out of town by mobs. The British-appointed governor of Massachusetts, Sir Francis Bernard (1712–1779), could not call in British soldiers without the approval of the Massachusetts council. Bernard knew his council would never approve of British soldiers patrolling the streets of Boston. Bernard's council was elected by the Massachusetts Assembly; many members of the assembly sympathized with Boston's rebels. In fact, Samuel Adams, the leader of the rebel group the Sons of Liberty, was a member of the Massachusetts Assembly. He may very well have been one of the members of the mob.

- It was extremely upsetting to Hutchinson that Parliament seemed to be allowing the chaos in the colonies to go on and on. In fact, he complained, some members of Parliament were actually encouraging the lawlessness by supporting colonial resistance to taxes. The worst part, Hutchinson thought, was that the people of Massachusetts saw Parliament as too timid to assert its authority.

- Colonists who objected to British taxes liked to argue that they were Englishmen, too, and entitled to the same rights that Englishmen enjoyed in England—such as having representatives in Parliament. Hutchinson expressed his opinion about that argument in his second letter. He said he doubted that it was possible for people who lived so far from the parent country to enjoy the same liberties as people in the parent country. In fact, he said, he would rather see "some further restraint of liberty" than to have the connection between America and Great Britain broken.

Letter of Thomas Hutchinson, June 18, 1768

SIR,

*As you allow me the honour of your correspondence, **I may not omit acquainting you with** so remarkable an event as the **withdrawal** of the **Commissioners of the Customs,** and most of the other officers under them, from the town on board the [ship] Romney, with **an intent to remove from thence to the Castle.***

*In the evening of the 10th, a **sloop** belonging to Mr. Hancock, a Representative for Boston, and a wealthy merchant of great influence over the **populace,** was seized by the Collector and **Comptroller** for a very **notorious breach of the acts of trade,** and, after seizure, **taken into custody** by the officer of the Romney **man of war,** and **removed under command of her guns.** It is pretended that the removal, and not the seizure, **incensed** the people. It seems **not very material** which it was.—A mob was immediately raised, the officers insulted, bruised, and much hurt, and the windows of some of their houses broke; a boat belonging to the Collector burnt in triumph, and many*

I may not omit acquainting you with: I must tell you about.

Withdrawal: Retreat.

Commissioners of the Customs: Officers in charge of collecting taxes on imports and exports.

An intent to remove from thence to the Castle: A plan to go to Castle William in Boston harbor.

Sloop: A type of boat with sails.

Populace: The common people.

Comptroller: Controller; a financial officer.

Notorious breach of the acts of trade: Obvious and public violation of the trade acts.

Taken into custody: Held under guard.

Man of war: Warship.

Removed under command of her guns: Taken away at gunpoint.

Incensed: Angered.

Not very material: Insignificant.

Extravagance in the time of it: The great deal of time they spent doing it.

Endeavours: Efforts.

Higher: More excited.

Destitute: Totally lacking.

Hold their board: Set up housekeeping.

Custom-house: The place for collecting taxes on imported and exported goods.

Declined and evaded: Said no and tried to get out of (giving advice).

Brush: A brief thing.

Obliged to quit the place of their residence: Forced to leave home.

Grievance: Hardship.

Discountenance the promoters of the late proceedings: Show disapproval of the actions of those who abused the King's Commissioners.

On the contrary, appointed one or more of the actors or abettors: Instead named one or more of the abusers or their helpers.

Wait on: Meet with.

Desire: Ask.

Influence all public measures: Have an effect on the actions of the people.

Anarchy: Disorder and confusion.

Be the bearer of this: Be carrying this letter.

A more full account: More details of the incidents.

*threats uttered against the Commissioners and their officers: no notice being taken of their **extravagance in the time of it**, nor any **endeavours** by any authority, except the governor, the next day, to discover and punish the offenders; and there being a rumour of a **higher** mob intended Monday (the 13th) in the evening, the Commissioners, four of them, thought themselves altogether unsafe, being **destitute** of protection, and removed with their families to the Romney, and there remain and **hold their board**, and next week intend to do the same, and also open the **custom-house** at the Castle. The Governor pressed the council to assist him with their advice, but they **declined and evaded**, calling it a **brush**, or small disturbance by boys and negroes, not considering how much it must be resented in England that the officers of the Crown should think themselves **obliged to quit the place of their residence**, and go on board a king's ship for safety, and all the internal authority of the province take no notice of it.— The town of Boston have had repeated meetings, and by their votes declared the Commissioners and their officers a great **grievance**, and yesterday instructed their Representatives to endeavour, that enquiry should be made by the Assembly whether any person by writing or in any other way, had encouraged the sending troops here, there being some alarming reports that troops are expected, but have not taken any measures to **discountenance the promoters of the late proceedings**; but **on the contrary, appointed one or more of the actors or abettors** on a committee appointed to **wait on** the Governor, and to **desire** him to order the man of war out of the harbour.*

*Ignorant as they be, yet the heads of a Boston town-meeting **influence all public measures**.*

*It is not possible this **anarchy** should last always. Mr. Hallowell, who will **be the bearer of this**, tells me he has the honour of being personally known to you. I beg leave to refer you to him for **a more full account**.*

I am, with great esteem, Sir,

Your most humble and obedient servant.

THO. HUTCHINSON (Hosmer, pp. 429–30)

Letter of Thomas Hutchinson, January 20, 1769

DEAR SIR,

You have laid me under very great obligations by this very clear and full account of proceedings in parliament, which I received from you by Capt. Scott. You have also done much service to the people of the province. For a day or two after the ship arrived, the enemies of government **gave out** that their friends in parliament were increasing, and all things would be soon **on the old footing;** in other words, that all acts imposing duties would be repealed, the commissioners' board dissolved, the customs put on the old footing, and **illicit trade** carried on with little or no hazard. It was very fortunate that I had it in my power to prevent such a **false representation** from spreading through the province. I have been very cautious of using your name, but I have been very free in publishing abroad the substance of your letter, and declaring that I had my **intelligence** from the best authority, and have in a great measure defeated the **ill design** in raising and attempting to spread so **groundless** a report. **What marks of resentment the parliament will show whether they will be upon the province in general or particular persons,** is uncertain, but that they will be placed somewhere is most certain, and I add because I think it ought to be so, that those who have been most steady in preserving the constitution and opposing the **licentiousness** of such as call themselves sons of liberty will certainly meet with favor and encouragement.

This is most certainly a crisis. I really wish that there may not have been the least degree of **severity** beyond what is absolutely necessary to **maintain,** I think I may say to you the dependance which a colony ought to have upon the parent state; but if no measures shall have been taken to secure this dependance, or nothing more than some declaratory acts or resolves, it is all over with us. The friends of government will be utterly disheartened, and the friends of **anarchy** will be afraid of nothing **be it ever so extravagant.**

The last **vessel** from London **had a quick passage.** We expect to be in suspense for the three or four next weeks and then to **hear our fate.** I never think of the measures necessary for the peace and good order of the colonies without pain. There must be an **abridgment** of what are called English liberties. I relieve myself by considering that in a remove from the state of nature to the most perfect state of government there must be a great **restraint** of natural liberty. I doubt whether it is possible to project a system of government in which a

---

You have laid me under very great obligations: I owe you a lot.

Gave out: Told everyone.

On the old footing: Just like before.

Illicit trade: Smuggling.

False representation: An untrue version of the matter.

Intelligence: News.

Ill design: Bad intentions.

Groundless: Untrue.

What marks of resentment the parliament will show whether they will be upon the province in general or particular persons: Whether Parliament will punish the province or only certain people.

Licentiousness: Total disregard for rules.

Severity: Punishment.

Maintain: Keep the colony dependent.

Anarchy: Total disorder.

Be it ever so extravagant: No matter how outrageous.

Vessel: Ship.

Had a quick passage: Got here quickly.

Hear our fate: Learn what steps Parliament is taking to ease the current tension.

Abridgment: Reduction.

Restraint: Loss.

*colony 3000 miles distant from the parent state shall enjoy all the liberty of the parent state. I am certain I have never yet seen the projection. I wish the good of the colony when I wish to see some further restraint of liberty rather than the connexion with the parent state should be broken; for I am sure such a breach must prove the ruin of the colony. Pardon me this **excursion**, it really proceeds from the state of mind into which our **perplexed** affairs often throws me.*

THO. HUTCHINSON (Hosmer, pp. 436–37)

What happened next . . .

The *Liberty* affair thrust John Hancock into the spotlight. He became a friend of the Sons of Liberty as well as its leader, Samuel Adams.

After the trouble over Hancock's boat, Boston customs officials were thoroughly frightened and requested that more British soldiers be sent to Boston to protect them. A large number of soldiers arrived in September 1768; Hutchinson remarked that with their arrival, he slept better than he had in years. It was Hutchinson's job to find places for the soldiers to live and to pay for their upkeep out of public funds. This did not endear him to either the citizens or the mobs, and Hutchinson's home became the target of several instances of mob violence. Boston patriot Samuel Adams and his radical revolutionary group, the Sons of Liberty, were usually responsible for inciting the mobs. They used the presence of British soldiers to stir people up with frantic talk of an emergency and the need to collect arms to protect themselves.

Unrest continued in Massachusetts. Governor Bernard was unable to quell the rioting, and in August 1769 he was recalled to London. Thomas Hutchinson then took over as acting governor of Massachusetts (he was not yet the permanent governor). Bernard did not return, and Hutchinson was named governor in 1771.

The British did not give up on their plan to collect taxes in the colonies, and tension was high, especially in

Boston. People were annoyed by the presence of so many British soldiers in the town. Everything finally came to a head with the Boston Massacre of 1770, when five people were killed in a clash between British soldiers and townspeople. Parliament was so shocked by the violence in Boston that it backed down and repealed the Townshend Acts in April 1770. For the next three years, Parliament was busy with other matters and things were fairly calm in the American colonies. Then the Tea Act was passed in 1773.

The Tea Act was passed because Parliament was trying to save the British-owned East India Company from going out of business. It was ailing because Americans were refusing to import British goods. Parliament thought it could trick the colonists into paying small, secret taxes on East India tea (the taxes would have been paid in London before the tea reached the colonies). Parliament thought that even with the secret tax, the tea would still be so cheap Americans would prefer to buy it rather than pay for the more expensive tea they were smuggling in from elsewhere.

Thomas Hutchinson, always ambitious, saw the Tea Act as a chance to make money from East India tea profits for himself and his sons. He arranged to have his sons appointed as agents to sell the tea. Unfortunately for Hutchinson's plan, on December 16, 1773, Samuel Adams and his Sons of Liberty dumped the tea into Boston Harbor in an event known as the Boston Tea Party.

The Boston Tea Party demonstrated to Parliament that Hutchinson was incapable of keeping order in Boston. Unknown to Hutchinson, his days as governor were nearly at an end. Later, Benjamin Franklin would stir up a scandal in London that would help put an end to Hutchinson's government career (see next entry in this chapter).

Did you know . . .

- Thomas Hutchinson was appointed chief justice of Massachusetts in 1760. At the time, he also held four other appointed positions. Many people viewed Hutchinson as very greedy because of his many appointments.

- Founding father John Adams (1735–1826) and other well-known Massachusetts lawyers (some of them early patri-

Mobs often gathered to protest the Stamp Act of 1765. One such mob attacked and damaged Thomas Hutchinson's home, thinking that he supported the Act. *Reproduced by permission of Archive Photos.*

ots) were extremely upset when Thomas Hutchinson was appointed chief justice. They considered him completely unqualified because he was not even a lawyer, and some of them wanted the job for themselves. For years after Hutchinson's appointment, vicious attacks on his character appeared almost weekly in newspapers. One article called him a man with "unreasonable and unbounded desires of power and profit."

- On August 2, 1765, a violent mob attacked Hutchinson's Boston home, which had been built by his grandfather a century earlier. As his family fled from the dining table, the mob smashed in the doors and ran through the home, damaging walls and furnishings and stealing family possessions. Most of his books and papers were destroyed, but volume 1 of his great work *History of Massachusetts-Bay* was rescued by a friend. The mob rummaged through the house all night long; if the house had not been so sturdy, it would have been torn to the ground.

- The mob that damaged Hutchinson's house thought he supported the Stamp Act of 1765 (taxes on printed matter such as newspapers, legal documents, and even dice and playing cards). But Hutchinson actually thought the act was a terrible idea and did not understand how Parliament could have passed it. But he also knew that a loud outcry from the colonies would make it harder to convince Parliament to back down and do away with the act. He urged the people of Massachusetts to calm down. Although he thought he was being sensible and wise, his actions gained him a reputation as an enemy of liberty.

Where to Learn More

Bailyn, Bernard. *The Ordeal of Thomas Hutchinson.* Cambridge: Belknap Press, 1974.

Boatner, Mark M. "Thomas Hutchinson" and "Hutchinson Letters Affair" in *Encyclopedia of the American Revolution.* Mechanicsburg, PA: Stackpole Books, 1994.

Fradin, Dennis Brindell. *Samuel Adams: The Father of American Independence.* New York: Clarion Books, 1998.

Galvin, John R. *Three Men of Boston: Leadership and Conflict at the Start of the American Revolution.* Washington, D.C.: Brasseys, 1997.

Hosmer, James K. *The Life of Thomas Hutchinson, Royal Governor of the Province of Massachusetts Bay.* Cambridge: Riverside Press, 1896.

McFarland, Philip. *The Brave Bostonians: Hutchinson, Quincy, Franklin, and the Coming of the American Revolution.* Boulder: Westview Press, 1998.

Marrin, Albert: *The War for Independence: The Story of the American Revolution.* New York: Atheneum, 1988.

Meyeroff, Stephen. *The Call for Independence: The Story of the American Revolution and Its Causes.* Cherry Hill, NJ: Oak Tree Publishers, 1996.

Pencak, William. *America's Burke: The Mind of Thomas Hutchinson.* Washington, D.C.: University Press of America, 1982.

Sutton, Felix. *Sons of Liberty.* New York: J. Messner, 1969.

"Thomas Hutchinson" in *Encyclopedia of World Biography.* Volume 8. Detroit: Gale Research, 1998.

Walmsley, Andrew Stephen. *Thomas Hutchinson and the Origins of the American Revolution.* New York: New York University Press, 1999.

Benjamin Franklin

Letter to Massachusetts Speaker of the Assembly Thomas Cushing

Written on December 2, 1772; excerpted from
The Papers of Benjamin Franklin

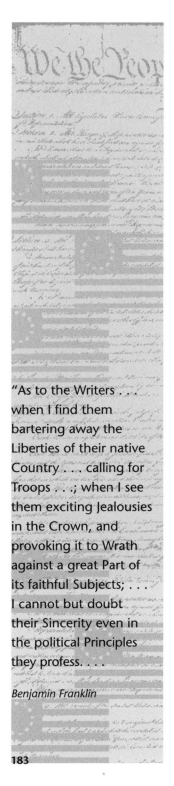

While Governor Thomas Hutchinson (1711–1780) was trying, without success, to keep the peace in Boston, Massachusetts, American statesman Benjamin Franklin (1706–1790) was serving in London, England, as a colonial agent for Massachusetts. Agents were men appointed by law-making bodies in the colonies to live in London, circulate among important people, and report back on what was happening in Parliament. The agents made sure Parliament knew what the colonies' needs and wishes were as Parliament prepared to make laws that affected the colonies.

Since the 1760s, Franklin had spent most of his time in London, watching as relations between England and America soured. He loved both countries and he could not understand why Parliament seemed so determined to upset and anger the colonies. One day in 1772, he thought he found the answer in a mysterious packet of letters given to him (he later wrote) by "A Gentleman of Character and Distinction (whom I am not at present permitted to name). Tho' astonished, I could not but confess myself convinced and I was ready as he desired to convince my Countrymen."

"As to the Writers . . . . when I find them bartering away the Liberties of their native Country . . . . calling for Troops . . . .; when I see them exciting Jealousies in the Crown, and provoking it to Wrath against a great Part of its faithful Subjects; . . . I cannot but doubt their Sincerity even in the political Principles they profess. . . .

Benjamin Franklin

What was Franklin convinced of by the letters? He was convinced that Parliament's actions against the colonies were the result of the bad advice written by evil men in the colonies, especially Governor Hutchinson. Franklin thought that the colonists should know that the bad policies of Parliament were not British ideas at all, but came from their own leaders. He thought that colonial resentment toward Great Britain would cool when this was revealed. Meanwhile, Parliament would have time to make better policies.

Franklin decided to share what he viewed as his wonderful discovery with the Massachusetts legislature, for whom he served as agent. Across the ocean and into the hands of Thomas Cushing (1725–1788), speaker of the assembly, came the packet of letters (the Massachusetts Assembly was the lower house of the legislature). The letters arrived in Boston in March 1773. In his cover letter, Franklin told Cushing how the letters fell into his hands. He said the handwriting on the letters would be shockingly familiar. He said that if the letter writers wanted good relations between the colonies and the mother country, they would not mind if he exposed the letters. Franklin described how his anger at Great Britain had subsided since reading the letters. He said that the writers had deliberately harmed relations between the colonies and Great Britain in order to enrich themselves. He complained that soldiers had been sent to America at the writers' request. He said that having to pay for luxuries for useless British soldiers was a great expense and annoyance. He said the presence of the soldiers was a big part of the unrest in the colonies. Franklin told Cushing not to publish the letters. Franklin thought the letters would be more effective if only a few people read them, then passed the word to many people for discussion. The effect he hoped for was harmony.

Things to remember while reading an excerpt from Benjamin Franklin's letter to Massachusetts speaker of the assembly Thomas Cushing:

- For several years, Franklin had been trying to soothe both Parliament and his rebellious fellow Americans, but his friends in Parliament continued to pass anti-American measures. Franklin was furious when he read the letters, especially Hutchinson's. Franklin thought Hutchinson was advising Parliament to carry out actions that would turn the colonies into enemies of Great Britain. But Franklin was relieved, too. Now that he thought he understood that British policies were the result of the bad advice in the letters, he felt more friendly toward the British government. He was sure his friends back home would feel the same way. And even though Hutchinson's reputation might be ruined by Franklin's action, it seemed a small price to pay if harmony was the result.

Excerpt from Benjamin Franklin's letter to Thomas Cushing

Sir,

*. . . On this Occasion I think it fit to acquaint you that there has lately fallen into my Hands Part of a Correspondence, that I have reason to believe laid the Foundation of most if not all our present **Grievances.** I am not at liberty to tell thro' what Channel I receiv'd it; and I have **engag'd** that it shall not be printed, nor any Copies taken of the whole or any part of it; but I am allow'd and desired to let it be seen by some Men of Worth in the Province for their Satisfaction only. . . . The **Hands** of the Gentlemen will be well known. (If these men want good relations between the colonies and the mother country, they will not mind if I expose this information.) **For my own Part, I cannot but acknowledge,** that my Resentment against this Country [Great Britain], for its **arbitrary Measures** in governing us . . . has [fallen away], since **my Conviction by these Papers,** that those Measures were projected, advised and called for by Men of Character among ourselves. . . .*

*As to the Writers . . . when I find them **bartering** away the Liberties of their native Country [for their own profit] . . . and . . . calling for Troops . . .; when I see them exciting Jealousies in the Crown, and **provoking it to Wrath** against a great Part of its faithful Subjects; creating **Enmities** between the different Countries of which the Empire*

Grievances: Complaints.

Engag'd: Promised.

Hands: Handwriting.

For my own Part, I cannot but acknowledge: As for me, I have to say.

Arbitrary Measures: Impulsive acts, not adopted for good reasons.

My Conviction by these Papers: I was convinced by reading these papers.

Bartering: Trading.

Provoking it to Wrath: Making the king angry.

Enmities: Hatreds.

Occasioning a great Expence: The letters led to the passage of the Townshend Acts, which ran up big tax bills for colonists.

Gratifications: Things that are pleasing.

Useless Officers and Enemies: Tax collectors.

Suppressing: Putting down.

I cannot but doubt their Sincerity: I have to doubt how sincere they are.

Deem: Think.

Emolument: (Pronounced im-MOL-ya-ment) Paycheck.

consists; ***occasioning a great Expence*** *to the new Country for the Payment of needless **Gratifications** to **useless Officers and Enemies;** and to the old for **Suppressing** or Preventing imaginary Rebellions in the new; **I cannot but doubt their Sincerity** even in the political Principles they profess; and **deem** them mere Time-servers, seeking their own private **Emolument** thro' any Quantity of Publick Mischief; Betrayers of the Interest, not of their Native Country only, but of the Government they pretend to serve, and of the whole English Empire. With the greatest Esteem and Respect, I have the Honour to be, Sir, Your most obedient and most humble Servant.*

    B FRANKLIN (Willcox, pp. 411–13)

What happened next . . .

If Franklin thought that harmony would result from his actions, he was sorely mistaken. The existence of the letters could not be kept quiet for long, and Franklin's plan backfired. Samuel Adams (1722–1803) got hold of the letters and had them published. Adams was a leader of the rebel group the Sons of Liberty and one of the earliest and loudest voices in favor of total independence from Great Britain. He was also a longtime enemy of Thomas Hutchinson.

The colonists were outraged over what they saw as Hutchinson's betrayal. Dummies representing Hutchinson were set on fire in Philadelphia, Pennsylvania, and Princeton, New Jersey. Poems were published comparing Hutchinson to evil rulers of ancient times; a popular play of the day accused him of selling "his native land." Massachusetts statesman John Adams (1735–1826) called him a "vile serpent," and declared that Hutchinson's letters bore "the evident marks of madness." The letters convinced many Americans that the rumors spread by the Sons of Liberty were true—there were plots against their liberties, and hopes for renewed friendship with Great Britain were not realistic.

The Hutchinson Letters

The packet given to Benjamin Franklin contained nineteen letters, written by seven different people and addressed to someone in London whose name had been erased (later revealed to be Thomas Whately, private secretary to a Member of Parliament but not in a position to influence government decisions). The letters had been written between 1767 and 1769, and they came from Massachusetts.

Some of the letters described a state of confusion and lawlessness in Boston and throughout New England, whipped up by rebel groups like the Sons of Liberty, over British taxation policies. Some letters expressed the opinion that armed soldiers should be sent from England to control the mobs who were rioting in the streets. Other letters spoke of the need for government reforms that would make Massachusetts more dependent on Parliament.

Hutchinson's letters said nothing that he had not said publicly, in speeches and essays. He wrote of his despair that the British government was not supporting his authority. He wrote of his belief that in the end Parliament would reward him for opposing mob violence. Hutchinson believed the British Empire would dissolve if steps were not taken to make firm the colonies' dependence on England. He insisted that the only way to avert such a disaster would be to gradually remove colonial government from popular control, even if it meant taking away certain liberties.

Hutchinson's letters were simply expressions of his beliefs and opinions. He never said that he wanted British soldiers to come and make the colonies submit, although he was accused by his enemies of doing so.

Hutchinson was an ambitious man who began his correspondence with Whately in part to describe his feelings about the state of politics in the colonies. He also hoped to forge a friendship with a man he respected. For the rest of his life, Hutchinson would insist that the publication of his letters was nothing more than a carefully laid plot to destroy him. For his part, Benjamin Franklin always claimed that he did the right thing in making the letters public. He said that he thought his act would stop a headlong rush to a confrontation between Great Britain and America.

Did you know . . .

- While Franklin believed that the solution to the conflict between the colonies and Great Britain lay in the healing effects of time, Hutchinson believed that the entire British

Sons of Liberty leader Samuel Adams (right) published Thomas Hutchinson's letters; the two were longtime enemies. *Reproduced by permission of Archive Photos.*

Empire would be destroyed if the colonies did not submit to Parliament's rules.

- Benjamin Franklin never revealed the identity of the person who had given him the famous letters in the first place. Historians still make guesses, but no one knows for sure.

Where to Learn More

Bailyn, Bernard. *The Ordeal of Thomas Hutchinson.* Cambridge: Belknap Press, 1974.

Boatner, Mark M. "Thomas Hutchinson" and "Hutchinson Letters Affair" in *Encyclopedia of the American Revolution.* Mechanicsburg, PA: Stackpole Books, 1994.

Franklin, Benjamin. *Writings.* New York: Library of America, 1987.

Lemay, J. A. Leo, and P. M. Zall, eds. *Benjamin Franklin's Autobiography: An Authoritative Text.* New York: W. W. Norton, 1986.

McFarland, Philip. *The Brave Bostonians: Hutchinson, Quincy, Franklin, and the Coming of the American Revolution.* Boulder: Westview Press, 1998.

Pencak, William. *America's Burke: The Mind of Thomas Hutchinson.* Washington, D.C.: University Press of America, 1982.

"Thomas Hutchinson" in *Encyclopedia of World Biography.* Volume 8. Detroit: Gale Research, 1998.

Walmsley, Andrew Stephen. *Thomas Hutchinson and the Origins of the American Revolution.* New York: New York University Press, 1999.

Willcox, William B., ed. *The Papers of Benjamin Franklin.* New Haven, CT: Yale University Press, 1978.

Resolves of the House of Representatives . . .

Adopted by the Massachusetts Assembly

Enacted June 16, 1773; excerpted from *The Life of Thomas Hutchinson, Royal Governor of the Province of Massachusetts Bay*

In the spring of 1773, the so-called Hutchinson letters (discussed earlier) were read at a meeting of the Massachusetts Assembly (also known as the House of Representatives). The letters had been written between 1767 and 1769 by Governor Thomas Hutchinson (1711–1780), Lieutenant Governor Andrew Oliver (1706–1774), and others, to friends in England. The letters commented on colonial reactions to British taxation policies.

When they heard the letters, the Massachusetts representatives were just as outraged as the public had been. Especially outrageous was Hutchinson's statement that "there must be a great restraint of natural liberty!" How dare Hutchinson urge British authorities to take away American freedoms? On June 23, 1773, the Massachusetts Assembly adopted a petition begging Parliament for the removal of Hutchinson and Oliver from their offices. The petition was based on the grounds that the Assembly and the people of Massachusetts no longer had confidence in Hutchinson and Oliver. The petition was called Resolves of the House of Representatives, Respecting the Letters of the Governor, Lieutenant Governor, and Others.

The petition began by stating that the letters gave a false view of what was going on in the colonies, a view that

"... The writer of these letters, signed Thomas Hutchinson, has been thus exerting himself, by his 'secret confidential correspondence,' to introduce measures, destructive of our constitutional liberty, he has been practising every method among the people of this province, to fix in their minds an exalted opinion of his warmest affection for them. ..."

From Resolves of the House of Representatives . . .

Thomas Hutchinson, whose letters led to a petition by the Massachusetts Assembly for his removal as royal governor of Massachusetts.
Reproduced by permission of Archive Photos.

showed the colonies to Parliament in the worst possible light. The petition denied Hutchinson's claim that the letters were personal correspondence written to a private citizen. The petition said the letters contained suggestions for how King George III (1738–1820) and Parliament should deal with the colonies. The petition went on to say that the misleading letters must certainly have so angered the king and Parliament that they dealt harshly with the colonies.

The petition claimed that one purpose of the letters was to have British soldiers sent to America to enforce the payment of taxes. Now the soldiers were in America disrupting the peace and promoting misery and bloodshed. The petition claimed that the letter writers had a special interest in seeing that taxes were collected, because their salaries were paid from the taxes. The petition claimed that Hutchinson tried to get colonial liberties quashed while he was going about pretending to have the colonists' best interests at heart. Hutchinson and the other letter writers were accused of trying to enrich themselves while denying liberties to other Americans.

As a matter of fact, the assembly complained, all the bad acts that ever came out of Great Britain were the fault of evil people making false claims about the colonies. The assembly complained that its petitions to King George had not been shown to him (the petitions had listed colonial grievances and begged for relief). King George had only seen letters written by people who had something to gain (their salaries) from the taxes placed on Americans. Those taxes had taken away American liberties and rights. The assembly expressed its confidence that the king must now agree: It was best for him and for the cause of peace if the letter writers did not continue in positions of authority.

Finally, the Massachusetts Assembly claimed it was its duty to King George and the citizens of Massachusetts to ask for the removal of Hutchinson and Oliver from office.

Things to remember while reading excerpts from the Resolves of the House of Representatives:

- Hutchinson's letters were written to a friend of Hutchinson's, Thomas Whately. However, Whately's name had been erased, so the Assembly did not know to whom the letters were written. Hutchinson's letters were actually private correspondence to a friend who was *not* in a position to influence British policy. The assembly refused to take Hutchinson's word for it.

- When Benjamin Franklin sent the letters to the speaker of the Massachusetts Assembly, he sent a cover letter. Franklin's letter said that the letters had been written to influence the king against the colonies. The assembly chose to believe Franklin over Hutchinson. Did Franklin really believe that Hutchinson and Oliver were trying to influence British policy? Did he really believe that King George and Parliament would have based their colonial policy on the opinions of Hutchinson and Oliver? Historians have questioned Franklin's sincerity throughout the whole Hutchinson letters affair. They doubt that he really believed the letters would be kept confidential. After all, it was Franklin who had written in his famous book, *Poor Richard's Almanac*: "Three may keep a secret if two of them are dead." Perhaps Franklin thought a greater good would come from his revelation of the letters. If harmony could be restored between England and America, that was a greater good than maintaining Hutchinson's reputation.

Excerpt from Resolves of the House of Representatives, Respecting the Letters of the Governor, Lieutenant Governor, and Others

*Resolved, That the letters signed Thomas Hutchinson, and those signed Andrew Oliver, now **under consideration of** this House, appear to be the **genuine** letters of the present Governor and Lieu-*

Resolved: It has been decided by this law-making body.

Under consideration of: Being examined by.

Genuine: Real; authentic.

Aggravated: Exaggerated.

Manifest design: Obvious purpose.

Represent the matters they treat of: Describe their subject.

Injurious: Harmful.

Aforesaid: Mentioned before.

Came to the chair: Became governor.

Represented abroad: Described everywhere.

Eminent: Outstanding.

Exalted station: High office.

Solid intelligence: Reliable news.

Have, and really had, a public operation: Be official government documents.

Revenue: A government's income.

Fleet: A number of warships operating together under one commander.

Esteemed: Looked upon as.

Appointed: Decided upon.

Repugnant to the charter: Offensive list of rules.

Subversive: Intending to overthrow.

Design: Intent.

Promoted the enacting said revenue acts, and the establishments founded on the same: Helped get tax acts passed and helped set up agencies to collect taxes.

Confidential: Private.

tenant Governor of this province, whose hand writing and signatures are well known to many of the Members of this House; and, that they contain **aggravated** accounts of facts, and misrepresentations; and, that one **manifest design** of them, was, to **represent the matters they treat of** in a light, highly **injurious** to this province, and the persons against whom they were wrote.

Resolved, That, though the letters **aforesaid,** signed Thomas Hutchinson, are said by the Governor, in his message to this House, of June 9th, to be private letters, wrote to a gentleman in London, since deceased, and that all, except the last, were wrote many months before he **came to the chair,** yet, they were wrote by the present Governor, when he was Lieutenant Governor and Chief Justice of this province, who has been **represented abroad,** as **eminent** for his abilities, as for his **exalted station;** and was under no official obligation to transmit intelligence of such matters as are contained in said letters; and, that they, therefore, must be considered by the person to whom they were sent, as documents of **solid intelligence;** and, that this gentleman in London, to whom they were wrote, was then a Member of the British Parliament, and one who was very active in American affairs; and therefore, that these letters, however secretly wrote, must naturally be supposed to **have, and really had, a public operation.** . . .

Resolved, As the opinion of this House, that it clearly appears from the letters aforesaid, signed Thomas Hutchinson, and Andrew Oliver, that it was the desire and endeavor of the writers of them, that certain acts of the British Parliament, for raising a **revenue** in America, might be carried into effect by military force; and by introducing a **fleet** and army into his Majesty's loyal province, to intimidate the minds of his subjects here, and prevent every constitutional measure to obtain the repeal of those acts, so justly **esteemed** a grievance to us, and to suppress the very spirit of freedom.

Resolved, That it is the opinion of this House, that, as the salaries lately **appointed** for the Governor, Lieutenant Governor, and Judges of this province, directly **repugnant to the charter** of this province, and **subversive** of justice, are founded on this revenue; and, as those letters were wrote with a **design,** and had a tendency to promote and support that revenue, therefore, there is great reason to suppose the writers of those letters, were well knowing to, suggested, and **promoted the enacting said revenue acts, and the establishments founded on the same.**

Resolved, That while the writer of these letters, signed Thomas Hutchinson, has been thus exerting himself, by his "secret **confiden-**

tial correspondence," to introduce measures, destructive of our constitutional liberty, he has been practising every method among the people of this province, to fix in their minds an exalted opinion of his warmest affection for them, and his **unremitted endeavors** to promote their best interest at the Court of Great Britain.

Resolved, As the opinion of this House,. . . that it is manifest, that there has been, for many years past, measures contemplated, and a plan formed, by a set of men, born and educated among us, to raise their own fortunes, and advance themselves to posts of honor and profit, not only to the destruction of the charter and constitution of this province, but at the expense of the rights and liberties of the American colonies. And, it is further the opinion of this House, that the said persons have been [largely responsible for introducing a military force here to carry out their plans, and so have disrupted the peace between England and the colonies and promoted the misery and bloodshed that followed].

Whereas, for many years past, measures have been taken by the British administration, very **grievous** to the good people of this province, which this House have now reason to suppose, were promoted, if not originally suggested, by the writers of these letters; and many efforts have been made, by the people, to **obtain the redress of their grievances.** . . .

Resolved, That it has been the misfortune of this government, from the earliest period of it, from time to time, to be secretly **traduced, and maliciously represented** to the **British Ministry**, by persons who were neither friendly to this colony, nor to the English constitution:

Resolved, That this House is bound, in duty to the King and their **constituents, humbly to remonstrate** to his Majesty, the conduct of his Excellency Thomas Hutchinson, **Esquire**, Governor, and the Honorable Andrew Oliver, Esquire, Lieutenant Governor of this province; and to pray that his Majesty would be pleased to remove them forever from the government thereof. (Hosmer, pp. 438–42)

Unremitted endeavors: Persistent efforts.

Grievous: Painful.

Obtain the redress of their grievances: Have their complaints resolved.

Traduced, and maliciously represented: Embarrassed by false statements and portrayed in a very mean way.

British Ministry: British government.

Constituents: People represented by elected officials.

Humbly to remonstrate: To plead with in a meek and mild way.

Esquire: a British title showing respect.

What happened next . . .

By the time the petition to remove Hutchinson and Oliver from office was adopted by the Massachusetts Assembly in June 1773, Governor Hutchinson was worn out from waiting for Parliament to act against the rebels. He requested permission from King George to go to England so that he could discuss taking on a different job. In June 1774, sixty-two-year-old Thomas Hutchinson, respected son of an old and famous Massachusetts family, sailed for England, never to return.

In London, six weeks after the petition was passed, Benjamin Franklin presented it to Lord Dartmouth (1731–1801), British secretary for the American colonies. It would be Dartmouth's job to present this very unusual document to King George's advisers, the Privy (pronounced PRIH-vee) Council. But the matter was never resolved. When Franklin was identified as the person who made the Hutchinson letters public—and was accused of stealing the letters in the first place—he was banished by the British government.

Where to Learn More

Bailyn, Bernard. *The Ordeal of Thomas Hutchinson.* Cambridge: Belknap Press, 1974.

Boatner, Mark M. "Thomas Hutchinson" and "Hutchinson Letters Affair" in *Encyclopedia of the American Revolution.* Mechanicsburg, PA: Stackpole Books, 1994.

Franklin, Benjamin. *Writings.* New York: Library of America, 1987.

Hosmer, James K. *The Life of Thomas Hutchinson, Royal Governor of the Province of Massachusetts Bay.* Cambridge: Riverside Press, 1896.

Lemay, J. A. Leo, and P. M. Zall, eds. *Benjamin Franklin's Autobiography: An Authoritative Text.* New York: W. W. Norton, 1986.

McFarland, Philip. *The Brave Bostonians: Hutchinson, Quincy, Franklin, and the Coming of the American Revolution.* Boulder: Westview Press, 1998.

Pencak, William. *America's Burke: The Mind of Thomas Hutchinson.* Washington, D.C.: University Press of America, 1982.

"Thomas Hutchinson" in *Encyclopedia of World Biography.* Volume 8. Detroit: Gale Research, 1998.

Walmsley, Andrew Stephen. *Thomas Hutchinson and the Origins of the American Revolution.* New York: New York University Press, 1999.

Benjamin Franklin

Public Statement on the Hutchinson Letters

December 25, 1773; excerpted from Benjamin Franklin's *Writings*

While Benjamin Franklin (1706–1790) waited for King George III's (1738–1820) Privy Council to discuss the Massachusetts petition to remove Governor Thomas Hutchinson (1711–1780) and Lieutenant Governor Andrew Oliver (1706–1774) from office (discussed in previous entry), a duel took place in England. Remember that the Hutchinson letters had been written to Thomas Whately, now dead. How Franklin came to have the letters, no one knows; someone probably stole them and gave them to Franklin. The brother of the dead Mr. Whately accused a man named John Temple of stealing the Hutchinson letters and giving them to Franklin. In the duel between Whately and Temple on December 11, 1773, Whately was wounded. Horrified, Franklin caused a notice to be published in the newspaper.

The notice explained that after hearing about the duel over the letters, Franklin felt compelled to accept sole responsibility for acquiring the letters and sending them to Boston. He said he did so in order to avoid further "mischief." Franklin did not stop there. He went on to explain his interpretation of the letters—that their purpose was to make Great Britain angry

"Finding that two Gentlemen have been unfortunately engaged in a Duel, about a transaction and its circumstances of which both of them are totally ignorant and innocent, I think it incumbent on me to declare . . . that I alone am the person who obtained and transmitted to Boston the letters in question."

Benjamin Franklin

Benjamin Franklin, a major player in the Hutchinson letters affair.
Reproduced by permission of the National Portrait Gallery, Smithsonian Institution.

at the colonies. He claimed that the letter writers had tried to keep the letters a secret for fear that their contents would become known in the colonies. Indeed, their fears were justified, because once Franklin had the letters, he felt himself duty-bound to send them to America.

Things to remember while reading Benjamin Franklin's public statement on the Hutchinson letters:

• In his statement, Franklin claimed that the letters were "not of the nature of 'private letters between friends,'" but were in fact letters written to public officials urging drastic action against the colonies. Hutchinson claimed to the end of his life that his letters were simply his observations and opinions about what was going on in Massachusetts, written to a friend (Whately). Historians still wonder how truthful Franklin was being when he explained his motives in the Hutchinson letters affair. He may have believed that his misleading statements would help restore harmony between Great Britain and America.

Benjamin Franklin's Public Statement on the Hutchinson Letters

SIR,

*Finding that two Gentlemen have been unfortunately engaged in a Duel, about a **transaction and its circumstances** of which both of them are totally ignorant and innocent, I think it **incumbent on** me*

Transaction and its circumstances: The sending of the letters to officials in Massachusetts and its aftermath.

Incumbent on: Necessary for.

to declare (for the prevention of farther mischief, as far as such a declaration may contribute to prevent it) that I alone am the person who obtained and transmitted to Boston the letters in question.—Mr. W. could not communicate them, because they were never in his possession; and for the same reason, they could not be taken from him by Mr. T.—They were not of the nature of "private letters between friends:" They were written by public officers to persons in public station, on public affairs, and intended to **procure public measures;** they were therefore handed to other public persons who might be influenced by them to produce those measures. Their **tendency** was to **incense** the Mother Country against her Colonies, and, by the steps recommended, to widen the **breach**, which they **effected.** The chief Caution expressed with regard to Privacy, was, to keep their contents from the Colony Agents, who the writers **apprehended** might return them, or copies of them, to America. That apprehension was, it seems, well founded; for the first Agent who laid his hands on them, thought it his duty to transmit them to his **Constituents.**

B. Franklin, Agent for the House of Representatives of the Massachusetts-Bay. (Franklin, pp. 703–4)

Procure public measures: Get acts passed that would affect the public.

Tendency: Purpose.

Incense: Anger.

Breach: Gap.

Effected: Accomplished; brought about.

Apprehended: Understood.

Constituents: People represented by elected officials.

What happened next . . .

Franklin's announcement was the first admission that he was the man who had made public the Hutchinson letters. Franklin was scheduled to appear before the king's Privy Council a month later, in January 1774, to discuss the Massachusetts Assembly's petition to remove Hutchinson from his governorship. Naturally, Parliament had heard about the duel and Franklin's admission of his role in making the Hutchinson letters public. If that was not enough to anger British authorities, the next piece of news to reach England was that the Boston Tea Party had taken place on December 16, 1773. In that incident, Boston rebels protesting British taxes had dumped 342 chests of British tea into Boston Harbor. When Franklin appeared before the Privy Council in January 1774, the Council was not very happy to see him.

Writer Philip McFarland described the scene in Parliament:

The Privy Council was not long in concluding that the Assembly's request was based on "False and erroneous allegations [charges]," and hence was "groundless, Vexatious [pronounced vex-A-shus; annoying] and Scandalous and calculated only for the . . . Purpose of keeping up a Spirit of Clamour [loud outcry] and Discontent." But much of the hearing was directed . . . not toward the petition but toward the agent who had submitted it. For the first time in all his years in England, Dr. Franklin was treated with something less than courtesy. He was, in fact, to be humiliated, an old man approaching seventy . . . while thirty-four lords of the Privy Council among crowds of spectators sniggered [laughed with contempt] and applauded in approval. . . .

. . . the solicitor general, having charged him with being a thief, advised the prudent [careful] to hide their papers and lock up their [desks] when this gentleman came among them.

The next day, Franklin's job as deputy postmaster of the colonies was taken from him by the British government as punishment for his part in the Hutchinson letters affair. Few of his friends in London thanked Franklin for his decision about the letters. He was abused in the newspapers, and those he thought were his friends turned on him. Franklin was bitter, but not sorry; he thought his act was one of the best things he had ever done.

Although the Massachusetts petition to remove Hutchinson and Oliver from office was rejected by the king's Privy Council, Hutchinson's career in Massachusetts was nearly over. He went to England to ask for another job. In July 1774, he spoke personally with King George III. He urged the king to reconcile with the colonies, a plea he had never made when he was governor. Meanwhile, the British passed the Intolerable Acts to punish Boston for the Boston Tea Party. The Intolerable Acts closed the Port of Boston, gave the British-appointed governor of Massachusetts complete control of town meetings, ordered that British officials who committed major crimes in the colonies would be tried in Great Britain, and required that the colonists house British soldiers in dwellings belonging to private citizens. To make sure the Intolerable Acts were enforced, General Thomas Gage (1721–1787) was sent from England to America to serve as commander in chief of British forces. He was also appointed governor of Massachusetts in Hutchinson's place.

Did you know . . .

- Benjamin Franklin was so anxious to have peace restored between Great Britain and the colonies that he offered to pay the East India Company for the tea dumped into Boston Harbor at the Boston Tea Party.

- Benjamin Franklin grew up only six blocks from Thomas Hutchinson. Franklin's modest boyhood home in Boston was in sharp contrast to the Hutchinson family's elegant mansion.

Where to Learn More

Bailyn, Bernard. *The Ordeal of Thomas Hutchinson.* Cambridge: Belknap Press, 1974.

Boatner, Mark M. "Thomas Hutchinson" and "Hutchinson Letters Affair" in *Encyclopedia of the American Revolution.* Mechanicsburg, PA: Stackpole Books, 1994.

Franklin, Benjamin. *Writings.* New York: Library of America, 1987.

Lemay, J. A. Leo, and P. M. Zall, eds. *Benjamin Franklin's Autobiography: An Authoritative Text.* New York: W. W. Norton, 1986.

McFarland, Philip. *The Brave Bostonians: Hutchinson, Quincy, Franklin, and the Coming of the American Revolution.* Boulder: Westview Press, 1998.

Pencak, William. *America's Burke: The Mind of Thomas Hutchinson.* Washington, D.C.: University Press of America, 1982.

"Thomas Hutchinson" in *Encyclopedia of World Biography.* Volume 8. Detroit: Gale Research, 1998.

Walmsley, Andrew Stephen. *Thomas Hutchinson and the Origins of the American Revolution.* New York: New York University Press, 1999.

Americans' Reactions to Benedict Arnold's Treason
1780

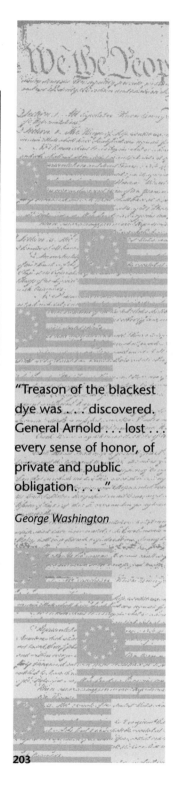

In colonial America, there were many men who were just as eager to get ahead as Thomas Hutchinson (1711–1780; see earlier entries in this chapter). For a man like Benedict Arnold (1741–1801), whose father had left him no money, one of the best and fastest ways to get noticed was by advancing through the military ranks. More than a few Revolutionary-era figures first came to national attention in that way, but not many were as famous as Arnold, both before and after his betrayal of his country.

By all accounts, Arnold was an outstanding military leader. He was loved by his men and exhibited tremendous courage and daring in battle. In 1775, he nearly took Quebec (Canada) with the intention of making it a fourteenth colony. That campaign involved a terrible march through the freezing wilderness; at one point his starving men were reduced to eating boiled candles. After that failure, he went on to save America from defeat at the hands of the British on several occasions. He played an important part in the American victory at Saratoga, New York, in 1777. That victory marked the beginning of the end of British control of the colonies, but it left Arnold with a shattered leg from a bullet wound.

> "Treason of the blackest dye was . . . discovered. General Arnold . . . lost . . . every sense of honor, of private and public obligation. . . ."
>
> *George Washington*

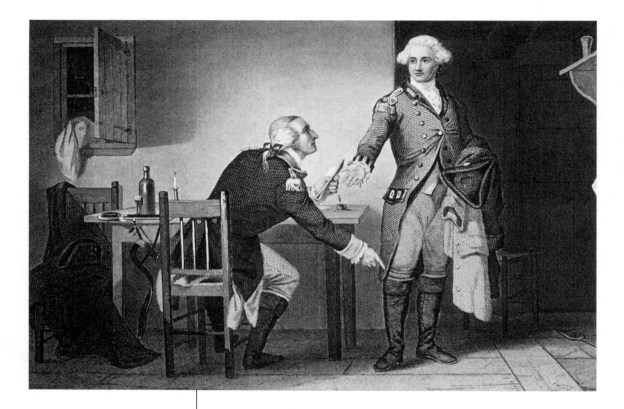

Benedict Arnold persuades British major John André to hide important papers in his boot.
Reproduced by permission of Archive Photos.

In 1780, General George Washington (1732–1799), who liked and admired Arnold, placed him in command of West Point, New York. By then, Arnold was a bitter man because he was passed up repeatedly for promotion (see sidebar entry on Arnold on p. 208). When British Major John André (1750–1780) approached him about betraying the American cause for money and a high military position in the British army, Arnold agreed to turn over West Point to the British. But André was captured by the Americans and hanged as a spy. Arnold managed to escape. News of his betrayal spread like wildfire.

What follows are various Americans' reactions to the treason of Benedict Arnold. An American officer, Lieutenant John Whiting, comments on the impressions he had of Arnold prior to learning of Arnold's betrayal of his country. General Washington's announcement of Arnold's treason is read by Nathanael Greene (1742–1786), a general in the Continental Army and, later, head of the commission that court-martialed (tried in court for military offenses) André. An anonymous poet writes an "acrostic"—a poem in which the first letters in each line form a name or message, in this case, Benedict Arnold. And Washington summarizes the events of the Arnold affair.

Things to remember while reading excerpts from Americans' reactions to Benedict Arnold's treason:

- Before his betrayal (discovered in 1780), Benedict Arnold was a major American hero. After Arnold was wounded in 1777, George Washington named him military governor of Philadelphia, Pennsylvania, recently abandoned by the British. His duties were not heavy. After years of hardship, Arnold was ready to enjoy lighthearted pursuits, especially since he had recently married Peggy Shippen, a beautiful, lively, young woman, who came from a wealthy family.

- The Arnolds had a reputation for their love of luxury and Philadelphia society; they were living far beyond their means. Meanwhile, support for the American cause was fading; the war seemed to drag on and on, and people were tired of it.

British spy John André, who was later hanged for his actions.
Engraving by W. G. Jackman. Reproduced by permission of Archive Photos.

Comments of Lieutenant John Whiting on Arnold's treason

Many Persons say they were not deceived in Genl. Arnold: I confess I had a good opinion of him as an Officer in the Field, but ever

Possest: Possessed.

Avarice: (Pronounced AV-a-riss) Greed.

Profuse manner: Free-spending way.

Perfidious: (Pronounced per-FID-ee-us) Faithless.

thought him to be ambitious and **possest** of a great degree of **avarice** and luxury. Some imagine his **profuse manner** of living had so involved him in debt that poverty urged him to it. Enough upon so **perfidious** a person. Leave him to his fate and admire the Man who bears to be honest in the worst of times. (Morpurgo, p. 171)

General George Washington's announcement to the Continental Army of Arnold's treason

Treason of the blackest dye was yesterday discovered. General Arnold, who commanded at West Point, lost to every sense of honor, of private and public obligation, was about to deliver up that important post into the hands of the enemy. Such an event must have given the American cause a dangerous, if not a fatal wound; but the treason has been timely discovered, to prevent the fatal misfortune. The **providential train of circumstances which led to it** affords the most convincing proof that the liberties of America are the object of Divine protection. At the same time that the treason is to be regretted, the general cannot help congratulating the army on the happy discovery.

Providential train of circumstances which led to it: The path to the discovery of his treason, seemingly revealed by God.

Base art: Dirty trick.

Effect: Bring about.

Proof against all the arts and seductions of an insidious enemy: Resistant to every clever trick played by a sneaky enemy.

Our enemies, despairing of carrying their point by force, are practicing every **base art** to **effect** by bribery and corruption what they cannot accomplish in a manly way. Great honor is due to the American army that this is the first instance of treason of the kind, where many were to be expected from the nature of the dispute. The brightest ornament in the character of the American soldiers is their having been **proof against all the arts and seductions of an insidious enemy.** Arnold has made his escape to the enemy, but Major André . . . who came out as a spy, is our prisoner. (Wheeler, p. 352)

American Revolution: Primary Sources

"An Acrostic—On Arnold"

Born for a curse to virtue and Mankind,
Earth's broadest realms can't show so black a mind.
Night's sable veil your crimes can never hide,
Each one's so great—they **glut** the historic tide.
Defunct—your memory will live.
In all the glares that **infamy** can give.
Curses of ages will attend your name.
Traitors alone will glory in your shame.
Almighty justice sternly waits to roll
Rivers of sulphur on your traitorous soul.
Nature looks back, with conscious error sad,
On such a tainted blot that she has made,
Let Hell receive you **rivetted** in chains,
Damn'd to the hottest of its flames." (Martin, p. 9)

Acrostic: (Pronounced uh-KROSS-tik) A poem in which the first letters in each line form a name or message, in this case, Benedict Arnold.

Glut: Fill beyond capacity.

Defunct: Even when you are no longer alive.

Infamy: Evil reputation.

Rivers of sulphur: Fiery waters.

Rivetted: Securely fastened.

Closing lines of George Washington's summary of the treason story

André has met his fate . . . with that **fortitude** which was to be expected from an accomplished man and a gallant officer. But I [doubt] if Arnold is suffering . . . the torments of a mental hell. He [lacks] feeling. From some traits of his character which have lately come to my knowledge, he seems to have been so **hacknied** in crime, so lost to all sense of honor and shame, that while his **faculties** still enable him to continue his **sordid** pursuits, there will be no time for remorse. (American Journey [CD-ROM])

Fortitude: Strength of mind that allowed him to face pain with courage.

Hacknied: (Pronounced HAK-need) Worn out from overuse.

Faculties: Mental abilities.

Sordid: Filthy.

Benedict Arnold: American Traitor

Benedict Arnold was born on January 14, 1741, in Norwich, Connecticut, to a well-to-do merchant father, Benedict Arnold IV, and a wealthy widow, Hannah Waterman King. The Arnold family had a long and celebrated history in America; for instance, an earlier Benedict Arnold had served as governor of Rhode Island. But Benedict IV lost the family fortune and turned to drink, and young Arnold saw his dreams of higher education and a position in society turn to dust. At age fourteen, he left his comfortable home to go to a relative and learn to be a druggist. His mother died in 1759, and his father passed away two years later. By then, the elder Arnold's drinking had become a source of shame for Arnold and his sister Hannah, his only sibling. Their relatives and neighbors shunned them.

Arnold set up his own drugstore in 1761, and he supplemented his income by smuggling goods from the West Indies. In 1767, he married Margaret Mansfield, who bore him three sons in five years before she died at the age of thirty in 1776. At the time, Arnold was leading a failed march against Quebec in the early stages of the Revolution. To his personal tragedy was added the anger he felt when Congress refused to promote him to major general in 1777. In the next two years, five other soldiers were promoted to major general ahead of him, and Arnold's bitterness against Congress grew.

Arnold continued to receive public praise for his military exploits, but it never

Benedict Arnold, America's most famous traitor.
Courtesy of the Library of Congress.

seemed to be enough to satisfy him. He became convinced that corrupt politicians were denying him the honors he deserved. By the time he was approached by the British in 1780 about coming over to their side, he had a much younger wife (Peggy Shippen) to support. He also seemed to have concluded that the new nation was being run so poorly that it might as well be run by the British. These are some of the reasons historians have given for Arnold's decision to change sides. For years he expressed his loyalty to the American cause and proved it by giving up his business and risking his life. At some point, though, he changed his mind about the rightness of that cause, and his name has come to be a synonym for treason.

What happened next . . .

The shock to the public at the news of Arnold's treason was enormous. The popular cry became: "Treason! Treason! Treason! Black as Hell." Arnold's scheme to deliver a deadly blow to the cause of American independence was a failure. People agreed that Arnold had failed because God was on the American side, and support for the cause was rekindled.

Arnold fled down the Hudson River and into the arms of the British. He was supposed to assume a position of command, but British soldiers refused to serve under him. They had all liked and respected the hanged Major André, but they considered Arnold a man without honor and they never completely trusted him. After the war ended, Arnold moved to London, England, where he was booed in public. The shipping industry he started failed, and he died in 1801, his suffering made worse by the terrible pain in his twice-wounded leg.

Did you know . . .

- In 1997, Art Cohn, director of the Lake Champlain Maritime Museum in Vergennes, Vermont, was using sonar equipment to scan Vermont's Lake Champlain when he made a discovery he had long hoped for: a Revolutionary War gunboat that was part of a fleet commanded by Benedict Arnold before he committed treason against his country. The gunboat was sitting upright at the bottom of Lake Champlain. It had been astonishingly well-preserved by the cold, deep water for 220 years. Cohn said that when he went down on the first dive to the ship, "There was a voice screaming in my head, 'Oh my God, this is the gunboat! Benedict Arnold probably walked on this deck!'"

Where to Learn More

Brandt, Claire. *The Man in the Mirror: A Life of Benedict Arnold*. New York: Random House, 1994.

"Divers Discover Gunboat of Benedict Arnold." [Online] http://www.wcinet.com/th/News/070197/National/65559.htm (accessed on April 7, 2000).

Fritz, Jean. *Traitor: The Case of Benedict Arnold*. New York: Putnam Publishing Group, 1997.

King, David C. *Benedict Arnold and the American Revolution.* Woodbridge, CT: Blackbirch Press, 1998.

Martin, James Kirby. *Benedict Arnold, Revolutionary Hero: An American Warrior Reconsidered.* New York: New York University Press, 1997.

Morpurgo, J. E. *Treason at West Point: The Arnold-André Conspiracy.* New York: Mason/Charter, 1975.

"Planning Underway for Future of Newly Discovered Revolutionary War Gunboat." Lake Champlain Maritime Museum home page. [Online] http://www.lcmm.org/pages/NauticalSurvey9907a.html (accessed on April 7, 2000).

Randall, Willard Sterne. *Benedict Arnold: Patriot and Traitor.* New York: Morrow, 1990.

Wheeler, Richard. *Voices of 1776.* New York: Thomas Y. Crowell Co., 1972.

Notes from the Battlefronts

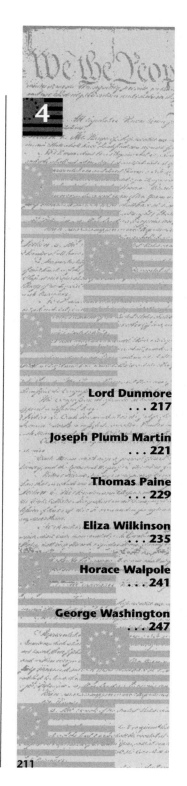

Ever since 1765, the British government (Parliament) had been trying to collect taxes in America to pay British bills. Americans protested right from the beginning that Parliament had no right to tax people who had no representation in Parliament. Some Americans voiced their objections to British taxation in newspapers and pamphlets. Others, like Samuel Adams (1722–1803) and his Sons of Liberty, protested violently and spoke early, openly, and illegally about independence from Great Britain. The last straw for the British was the Boston Tea Party of December 1773, when Boston patriots dumped 342 chests of British tea into Boston Harbor. To punish Boston, which was the center of the most violent protests, and to let Boston serve as an example to the other colonies, Parliament passed the Intolerable Acts in 1774. The Intolerable Acts closed the port of Boston, gave the British-appointed governor of Massachusetts complete control of town meetings, ordered that British officials who committed major crimes in the colonies would be tried in Great Britain, and required that the colonists house British soldiers in dwellings belonging to private citizens.

Lord Dunmore . . . 217

Joseph Plumb Martin . . . 221

Thomas Paine . . . 229

Eliza Wilkinson . . . 235

Horace Walpole . . . 241

George Washington . . . 247

Closing the port of Boston (as a result of the Boston Port Act) meant that no goods could go in or out of the city, and even fishing boats could not use the harbor. The idea was to starve Boston citizens into paying for the dumped tea. Their loss of control over town meetings (the Administration of Justice Act) took away the self-government that Massachusetts citizens had enjoyed since the founding of Plymouth Colony in 1621. To Bostonians, these were the most offensive of Great Britain's punitive acts.

Parliament then appointed General Thomas Gage (1721–1787) to be commander in chief of British forces in America as well as governor of Massachusetts. He arrived in May 1774 with instructions to set up a new Massachusetts capital in Salem (near Boston) and prepare to make sure the Intolerable Acts were enforced.

The other colonies were angry at the British for their punishment of Boston. They wondered what punishments might be in store for them. They were also moved by sympathy for the plight of the suffering citizens of Boston. Finally, twelve of the thirteen colonies decided to send representatives to a First Continental Congress to decide what to do about the problem. Congress met for the first time in September 1774.

Congress issued statements complaining about the Intolerable Acts and just about every other act of Parliament since 1765. Congress drew up several petitions to King George III (1738–1820), listing their complaints and asking for a remedy. Congress then agreed to discontinue trade with Great Britain until the problems were addressed. Congress promised to meet again in May 1775 if the problems had not been set right.

King George refused to have anything to do with Congress's petitions. He said Congress was an illegal body and any documents coming from it were also illegal. Meanwhile, the atmosphere in Boston grew more hostile, and General Gage was forced to move there from Salem to keep the peace. Bostonians resented the presence of so many soldiers in town, and they resented Gage's attempts to enforce the Intolerable Acts. During the winter of 1774–75, Massachusetts rebels began to train for war and to stockpile weapons and ammunition at Concord, Massachusetts.

The British government grew more determined to show Boston and the rest of the colonies who was boss. On April 14, 1775, General Gage received instructions to do *something* that would show he was in charge. Gage decided to send soldiers to Lexington, Massachusetts, to arrest Samuel Adams and his friend, John Hancock (1737–1793), another member of the Sons of Liberty, both of whom had been branded criminals by Parliament. From there, the soldiers were to march on to Concord to seize the rebel weapons stockpiled there. Alerted by patriots Paul Revere (1735–1818) and William Dawes (1745–1799), a band of between forty and seventy minutemen (citizen-soldiers, prepared to protect their town at a minute's notice) turned out to greet the British at Lexington on April 19. Shots were fired at Lexington and Concord, and the Revolutionary War unofficially began. Hancock and Adams escaped and made their way to Philadelphia for the May 10 meeting of the Second Continental Congress.

When shots rang out in Lexington, Massachusetts, the Revolutionary War unofficially began.
Drawing by Amos Doolittle. Courtesy of the National Archives and Records Administration.

Meanwhile, in the colony of Virginia, the British-appointed governor, John Murray (1732–1809), known as Lord Dunmore, was shocked by the April 1775 events at Lexington and Concord. These events occurred in addition to some serious trouble he was having at home with patriot Patrick Henry (1739–1799), who was urging armed resistance to the British. Dunmore finally declared martial law in Virginia in November 1775. Martial law is the temporary rule by military authorities, imposed in time of war or when regular rule ceases to function. Lord Dunmore's Declaration of Martial Law opens this chapter.

Although the fighting had already begun, it would be more than a year after the shootings at Lexington and Concord before Congress officially declared America's independence from Great Britain. One of the first accomplishments of the Second Continental Congress was the formation of a Continental Army with George Washington (1732–1799) as its leader. By November 1775, Washington had seventeen thousand men under his command, but their terms of service were due to expire at the end of the year. Washington put out a call for men to enlist. One young man who answered the call was a sixteen-year-old Connecticut farm boy named Joseph Plumb Martin (1760–1850). Long after the war ended, Martin wrote a book about his Revolutionary War experiences called *A Narrative of Some of the Adventures, Dangers, and Sufferings of a Revolutionary Soldier.* The book was later called, alternatively, *Private Yankee Doodle* and *Yankee Doodle Boy.* Some of Martin's wartime exploits are recounted in this chapter, in his own words.

By the winter of 1776, the war had turned against the Americans. Badly outnumbered and seeming to face defeat at every turn, General Washington needed something that would rally Americans whose patriotism was flagging. He found his answer in the stirring words of writer Thomas Paine's (1737–1809) *The Crisis.* An excerpt appears in this chapter. (A brief biography of Paine and a description of his earlier work, *Common Sense,* also appear in chapter 1.)

The first battles of the Revolutionary War took place mainly in the north. In 1778–79, the scene shifted to the south for some fierce fighting. Sixteen-year-old Eliza Wilkinson was present at the looting of her sister's South Carolina home by British soldiers. Her firsthand account of that dreadful experience has been preserved and an excerpt appears in this chapter.

The fighting in the south climaxed with the decisive American victory at Yorktown, Virginia, on October 18, 1781. This chapter contains writer and politician Horace Walpole's (1717–1797) comments on what he considered a "disgraceful" British surrender. Many Americans believed the war ended at Yorktown, but George Washington was not so sure. He did not trust the British and could not feel secure until a peace treaty had been signed. When that happy event finally occurred in 1783, Washington was able to say goodbye to his troops. His heartfelt farewell ends this chapter.

Lord Dunmore

Declaration of Martial Law in Virginia
Issued on November 7, 1775; excerpted from
Annals of America, **1968**

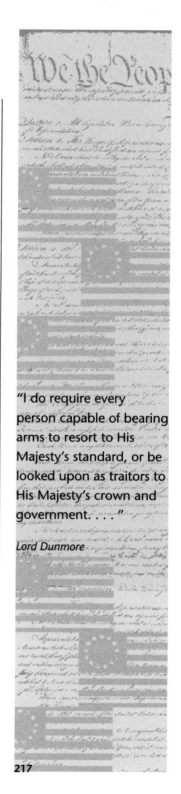

In March 1775, radical patriot Patrick Henry (1736–1799) stood up in front of the Virginia House of Burgesses (its lawmaking body) and made a passionate speech in support of his call for military preparations against the British. He ended his speech with the famous cry, "Give me liberty, or give me death." Virginia's House met illegally because the short-tempered royal governor of Virginia, John Murray (1732–1809), known as Lord Dunmore, had dissolved the legislature in 1773 and 1774 for the openly anti-British sentiments expressed by some of its members. It was still dissolved in 1775 when Henry gave his speech.

After Henry's speech, events in Virginia moved swiftly to armed conflict. As the Massachusetts patriots had done at Concord, Henry and others in Virginia had been stockpiling gunpowder in Williamsburg, Virginia. On May 2, 1775, just as he was about to leave for Philadelphia, Pennsylvania, to attend the Second Continental Congress, Henry learned that Dunmore had seized the stockpile at Williamsburg. Henry and a group of militia men marched on Williamsburg and provoked an armed confrontation with Dunmore. Dunmore was defiant, shouting that "by the living God if an insult is offered to me

"I do require every person capable of bearing arms to resort to His Majesty's standard, or be looked upon as traitors to His Majesty's crown and government. . . . "

Lord Dunmore

or to those who have obeyed my orders, I will declare freedom to the slaves and lay the town in ashes!" But Dunmore backed down, and on May 4 he paid for the gunpowder he had seized.

Dunmore was forced to flee for safety to a British warship anchored off the coast of Virginia. From there, he carried out military maneuvers against the colonists, finally ordering the destruction of Hampton, Virginia, in October 1775. Upset by his failure to destroy Hampton, on November 7, Governor Dunmore declared martial (pronounced MAR-shul) law in Virginia. Martial law is temporary rule by military authorities, imposed in time of war or when regular rule ceases to function. Declaring martial law is a very extreme step, and it was shocking to the citizens of Virginia. Even more shocking was that Dunmore made good on his earlier threat and offered freedom to any slave who deserted his master to bear arms for the British cause.

Things to remember while reading an excerpt from Lord Dunmore's Declaration of Martial Law in Virginia:

- Lord Dunmore was the most assertive of all the colonial governors. He governed a colony with more patriots than any other except Massachusetts. Dunmore did more than any other colonial governor to try to put down the revolutionaries.

- Virginia had far more slaves than patriots. In fact, more than one-third of the population of Virginia was slaves. That is why Virginians were so shocked by Dunmore's offer to free the slaves. For the entire duration of the Revolutionary War, southern slave owners lived in fear of an uprising by armed runaway slaves.

Excerpt from Declaration of Martial Law in Virginia

*And **to the end** that peace and good order may the sooner be restored, I do require every person capable of bearing arms to **resort***

To the end: With this goal in mind.

to His Majesty's standard, or be looked upon as traitors to His Majesty's crown and government, and thereby become **liable** to the penalty the law inflects upon such offenses; such as **forfeiture** of life, **confiscation** of lands, etc.

And I do hereby further declare all **indentured** servants, Negroes, or others . . . free, that are able and willing to bear arms, they joining His Majesty's troops as soon as may be, for the more speedily reducing his colony to a proper sense of their duty to His Majesty's crown and dignity. *(Annals of America, p. 361)*

What happened next . . .

By December 1775, about three hundred runaway slaves had joined Lord Dunmore's Ethiopian Regiment, as his military unit was called (Ethiopian is an outdated term for black Africans). By the following summer, at least eight hundred slaves had joined Dunmore. Rebel Virginia lawmakers responded by ordering the death penalty to "all Negro or other Slaves, conspiring to rebel."

The British joined Lord Dunmore in offering freedom to slaves who served them. While Dunmore's men were armed and fought in battles, the British used the runaway slaves for the least desirable kind of work. This work included digging pit toilets, washing clothes in huge, steaming kettles of water, and tending to the livestock. These slaves were underfed and underclothed, and when a smallpox epidemic broke out among the British Army in Virginia in 1781, the blacks were badly affected and large numbers died. The British left their bodies strewn about the countryside, hoping to spread the disease to local rebels.

Did you know . . .

- As the war dragged on, some runaway slaves were betrayed by British soldiers, who sent them off to be sold in the West Indies (a group of islands between North and South America). The British finally put an end to recruiting slaves

Resort to His Majesty's standard: Return to the king's flag.

Liable: Subject.

Forfeiture: (Pronounced FOR-fit-cher) Surrender.

Confiscation: Seizure (of private property) for the public treasury.

Indentured: Required by law to serve for a set period of time.

for King George III's (1738–1820) army. Still, at the end of the war, the British had to deal with several thousand pro-British former slaves, who could not stay in America, where they were special objects of hatred for siding with the British. Some two to three thousand former slaves were taken to Nova Scotia, in British-owned Canada. Some former slaves were taken to British army headquarters in New York City (the British stayed in New York for about eighteen months after the surrender at Yorktown). Before the British decided what to do with them, many former slaves were seized by their former owners and re-enslaved.

- Many slaves who might have gone over to the British side were prevented by living too far from British posts. They would have had to cross through a lot of American-held territory before they could get to the British. Others were prevented by the fact that they had children living on with other masters, and they would not leave without their children.

Where to Learn More

"Africans in America." America's journey through slavery presented in four parts by PBS and WGBH. Part two: Revolution: 1750–1805. With narratives, a resource bank (list of documents, essays, etc.), and a teacher's guide. [Online] http://web-cr05.pbs.org/wgbh/aia/part2/title.html (accessed on March 25, 2000).

Annals of America. New York: Encyclopedia Britannica, Inc., 1968.

Boatner, Mark M. "Negroes in the American Revolution" in *Encyclopedia of the American Revolution*. Mechanicsburg, PA: Stackpole Books, 1994.

Nardo, Don, and Martin Luther King, Jr. *Braving the New World: 1619–1784: From the Arrival of the Enslaved Africans to the End of the American Revolution (Milestones in Black American History)*. New York: Chelsea House, 1995.

Joseph Plumb Martin

A Narrative of Some of the Adventures, Dangers, and Sufferings of a Revolutionary Soldier

Originally published in 1830 and most recently republished as *Yankee Doodle Boy* in 1995
Excerpted from *Witnessing America*, 1996

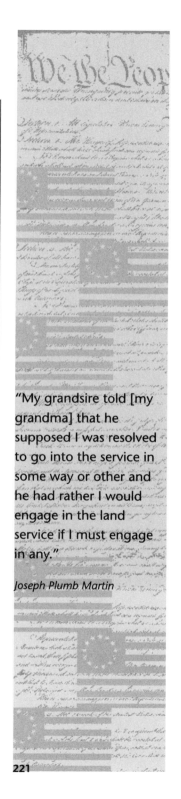

A young Connecticut farm boy, Joseph Plumb Martin (1760–1850), had been aware since 1774 that war with Great Britain was a strong possibility. At first, he vowed to himself to have nothing to do with it. But army recruiters came to his town in the spring of 1775, just after the war had unofficially begun in Lexington and Concord, Massachusetts. The recruiters offered a payment to anyone who would enlist to fight the British. Some of the new recruits stayed at Martin's grandfather's home before they departed to fight in Boston or New York City. Fired up by the conversations he heard and the chance to earn some money, Martin changed his mind and resolved to become a soldier. He was too young then, but in the summer of 1776, Martin enlisted.

For seven years, Martin served in the Continental Army, led by General George Washington (1732–1799). He stayed with Washington for two years after the British surrender at Yorktown, right up until Washington said farewell to his troops (see entry on p. 247). Martin saw action in many of the major battles and in dozens of smaller skirmishes, and he wrote about his experiences after the war was over. Martin's book was published

"My grandsire told [my grandma] that he supposed I was resolved to go into the service in some way or other and he had rather I would engage in the land service if I must engage in any."

Joseph Plumb Martin

Joseph Plumb Martin, Proud Yankee Soldier

Joseph Plumb Martin was born on November 21, 1760, in Becket, Massachusetts. Ebenezer Martin, his father, was minister of a new Congregational Church. He had married Susanna Plumb, daughter of a wealthy Connecticut farmer, while attending Yale College in New Haven, Connecticut. When Joseph was about seven years old, his father left the family. Joseph was left in the care of Susanna's parents, Joseph and Rebecca Plumb.

Joseph never received any formal schooling. Instead, he worked hard on his grandparents' farm, but somehow developed a love for reading and expressing himself by writing. He was only fourteen when the Revolutionary War started in 1775, too young to enlist. He did enlist in June 1776, signing on for a six-month term. He was discharged in December 1776 and returned home, thinking he had had enough of being a soldier. But life on the farm was not as satisfying as it had been, and in April 1777 he joined the Continental Army, where he served until the army was disbanded in 1783.

After the war, Martin worked as a farmer and laborer, but he never prospered. He married Lucy Clewley in 1794, and they had five children. Although his life was hard, Martin retained his sense of humor and his interest in reading and writing.

A Narrative of Some of the Adventures, Dangers, and Sufferings of a Revolutionary Soldier was written when Martin was seventy years old. He described in detail the daily hardships of a common soldier—the fear, pain, and deaths of comrades in battle. It is perhaps the best and liveliest eyewitness account of the American Revolution written from the point of view of a Continental soldier. Martin died in 1850.

in 1830 under the title *A Narrative of Some of the Adventures, Dangers, and Sufferings of a Revolutionary Soldier, Interspersed with Anecdotes of Incidents That Occurred Within His Own Observation.* Two of Martin's war stories follow.

In the first story, the young soldier-to-be described his grandparents' reaction to his decision to enlist in the Continental Army in the spring of 1776. They were reluctant to have him go but realized he was determined to do it.

In the second story, Martin described an incident that occurred while he was on sentry (guard) duty during the 1776 campaign. He was with the Continental Army on the northern

end of Manhattan Island, New York. The British and American lines were very close to each other, and the soldiers were quite jumpy. It was late, Martin was tired, and thinking that his shift must be at an end, he approached a nervous guard to find out what time it was. The guard mistook him for an enemy and fired his weapon; this excited the other men on guard duty. When their commanding officers came to investigate, Martin denied knowing the cause of the disturbance. Word spread

American soldiers battle the British in the Revolutionary War.
Reproduced by permission of Millbrook Press.

that a spy was loose, requiring extra attention. So Martin's guard unit was forced to remain on duty through the night. Despite his fatigue, Martin managed to find humor in the way the spy story spread so quickly.

Things to remember while reading excerpts from *A Narrative of Some of the Adventures, Dangers, and Sufferings of a Revolutionary Soldier:*

- The Continental Army was made up of members of state militias (pronounced muh-LISH-uz). The militia men were not trained, professional soldiers. In addition to being untrained, the nineteen thousand Americans who fought in the New York campaign were poorly armed and were primarily led by amateurs. In contrast, they faced more than forty thousand professional soldiers and sailors, well armed and well supplied, supported by nearly three hundred battleships. It is no wonder that Martin and his fellow sentries were jumpy.

- Manhattan Island was surrounded by deep water, easily navigated by British ships (the Americans had no navy). General Charles Lee (1731–1782), who had arrived there ahead of Washington, wrote to Washington that "whoever commands the sea must command the town." In fact, the Americans knew that the defense of New York was a hopeless cause. They only defended it because it would have hurt American morale to hand over such an important city without a fight.

Excerpts from A Narrative of Some of the Adventures, Dangers, and Sufferings of a Revolutionary Soldier

[First excerpt]

One evening, very early in the spring of this year, I chanced to overhear my grandma'am telling my grandsire that I had threatened to **engage on board a man-of-war.** I had told her that I would enter on board a **privateer** then **fitting out** in our neighborhood. The good old lady thought it a man-of-war, that and privateer being **synonymous terms** with her. She said she could not bear the thought of my being on board of a man-of-war; my grandsire told her that he supposed I was resolved to go into the service in some way or other and he had rather I would engage in the land service if I must engage in any. This I thought to be a sort of **tacit** consent for me to go, and I determined to take advantage of it as quick as possible.

Soldiers were at this time enlisting for a year's service. I did not like that; it was too long a time for me at the first trial; I wished only to **take a priming** before I took upon me the whole coat of paint for a soldier. (Martin, pp. 14–15)

[Second excerpt]

A simple affair happened, while I was upon guard at a time while we were here, which made considerable disturbance amongst the guard and caused me some extra hours of **fatigue** at the time. As I was the cause of it at first, I will relate it. The guard consisted of nearly two hundred men, commanded by a field officer. We kept a long chain of **sentinels** placed almost within speaking distance of each other, and being in close neighborhood with the enemy **we were necessitated to** be pretty alert. I was upon my post as sentinel about the middle of the night. Thinking we had **overgone** the time in which we ought to have been relieved, I stepped a little off my spot towards one of the next sentries, it being quite dark, and asked him in a low voice how long he had been on sentry. He **started** as if attacked by the enemy and roared out, "Who comes there?" I saw I had alarmed him and stole back to my spot as quick as possible. He still kept up his cry, "Who comes there?," and receiving no answer, he **discharged his piece,** which alarmed the whole guard, who immediately formed and prepared for action and sent off a **non-commissioned officer** and file of men to **ascertain** the cause of alarm.

They came first to the man who had fired and asked him what was the matter. He said that someone had made an abrupt advance upon his premises and demanded, "How comes you on, sentry?" They next came to me, inquiring what I had seen. I told them that I had not seen or heard anything to alarm me but what the other sentinel had caused. The men turned to the guard, and we were soon relieved, which was all I had wanted.

Engage on board a man-of-war: Sign up to serve on a warship.

Privateer: A privately owned ship authorized by the government during wartime to attack and capture enemy vessels.

Fitting out: Being filled with necessary supplies.

Synonymous terms: Words meaning the same thing.

Tacit: Understood without being said aloud.

Take a priming: A primer is an undercoat for paint; Martin means he will try it out.

Fatigue: Extreme tiredness.

Sentinels: Guards.

We were necessitated to: We had to.

Overgone: Gone over.

Started: Acted startled.

Discharged his piece: Shot off his weapon.

Non-commissioned officer: An enlisted man who is appointed to a rank that gives him leadership over other enlisted men.

Ascertain: Find out.

*Upon our return to the guard I found, as was to be expected, that the alarm was the subject of general conversation among them. They were confident that a spy or something worse had been amongst us and consequently greater **vigilance** was necessary. We were accordingly kept the rest of the night **under arms**, and I cursed my **indiscretion** for causing the disturbance, as I could get no more rest during the night. I could have set all to rights by speaking a word, but it would not do for me to betray my own secret. But it was **diverting** to me to see how much the story gained by being carried about, both among the guard and after its arrival in the camp. (Rae, pp. 164–65)*

What happened next . . .

As expected, the British captured New York City in September 1776. The city became British headquarters for the duration of the war. The Continental Army, under the command of General Washington, then was forced to retreat across New Jersey and into Pennsylvania. Joseph Plumb Martin stayed with Washington for the rest of the war. He saw the British Army surrender at Yorktown, Virginia, in 1781. He remained with Washington until after the peace treaty was signed, ending the war in 1783.

Did you know . . .

- The term "Yankee" originally was used for New Englanders (people from Massachusetts, Rhode Island, New Hampshire, Connecticut, and Vermont). The British used the word Yankee as an insult, but patriotic Revolutionary War soldiers adopted the term to show their rebel pride.

- "Yankee Doodle" was a Revolutionary-era song whose tune came from an old British drinking song. The legend is that in 1775, a British doctor made up new words to the drinking song to poke fun at American soldiers, who were regarded by the British as "country bumpkins."

- When George Washington arrived in New York in 1776 and began training an army, he faced many problems, including infighting among his men. The problems arose in part from an old boundary dispute, which had pitted the citizens of New York (called "Yorkers") against New Englanders ("Yankees"). Remembering their old hostility, "Yankee" volunteers often fought with "Yorker" soldiers.

Where to Learn More

Diamant, Lincoln. *Yankee Doodle Days: Exploring the American Revolution.* Fleischmanns, NY: Purple Mountain Press, 1996.

Martin, Joseph Plumb. *Private Yankee Doodle: Being a Narrative of Some of the Adventures, Dangers, and Sufferings of a Revolutionary Soldier.* Edited by George F. Scheer. Boston: Little, Brown, 1962.

Martin, Joseph Plumb. *Yankee Doodle Boy: A Young Soldier's Adventures in the American Revolution Told by Himself.* Edited by George F. Scheer. Holiday House, reissued 1995.

Rae, Noel, ed. *Witnessing America: The Library of Congress Book of Firsthand Accounts of Life in America 1600–1900.* New York: Penguin, 1996.

Wilbur, C. Keith. *Pirates and Patriots of the Revolution.* Broomall, PA: Chelsea House, 1996.

Wilbur, C. Keith. *The Revolutionary Soldier: 1775–1783.* Broomall, PA: Chelsea House, 1999.

Thomas Paine

The Crisis

First published on December 19, 1776; excerpted from *Common Sense and Other Political Writings*, 1953

One of the greatest writers of the Revolutionary era was Thomas Paine (1737–1809), whose *Common Sense* is described in chapter 1. Paine was born and raised in England. He tried his hand at several different jobs before he turned to writing. He had only been in America for a few months when he was first asked to use his writing talent in the cause of American independence. His first effort, *Common Sense,* was quite successful. Two years after his arrival in America, Paine wrote the first of *The Crisis* papers.

Paine joined General George Washington's (1732–1799) army in New Jersey in December 1776. By then, Washington was a desperate man. He had just been soundly defeated in New York and forced to flee across New Jersey, with British soldiers hot on his heels. As they passed through New Jersey, both British and American soldiers looted and pillaged New Jersey farms and homes. On December 8, Washington's army crossed the Delaware River and set up camp on the Pennsylvania shore.

Americans were shocked, disgusted, and angry at the reports they heard about the defeat in New York and the soldiers' activities in New Jersey. Public support for the war for independence was on the verge of collapse.

"These are the times that try men's souls."

Thomas Paine

George Washington and soldiers cross the Delaware River, prior to the surprise attack on British-hired German soldiers.

It was winter and conditions were very bad for the soldiers. Thousands deserted what they saw as a lost cause; those who remained were poorly armed and clothed. A few lucky ones slaughtered cows and covered their feet with bloody cow hides, but most of the men were virtually shoeless. The soldiers' terms of duty would expire at the end of December (they only signed on for six months or a year). If Washington could not rally his dejected army, he could not count on anyone signing up again. On December 17, 1776, Washington wrote to his brother: "Your imagination can scarce extend to a situation more distressing than mine. . . . I think the game is pretty near up. . . ."

The American cause seemed doomed. But Washington had formed a daring plan, one that very few people thought could succeed. He would transport his army in boats across the Delaware River for a surprise attack on King George III's (1738–1820) hired German soldiers, who were camped in Trenton, New Jersey. As the soldiers prepared, Paine, at Washington's request, at once began writing the series of essays called

The Crisis. Their purpose was to inspire hope and to remind people of what they were fighting for: freedom. Paine then hurried to nearby Philadelphia, Pennsylvania, where his first paper was published in the *Pa. Journal* on December 19, 1776.

On December 23, in a freezing snowstorm, just as Washington's men were climbing into boats for the crossing of the Delaware River, Washington had Paine's inspiring words read to his men. The following excerpt of *The Crisis* reminded Washington's soldiers and all Americans that even though times were desperate, those who rallied now would deserve the highest "love and thanks" of every man and woman. Paine reminded soldiers that they were fighting against the worst kind of tyranny, and that the harder the fight, the greater the triumph. He further reminded them that to submit to British taxes and to the British army sent to enforce the payment of those taxes, would make Americans nothing more than slaves.

Things to remember while reading an excerpt from *The Crisis:*

- Paine truly believed that America would form a superior system of government and that America could not be conquered. His conviction is clear in his encouraging words to the American people. Throughout *The Crisis* papers, Paine repeatedly attacked the fainthearted, the "summer soldiers" and "sunshine patriots."

- More than any other Revolutionary-era writer, Paine expressed his ideas in language for the common people. He liked to portray the struggle for independence as a simple struggle between good and evil. Naturally, the colonists were on the good side.

Excerpt from The Crisis

*These are the times that try men's souls. The **summer soldier and the sunshine patriot** will, in this crisis, shrink from the service of their country, but he that stands it now deserves the love and thanks of*

Summer soldier and the sunshine patriot: Those who support the cause only when times are good.

Tyranny: A government in which absolute power rests in a single ruler.

"To bind us in all cases whatsoever": This phrase refers to the Declaratory Act of 1766, which affirmed the right of Parliament to make laws that would bind the colonists "in all cases whatsoever."

*man and woman. **Tyranny**, like hell, is not easily conquered; yet we have this consolation with us that, the harder the conflict, the more glorious the triumph. . . . Britain, with an army to enforce her tyranny, has declared that she has a right (not only to tax) but "**to bind us in all cases whatsoever**," and if being bound in that manner is not slavery, then is there not such a thing as slavery upon earth. (Paine, p. 55)*

What happened next . . .

Paine's first *Crisis* paper had a bracing effect on Washington's men. On December 25, in freezing sleet and rain, twenty-four hundred soldiers marched to Trenton and surrounded the town as the German soldiers lay sleeping, worn out from their Christmas celebrations. The Germans were soon forced to surrender. General Washington called the victory "a glorious day for our country." On January 3, 1777, Washington followed up his stunning success by taking Princeton, New Jersey. He then retired for the winter in Morristown, New Jersey.

Paine continued to write his *Crisis* papers until 1783, when a peace treaty was signed ending the Revolutionary War. The topics he covered in the papers were wide ranging. He suggested that the property of people who remained loyal to the British be taken away and sold for the benefit of the new American nation. He also suggested that people take oaths of loyalty to the new American government.

Paine showed his solidarity with Continental soldiers in deeds as well as words. In 1779, seeing that the soldiers were at the end of their rope because of lack of adequate food and supplies, Paine took five hundred dollars out of his own pocket to start a fund for the neediest soldiers. In 1781, he went on a mission to France to get help for the Continental Army. The clothing and ammunition he brought back were a tremendous morale booster.

Did you know . . .

- Thomas Paine would not take any money for *The Crisis*. He believed passionately in the American cause, and although he was very poor, he said taking money for writing his essays would take away from their worth.

- In 1787, four years after the Treaty of Paris ended the Revolutionary War, Paine traveled to England and France. He hoped to get foreign money to build an iron bridge (his own invention) over a river in Pennsylvania, but instead he found himself caught up in politics abroad, especially the French Revolution (1789–99). By the time he returned to America in 1802, he had been almost forgotten by the American people. He died in 1809 in poverty and was buried on the grounds of his farm in New Rochelle, New York. The farm had been a gift from the state of New York for his contributions to the American Revolution.

Where to Learn More

Commager, Henry Steele, and Richard B. Morris, eds. *The Spirit of Seventy-Six: The Story of the American Revolution as Told by Participants.* New York: Da Capo Press, 1995.

"The Crossing" (video). A dramatization of George Washington's perilous gamble of crossing the Delaware River and attacking the British forces at Trenton. Based on the novel by Howard Fast. Made for cable television, 2000.

Davis, Burke. *George Washington and the American Revolution.* New York: Random House, 1975.

"Documents on the American Revolution." Including descriptions of battles, camp life, naval operations, and action on the western frontier. [Online] http://www.hillsdale.edu/dept/History/Documents/War/EMAmRev.htm (accessed on April 6, 2000).

Fruchtman, Jack, Jr. *Thomas Paine: Apostle of Freedom.* New York: Four Walls Eight Windows, 1994.

Meltzer, Milton. *Tom Paine: Voice of Revolution.* New York: Franklin Watts, 1996.

Meltzer, Milton, ed. *The American Revolutionaries: A History in Their Own Words, 1750–1800.* New York: HarperTrophy, reprint edition, 1993.

Paine, Thomas. *Common Sense and Other Political Writings.* Edited by Nelson F. Adkins. New York: Macmillan, 1953.

Paine, Thomas. *Paine: Collected Writings.* Edited by Eric Foner. New York: Library of America, 1995.

Thomas Paine National Historical Association. [Online] www.thomas-paine.com/tpnha (accessed on March 14, 2000).

"The Turn of the Tide" in *The Spirit of Seventy-Six: The Story of the American Revolution as Told by Participants*. Bicentennial edition. Edited by Henry Steele Commager and Richard B. Morris. New York: Harper-Row, 1975.

Eliza Wilkinson

Account of the Looting of Her Sister's Home by British Soldiers

Originally published in 1839; most recently published in 1969
Excerpted from *Voices of 1776*, 1972

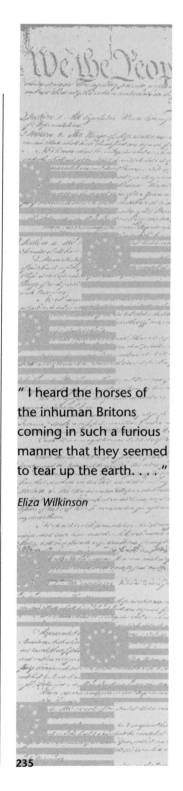

Until 1779, the American Revolution was fought mostly in the north. Then it moved far to the south, where some of the fiercest fighting of the war took place. The south, especially Georgia and South Carolina, was home to more Loyalists (colonists who were loyal to King George III [1738–1820]) than the north. Part of the overall British plan to win the war was to secure the support of those Loyalists, making full use of black slaves. Once the south was in their hands, the British planned to use it as a base to conquer the north.

General Sir Henry Clinton (1738–1795) was placed in command of British forces for the southern operation. One of his first actions was to make an announcement similar to the Declaration of Martial Law in Virginia by John Murray (1732–1809), known as Lord Dunmore (see entry on p. 217), but applying to the entire south. The British promised freedom to slaves who came over to their side.

Tens of thousands of slaves reported voluntarily to the British, thinking they would be granted their freedom. Others were seized and forced to fight. Plantation owners throughout the south complained bitterly about this turn of events.

" I heard the horses of the inhuman Britons coming in such a furious manner that they seemed to tear up the earth. . . . "

Eliza Wilkinson

An American soldier recovers the fallen American flag following Britain's capture of Charleston, South Carolina.
Reproduced by permission of Archive Photos.

When the war turned to the south, patriot Eliza Wilkinson was a sixteen-year-old widow living on her father's plantation (large farm) just south of Charleston, South Carolina. In 1779, General Clinton posted British troops all along the nearby Savannah River in preparation for taking Charleston, and local patriots were frightened. Wilkinson fled to the nearby plantation of her sister, hoping to get out of harm's way, but on June 3, 1780, British soldiers arrived at the door.

Things to remember while reading an excerpt from Eliza Wilkinson's account of the looting of her sister's home by British soldiers:

- The South Carolina economy revolved around farming. The wealthiest southerners lived on large farms, called plantations, which were worked by black slaves. For a long time, southern plantation owners had maintained their lavish lifestyle by trading with Great Britain. The British thought the south would be full of people who were loyal to King George and to the way of life that had made them rich. To their surprise, the British did not find as much support from southerners as they had expected. The behavior Eliza Wilkinson described in her story below is one reason why southerners did not support the British.

Excerpt from Eliza Wilkinson's account of the looting of her sister's home by British soldiers

. . . a Negro girl ran in, exclaiming, "O! The king's people are coming! It must be them, for they are all in red!" . . . I heard the horses of the inhuman **Britons** coming in such a furious manner that they seemed to tear up the earth. . . . They were up to the house—entered with drawn swords and pistols in their hands. Indeed, they rushed in . . . crying out, "Where're these women rebels?"

. . . The moment they espied us, off went our caps. . . . And for what. . .? Why, only to get a **paltry** stone and wax pin which kept them on our heads, at the same time uttering the most abusive language imaginable and making as if they'd **hew** us to pieces with their swords. But it's not in my power to describe the scene. It was terrible to the last degree. . . . They then began to **plunder** the house of everything they thought valuable or worth taking. Our trunks were split to pieces, and each mean, pitiful wretch crammed his bosom with the contents, which were our apparel. . . . I ventured to speak to the inhuman monster who had my clothes. I represented to him the times were such we could not replace what they'd taken from us, and

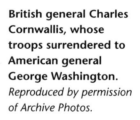

British general Charles Cornwallis, whose troops surrendered to American general George Washington. *Reproduced by permission of Archive Photos.*

Britons: Natives of Britain.

Paltry: Of little value.

Hew: Cut.

Plunder: Violently rob.

begged him to spare me only a suit or two. But I got nothing but a hearty curse for my pains. Nay, so far was his callous heart from relenting that, casting his eyes towards my shoes, "I want them buckles," said he, and immediately knelt at my feet to take them out. . . . [W]hile he was busy . . . a brother villain, whose enormous mouth extended from ear to ear, bawled out, "Shares there, I say! Shares!" So they divided my buckles between them.

*. . . And, after bundling up all their booty, they [left the house and] mounted their horses. But such **despicable** figures! Each wretch's bosom stuffed so full, they appeared to be all afflicted with some **dropsical disorder.** (Wheeler, p. 290)*

What happened next . . .

The British were easily able to take the south. General Clinton captured Charleston in 1780. Under the command of British general Lord Charles Cornwallis (1738–1805), the British occupied most of South Carolina and moved into North Carolina. Loyalists came forward offering their support, but never as many as Cornwallis expected. The fighting finally ended at Yorktown, Virginia, on October 19, 1781, with an American victory.

According to one version of the story, a band played "The World Turned Upside Down" as the king's troops surrendered to the patriots under General George Washington (1732–1799). Cornwallis did not lead his troops in the surrender; he claimed to be "sick." To add to the embarrassment of the scene, observers reported that many of the surrendering British soldiers were drunk.

Did you know . . .

- The war in the south was a different kind of war from that in the north. The landscape was different, ranging from swampy lowlands to mountainous wilderness. The people were different, ranging from uneducated backwoodsmen to sophisticated planters. There was a tremendous gulf between rich and poor, slaves and masters.

- A substitution system was adopted by several colonies during the war. The system allowed men to fulfill their military duty by sending their slaves to serve for them. This was regarded as a perfectly honorable way of carrying out one's soldierly duty.

- In 1779, there were only five cities in the thirteen colonies with a population of more than eight thousand. Only one of those cities, Charleston, was in the south.

Where to Learn More

Claghorn, Charles E. *Women Patriots of the American Revolution: A Biographical Dictionary.* Metuchen, NJ: Scarecrow Press, 1991.

Meyer, Edith Patterson. *Petticoat Patriots of the American Revolution.* New York: Vanguard Press, 1976.

Norton, Mary Beth. *Liberty's Daughters: The Revolutionary Experience of American Women, 1750–1800.* Ithaca, NY: Cornell University Press, 1996.

Wheeler, Richard. *Voices of 1776.* New York: Thomas Y. Crowell Co., 1972.

Wilkinson, Eliza. *The Letters of Eliza Wilkinson.* New York: Ayer, 1969.

Zeinert, Karen. *Those Remarkable Women of the American Revolution.* Brookfield, CT: Millbrook Press, 1996.

Horace Walpole

Letter to the Earl of Strafford about the Surrender of Cornwallis at Yorktown

Written on November 27, 1781; excerpted from *The Best Letters of Horace Walpole*, 1911

In 1779, the war's action moved from the north to the south. By then, the French had agreed to openly assist the American cause. With the help of the French navy, the Americans finally achieved a stunning victory at Yorktown, Virginia, on October 19, 1781.

Back in England, the news of the surrender at Yorktown came as a complete (and unwelcome) surprise. For two years, all London had been hearing was news of a string of southern victories. Parliament, the British lawmaking body, was scheduled to return from a recess on November 27, 1781. Everyone wanted to hear what would be said about the loss at Yorktown. But King George III (1738–1820) had written his speech before he received news of the loss, and he apparently saw no reason to change it. He spoke to Parliament without mentioning the surrender. At the time, King George planned to pursue the war, but he was soon forced to give up that plan, because Parliament and British public opinion had turned against the war.

Writer and politician Horace Walpole (1717–1797), who has been called the best letter writer in the English lan-

> "Oh, my Lord, I have no patience with my country, and shall leave it without regret! Can we be proud when all Europe scorns us?"
>
> *Horace Walpole*

Horace Walpole, often called the best letter writer in the English language. *Reproduced by permission of Archive Photos.*

guage, was disgusted at the news of the British surrender and at the spectacle of Parliament ignoring the news. He was moved to write a letter to a friend, an excerpt of which follows. In the letter, Walpole bemoaned the fact that England had never experienced such a humiliating defeat. He wondered if the defeat truly meant that the war was over. He complained (in a part of the letter not shown) that the newspapers talked of frivolous matters (such as what society people had worn to the opera the night before) while England was disgraced. He said the newspaper stories must be composed by young boys. He expressed his impatience with his country, which all Europe then scorned.

Things to remember while reading an excerpt from Horace Walpole's letter to the Earl of Strafford:

- Walpole began writing the letters for which he became famous in 1739. Throughout his life, Walpole wrote thousands of letters in which he made observations on politics, literature, major events that took place throughout Europe and America, and the gossip of his day. Specialists use his letters as an important reference to the eighteenth century. The letters commented on such diverse subjects as the discovery of the planet Uranus, Benjamin Franklin's experiments with electricity, ballooning, prison reform, and social customs. In his letters, Walpole also analyzed the chief figures of British politics.

- In addition to being a letter writer, Walpole was a politician. He entered Parliament in 1742 and served until 1769. Walpole opposed oppression and injustice, and he spoke out in Parliament against the black slave trade as well as restrictions on the freedoms of colonists in America.

- Walpole loved to travel and made frequent trips to Paris, France. It is possible that his reference to leaving the country referred to such a trip.

Excerpt from Horace Walpole's letter to the Earl of Strafford

*When did England see two whole armies lay down their arms and surrender themselves prisoners? Can **venal addresses efface such stigmas**, that will be recorded in every country in Europe? Or will such*

Venal addresses efface such stigmas: Speeches without honor wipe out such disgraces.

disgraces have no consequences? Is not America lost to us? Shall we offer up more human victims to the demon of **obstinacy**; *and shall we tax ourselves deeper to* **furnish out** *the sacrifice?*

Would not one think that our newspapers were penned by boys just come from school. . . . We are monkeys in conduct, and as clumsy as bears when we try to **gambol**. *Oh, my Lord, I have no patience with my country, and shall leave it without regret! Can we be proud when all Europe scorns us? It was* **wont to** *envy us, sometimes to hate us, but never despised us before. (McMahan, pp. 233–34)*

What happened next . . .

Walpole was an expert gardener and interior decorator, and he enjoyed writing about those subjects. In 1749, he had bought a building outside London called Strawberry Hill. He remodeled it in an architectural style that later became known as Victorian Gothic; the style became popular in Europe and the United States. Walpole's house featured towers, arches, painted glass, a chapel, a library, and a notched roof. Its interior featured collections of pictures, furniture, and decorative "curiosities," as well as books of all sorts. Strawberry Hill is also noteworthy because it contained the first printing press located in an English private house.

Walpole's *A Description of the Villa of Horace Walpole at Strawberry Hill* appeared in 1774. It was enlarged in 1784, then again in 1786. The book described Walpole's unique and rather whimsical house. He wrote in the preface, "It was built to please my own taste, and in some degree to realize my own visions." The next year Walpole printed *Hieroglyphic Tales.* Hieroglyphic (pronounced hy-uh-ruh-GLIH-fik) means hard to understand. The book was a collection of six stories of fantasy written to amuse the children of his friends.

In 1791, seventy-four-year-old Walpole became the fourth Lord Orford. By then, he was troubled by various ailments common to the elderly. His final years were saddened by the violent deaths of many of his friends in France who were killed by angry revolutionaries during the French Revolution

(1789–99). At the age of eighty, Walpole fell ill and died on March 2, 1797.

In March 1782, King George III finally admitted defeat and sent representatives to Paris to negotiate a treaty of peace with the Americans. The treaty was signed on September 3, 1783. In the peace treaty, Great Britain finally recognized American independence.

Did you know . . .

- In 1764, Horace Walpole published *The Castle of Otranto*, which is recognized as the first Gothic novel. It portrays everyday characters caught up in incidents that have supernatural elements. About the writing of this novel, Walpole commented that he "had a dream, of which all I could recover was that I had thought myself in an ancient castle . . . and that on the uppermost bannister of a great staircase I saw a gigantic hand in armour. In the evening I sat down, and began to write, without knowing in the least what I intended to . . . relate."

Where to Learn More

"Horace Walpole." Richmond upon Thames Local Studies Collection. [Online] http://www.richmond.gov.uk/depts/opps/leisure/libraries/history/notes/05.htm (accessed on April 6, 2000).

McMahan, Anna B., ed. *The Best Letters of Horace Walpole.* Chicago: A. C. McClurg, 1911.

Walpole, Horace. *The Castle of Otranto and Hieroglyphic Tales.* London: Everyman Paperback Classics, 1998.

Walpole, Horace. *The History of the Modern Taste in Gardening.* New York: Ursus Press, 1995.

George Washington

Farewell Address to the Armies of the United States

Issued on November 3, 1783; excerpted from George Washington's *Writings*, 1997

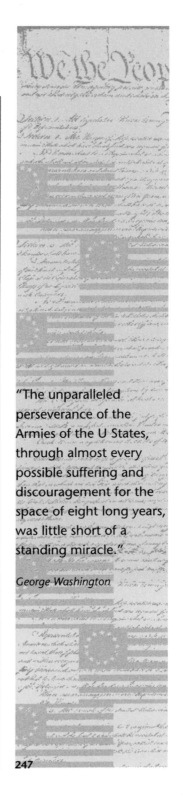

After the British surrendered at Yorktown, Virginia, on October 19, 1781, the village lay in ruins. Victorious American soldiers looted British stockpiles, seizing food, guns, ammunition, swords, and British and German flags (German soldiers were hired to fight alongside the British). Six thousand British and German soldiers were marched off to prison camps in Virginia and Maryland, but their commanding officers returned to England. There still remained a large number of British soldiers at their headquarters in New York City.

Americans were ecstatic over General George Washington's (1732–1799) spectacular victory at Yorktown. They considered the war over, but Washington was not so sure. All the news from England indicated that King George III (1738–1820) wanted to continue the war. Washington warned Congress that it should be ready for new confrontations in 1782. To be on the safe side, Congress ordered the Continental Army to stay together until a peace treaty was signed. Washington and his men set up camps around New York City to keep an eye on the British soldiers there. Also occupying New York City was a large number of Loyalists—Americans who had

"The unparalleled perseverance of the Armies of the U States, through almost every possible suffering and discouragement for the space of eight long years, was little short of a standing miracle."

George Washington

remained loyal to King George throughout the Revolutionary War. Now shunned by their former neighbors, they waited anxiously to see what was to become of them.

In August 1782, Washington learned from the British commander in New York that peace negotiations had begun in Paris. Washington feared a British trick. He suspected that the British planned to join in a conspiracy with the French against America. But while British soldiers in New York quietly awaited word of a peace treaty, Loyalists there were quite upset at the news. They started staging violent raids in New York and New Jersey. Washington and his soldiers found themselves involved in a brutal, bloody civil war. Finally, British general Guy Carleton (1724–1808) announced that he was putting an end to Loyalist raids, and they soon ceased.

The peace treaty would not be signed until September 1783. For seventeen months after Yorktown, Washington coped with a bored and restless army that grew increasingly irritable as time went on. The new American government was having problems with finances, because under the Articles of Confederation that served as the constitution, Congress did not have the power to tax. Therefore, it had no money and could not pay the Continental Army. The states were unwilling to tax themselves to pay for the army, because they considered the war over.

Washington tried to keep his men amused. He granted his officers long leaves of absence. But nothing he did was enough to keep the men happy for long. By the spring of 1783, Washington feared that the next outbreak of violence would come from America's own soldiers. Congress's inability to act led to the suggestion that Washington keep his army under control by establishing a military dictatorship with himself as king. Washington was appalled at the suggestion. After fighting so long and so hard for independence from an English king, he was not about to become America's king.

In an emotional meeting with the officers of the Continental Army on March 15, 1783, Washington urged them to have patience; Congress had promised that the army would be paid as soon as possible. During the course of his speech, Washington donned a pair of glasses, which he had never done before in the sight of his men. In explanation, he said: "Gentlemen, I have grown gray in your service, and now I am going blind." His men were moved to tears. Shortly after that, the officers drew up an address to Congress. They expressed their confidence in the justice of Congress and their country. They stated their conviction that the Continental Army would not be disbanded until the men who had fought so faithfully were justly compensated. Washington also continued to urge Congress to address the issue of army pay. He offered the suggestion that the men be paid in western land.

On April 19, 1783, exactly eight years after the first shots of the Revolution were fired at Lexington, Massachusetts, Washington announced to his men "the cessation of hostilities between the United States of America and the King of Great Britain." After a great deal more negotiating, the Treaty of Paris was signed on September 3, 1783. Washington received the news and, on November 3, 1783, said farewell to his men.

George Washington delivered his farewell address to his army on November 3, 1783. *Courtesy of the Library of Congress.*

In his speech, Washington said it was miraculous that the army had held out for eight long years against the superior forces of the British. As terrible as it had been, everyone ought to congratulate himself for the role he had played in the glorious cause, Washington said. Washington called down the blessings of heaven on the men who had brought such good to their countrymen. He then announced his retirement from the military forever.

Things to remember while reading an excerpt from George Washington's farewell address:

- As the time drew closer for Washington to deliver his speech, Robert Morris (1734–1806), America's finance director, announced that he had no cash to pay Washington's men. What was more, he had no cash to buy paper to print an IOU (a statement that indicates how much money is owed). Washington's men were angry. To try and help, Washington drew up a letter to all the states. He said it was the last official letter he would ever write because he was retiring forever. In the letter, Washington urged the states to put aside their differences and look to the best interests of the whole country. Such differences were preventing Congress from raising money to pay the army. He urged that the Articles of Confederation (then America's constitution) be expanded so that a strong central government could be created to address America's immediate problems. The letter was called "Washington's Legacy." Washington was actually hoping that a convention would be called to write a federal constitution. That did not happen until 1789.

- Washington's men did not actually gather to hear his speech in person. Congress had already released most of the army, still without having paid them. Washington sent the address from his headquarters at Rocky Hill, New York, to the men who remained at the military camp on the Hudson River near New York City. He also sent a letter urging the soldiers to return to civilian life, confident that their grievances would be addressed sometime.

Excerpt from George Washington's farewell address to the armies of the United States

*A contemplation of the compleat attainment . . . of the object for which we contended against so **formidable** a power cannot but inspire us with astonishment and gratitude. The **disadvantageous circumstances** on our part, under which the war was undertaken, can never be forgotten. . . . The **unparalleled perseverance** of the Armies of the U States, through almost every possible suffering and discouragement for the space of eight long years, was little short of a standing miracle.*

Every American Officer and Soldier must now console himself for any unpleasant circumstances which may have occurred by a recol-

Formidable: Dreadful.

Disadvantageous circumstances: Handicaps.

Unparalleled perseverance: Persistence never before seen.

lection of the uncommon scenes in which he has been called to Act no inglorious part, and the astonishing events of which he has been a witness, events which have seldom if ever before taken place on the stage of human action, nor can they probably ever happen again.

*. . . may the choicest of heaven's favours, both here and here-after, attend those who, under **the devine auspices**, have secured unnumerable blessings for others; with these wishes, and this **bene-diction**, the Commander in Chief is about to retire from Service. The Curtain of seperation will soon be drawn, and the military scene to him will be closed for ever. (Washington, pp. 543, 546)*

The devine auspices: God's protection.

Benediction: Blessing.

What happened next . . .

On November 25, 1783, British soldiers departed America forever, setting sail from New York Harbor. A few hours later, mounted on a fine gray horse, Washington led a few of his officers in a triumphant procession into New York City. Only a few citizens turned out to cheer; during the long occupation of New York by the British and Loyalists, most patriots had fled.

Washington retired from public life and concentrated on being a gentleman farmer at Mount Vernon, his Virginia estate. He experimented with breeding mules, hunted foxes, entertained his plantation friends, and wrote letters to many of the leaders of the new nation.

Before long, it became clear that the new nation would again need Washington's leadership. The Articles of Confederation, the document that held the states together during the Revolutionary War, was failing to hold the country together. In May 1787, Washington became one of the delegates to the Constitutional Convention in Philadelphia, Pennsylvania. The goal of the meeting was to draft a new document with rules for how the national government was to be run. The delegates unanimously elected Washington president of this convention.

The Constitution was put into effect in 1789. It called for the election of a president. Not surprisingly, Washington was Congress's choice as first president of the United States of America (today, citizens vote in presidential elections). Washington took the oath of office on April 30, 1789, at Federal Hall in New York City, then the capital of the United States.

Most states granted back pay to Revolutionary War soldiers who applied. But it was a long time before the issue of soldiers' pensions from the U.S. government was satisfactorily resolved. Finally, on June 7, 1832, Congress passed an act granting pensions.

Did you know . . .

- While Washington waited in New York for a peace treaty to be signed, he learned that a famous French dentist was in the country visiting nearby. The dentist was invited to visit Washington's headquarters, where a closed-door meeting was held. Historians speculate that the dentist later supplied Washington with false teeth. Contrary to popular belief, Washington's false teeth were not made of wood. They were made of a cow's tooth, Washington's own teeth, hippopotamus ivory, metal, and springs.

- Historians believe that Washington's March 1783 speech to his army officers averted the greatest threat that America has ever known. The officers were threatening a military takeover of the country if Congress did not get them their paychecks for their service in the Revolutionary War.

- When Washington entered New York City in triumph in November 1783, a third of the city lay in ruins, destroyed by a 1776 fire. At that time, the British had just captured the city and blamed Washington and his men for setting it on fire. No one knows how the fire actually started.

Where to Learn More

Bliven, Bruce, and J. Thomas, eds. *The American Revolution (Landmark Books)*. New York: Random House, 1987.

Cook, Don. *The Long Fuse: How England Lost the American Colonies, 1760–1785*. New York: Atlantic Monthly Press, 1995.

Marshall, George L., Jr. "The Rise and Fall of the Newburgh Conspiracy: How General Washington and his Spectacles Saved the Republic. [Online] http://earlyamerica.com/review/fall97/wshngton.html (accessed on April 6, 2000).

Meltzer, Milton. *George Washington and the Birth of Our Nation.* New York: Franklin Watts, 1986.

Mount Vernon Educational Resources. [Online] http://www.mountvernon. org/education/index.html (accessed on April 6, 2000).

"Revolutionary War Pensions Record Index, Cheraw District South Carolina: Declarations and Affidavits from the Pension Applications of Cheraw District Soldiers in the American Revolution." [Online] http://www.konnections.com/clpurvis/Revwar.htm (accessed on April 6, 2000).

Rosenburg, John. *First in Peace: George Washington, the Constitution, and the Presidency.* Brookfield, CT: Millbrook Press, 1998.

Washington, George. *Writings.* Edited by John Rhodehamel. New York: Library of America, 1997.

Where to Learn More

The following list focuses on general works about the Revolutionary era written for readers of middle school and high school age. Books aimed at adult audiences have been included when they are especially important in providing information or analysis that would otherwise be unavailable, or because they have become classics. Please note that the web site addresses were verified prior to publication, but are subject to change.

Books

Annals of America. New York: Encyclopedia Britannica, Inc., 1968.

Blanco, Richard L., ed. *The American Revolution, 1775–1783: An Encyclopedia*. New York: Garland Publishing, 1993.

Bliven, Bruce. *The American Revolution, 1760–1783*. New York: Random House, 1981.

Bliven, Bruce, and J. Thomas, eds. *The American Revolution (Landmark Books)*. New York: Random House, 1987.

Boatner, Mark M. *Encyclopedia of the American Revolution*. Mechanicsburg, PA: Stackpole Books, 1994.

Burnett, Edmund Cody. *The Continental Congress*. New York: Norton, 1964.

Claghorn, Charles E. *Women Patriots of the American Revolution: A Biographical Dictionary*. Metuchen, NJ: Scarecrow Press, 1991.

Clark, Dora Mae. *British Opinion and the American Revolution*. New York: Russell & Russell, 1966.

Commager, Henry Steele. *Documents of American History*. New York: Appleton-Century-Crofts, 1958.

Commager, Henry Steele, and Richard B. Morris, eds. *The Spirit of 'Seventy-Six: The Story of the American Revolution as Told by Participants*. New York: Da Capo Press, 1995.

Cook, Don. *The Long Fuse: How England Lost the American Colonies, 1760–1785*. New York: Atlantic Monthly Press, 1995.

Cox, Clinton. *Come All You Brave Soldiers: Blacks in the Revolutionary War*. New York: Scholastic, 1999.

Crompton, Samuel Willard. *100 Colonial Leaders Who Shaped North America*. San Mateo, CA: Bluewood Books, 1999.

Davis, Burke. *George Washington and the American Revolution*. New York: Random House, 1975.

Diamant, Lincoln. *Yankee Doodle Days: Exploring the American Revolution*. Fleischmanns, NY: Purple Mountain Press, 1996.

Dictionary of American Biography (21 volumes). New York: Scribner's, 1957.

Draper, Theodore. *A Struggle for Power: the American Revolution*. New York: Times Books, 1996.

Egger-Bovet, Howard, and Marlene Smith-Baranzini. *USKids History: Book of the American Revolution*. Boston: Little Brown, 1994.

Faragher, John Mack, ed. *The Encyclopedia of Colonial and Revolutionary America*. New York: Facts on File, 1990.

Fleming, Thomas. *Liberty! The American Revolution*. New York: Viking Penguin, 1997. (Companion volume to the PBS television series.)

Galvin, John R. *Three Men of Boston: Leadership and Conflict at the Start of the American Revolution*. Washington, DC: Brasseys, 1997.

Hakim, Joy. *From Colonies to Country*. New York: Oxford University Press, 1999.

Hibbert, Christopher. *Redcoats and Rebels: The American Revolution Through British Eyes*. New York: Avon, 1991.

Hull, Mary E. *The Boston Tea Party in American History*. Springfield, NJ: Enslow Publishers, 1999.

King, David C. *Lexington and Concord*. New York: Twenty-First Century Books, 1997.

Leckie, Robert. *George Washington's War: The Saga of the American Revolution.* New York: HarperCollins, 1992.

Lukes, Bonnie L. *The American Revolution.* World History Series. San Diego: Lucent Books, 1996.

Marrin, Albert. *The War for Independence: The Story of the American Revolution.* New York: Atheneum, 1988.

Meltzer, Milton. *George Washington and the Birth of Our Nation.* New York: Franklin Watts, 1986.

Meltzer, Milton, ed. *The American Revolutionaries: A History in Their Own Words, 1750–1800.* New York: HarperTrophy, reprint edition, 1993.

Meyer, Edith Patterson. *Petticoat Patriots of the American Revolution.* New York: Vanguard Press, 1976.

Meyeroff, Stephen. *The Call for Independence: The Story of the American Revolution and Its Causes.* Cherry Hill, NJ: Oak Tree Publishers, 1996.

Montross, Lynn. *The Reluctant Rebels: The Story of the Continental Congress, 1774–1789.* New York: Harper & Brothers, 1950.

Morgan, Edmund S., and Helen M. Morgan. *The Stamp Act Crisis: Prologue to Revolution.* New York: Collier Books, 1962.

Nardo, Don, ed. *The American Revolution.* Opposing Viewpoints Digests. San Diego: Greenhaven Press, 1998.

Norton, Mary Beth. *Liberty's Daughters: The Revolutionary Experience of American Women, 1750–1800.* Ithaca, NY: Cornell University Press, 1996.

Olesky, Walter. *The Boston Tea Party.* New York: Franklin Watts, 1993.

O'Neill, Laurie. *The Boston Tea Party.* Spotlight on American History. Brookfield, CT: Millbrook Press, 1996.

Purcell, L. Edward. *Who Was Who in the American Revolution.* New York: Facts on File, 1993.

Rae, Noel, ed. *Witnessing America: The Library of Congress Book of Firsthand Accounts of Life in America 1600–1900.* New York: Penguin, 1996.

Reit, Seymour. *Guns for General Washington: A Story of the American Revolution.* Great Episodes. San Diego: Harcourt Brace, 1992.

Rinaldi, Ann. *The Fifth of March: A Story of the Boston Massacre.* San Diego: Harcourt Brace, 1993.

Scheer, George F. *Rebels and Redcoats: The American Revolution Through the Eyes of Those Who Fought and Lived It.* New York: Da Capo Press, 1988.

Stein, R. Conrad. *Cornerstones of Freedom: The Story of Valley Forge.* Chicago: Children's Press, 1985.

Stokesbury, James L. *A Short History of the American Revolution.* New York: William Morrow & Co., 1992.

Sutton, Felix. *Sons of Liberty.* New York: J. Messner, 1969.

Wheeler, Richard. *Voices of 1776.* New York: Thomas Y. Crowell Co., 1972.

Wilbur, C. Keith. *Pirates and Patriots of the Revolution.* Broomall, PA: Chelsea House, 1996.

Wilbur, C. Keith. *The Revolutionary Soldier: 1775–1783.* Broomall, PA: Chelsea House, 1999.

Young, Alfred F. *The Shoemaker and the Tea Party: Memory and the American Revolution.* Boston: Beacon Press, 1999.

Zeinert, Karen. *Those Remarkable Women of the American Revolution.* Brookfield, CT: Millbrook Press, 1996.

World Wide Web

"Declaration of Independence." Surfing the Net with Kids. [Online] http://surfnetkids.com/declaration.htm (accessed on April 4, 2000).

"The Declaration of Independence: A History" and "The Writing and Publicizing of the Declaration of Independence, the Articles of Confederation, and the Constitution of the United States." National Archives and Records Administration, Exhibit Hall. [Online] http://www.nara.gov/exhall/exhibits.html (accessed on April 4, 2000).

"Documents on the American Revolution." Including descriptions of battles, camp life, naval operations, and action on the western frontier. [Online] http://www.hillsdale.edu/dept/History/Documents/War/EMAmRev.htm (accessed on April 6, 2000).

"Journals of the Continental Congress—In Thirty-Four Volumes." [Online] http://memory.loc.gov/ammem/amlaw/lwjclink.html (accessed on March 19, 2000).

Index

A

Acrostic, 205, 207
Adams, Abigail, 48, 125, 145
    (box), 145 (ill.), 146
Adams, Charles Francis, 132
Adams, John, 47 (ill.), 123 (box),
    124 (ill.)
    Adams, Abigail, 145
    Adams, Samuel, 17
    Articles of Confederation, 152,
      166–67
    Boston Massacre, 36
    British charge of treason, 87
    closing of Port of Boston, 48
    Declaration of Independence,
      135–36, 146
    Declaratory Act, 22
    Dickinson, John, 131, 132
    First Continental Congress,
      108, 124, 126
    Hancock, John, 148
    Hutchinson, Thomas, 179, 186
    Jefferson, Thomas, 137, 138
    Lee, Arthur, 43
    Paine, Thomas, 104–6
    Revolutionary War, 2
    writings of, 125 (box)
Adams, John Quincy, 123
Adams, Samuel, 4, 17, 32–33
    (box), 33 (ill.), 34, 188 (ill.)
    Boston Massacre, 35
    Boston Tea Party, 179
    British charge of treason,
      87–88
    call for American
      independence, 41
    Gage, Thomas, 213
    Hancock, John, 148
    Hutchinson letters affair, 172,
      174, 178, 186
    Lee, Arthur, 42, 43
    Townshend Acts, 29
Administration of Justice Act,
    39, 212
Admiralty courts, 8, 27
"African Slavery in America," 100
Amelia (princess), 59
American Civil War, 116, 147
American Department, 30
American Prohibition Act, 60–61

Bold type indicates
main entries and their page
numbers. Illustrations are
marked by (ill.). Sidebar
boxes are marked by (box).

American Revolutionary War, 127, 153, 155, 213 (ill.), 223 (ill.), 236 (ill.)
  documents, 154 (box)
  end of American Revolutionary War, 241, 245, 247–53
  Martin, Joseph Plumb, 221–27
  Native Americans, 164 (box)
André, John, 204, 204 (ill.), 205, 205 (ill.), 209
Annual Register, 51
Arnold, Benedict, 170, **203–10**, 204 (ill.), 208 (box)
Articles of Confederation, **151–68**, 251
Assembly of New York, 65

B

Baltimore, Lord, 84
Barré, Isaac, 17
Battle of Bunker Hill, 127
Battle of Lexington and Concord, 127, 128 (ill.), 213 (ill.)
Belcher, Jonathan, 35
Bernard, Francis, 15, 30, 31, 41, 44, 174, 178
Boston, Massachusetts, 40–41, 171–82, 183–89
Boston Massacre, 31 (ill.), 34, 35, 179
Boston Port Act, 39, 40, 41, 44–45, 212
Boston Tea Party, 33, 38 (ill.), 39, 179, 201
British Army, 31
British Royal Navy, 30
Burke, Edmund, **49–54**, 50 (ill.), 51 (box), 86–87, 104, 124

C

Calvert, George, 84
Carleton, Guy, 248
Castle of Otranto, 245
Charles II, 58
Charleston, South Carolina, 236, 236 (ill.)
Charlotte Sophia, 58
Civil War. *See* American Civil War
Clinton, Henry, 235, 236, 238
Cohn, Art, 209
Colonies, system of government in, 2

Committee of Five, 136, 146
Committees of correspondence, 32, 33, 113
Common Sense, 61, **97–106**, 99 (ill.), 229
Continental Army, 101, 214, 221, 222, 224
Continental Association, **111–26**
Continental Congress. *See* First Continental Congress; Second Continental Congress
Cornwallis, Charles, 237 (ill.), 238
Crisis, The, 98–99, **229–34**
Cushing, Thomas, 184, 185
Customs officials, 30 (ill.), 30

D

Dandridge, Francis, 12
Dartmouth, Lord, 196
Dawes, William, 213
Deane, Silas, 43, 139
Declaration of Independence, 59, **135–49**, 141 (ill.), 144 (ill.)
Declaration of Martial Law, 214, **217–20**
Declaration of Rights and Grievances, 15
Declaration of the Causes and Necessity of Taking Up Arms, **127–33**
Declaratory Act, **19–23**
Delaware River (crossing), 230 (ill.)
Dickinson College, 70
Dickinson, John, 42, 64 (ill.), 131 (box)
  Articles of Confederation, 151, 166, 167
  Declaration of Independence, 146
  Declaration of the Causes and Necessity of Taking Up Arms, 128
  Letters from a Farmer in Pennsylvania to the Inhabitants of the British Colonies, **63–70**, 132
  Olive Branch Petition, 128
Dunmore, Lord, 87, 89, 95, 214, **217–20**, 235

E

Earl of Strafford, 243–44
East India Company, 37, 39,
    179, 201
"Edict by the King of Prussia,
    An," **71–80**
Electricity, 74
Elizabeth II, 61
Ethopian Regiment, 219

F

Farewell Address to the Armies of
    the United States, **247–53**
First Continental Congress,
    57, 89, 97, 114–115 (box),
    122 (ill.)
  Adams, John, 124, 126
  Continental Association,
    111–26
  George III, 51, 108–10
  Franklin, Benjamin, 73 (ill.), 74
    (box), 78 (ill.), 198 (ill.)
  Articles of Confederation, 152
  Declaration of Independence,
    135–36
  Dickinson, John, 69
  "Edict by the King of Prussia,
    An," **71–80**
  Hutchinson letters affair, 170,
    183–89, 187, 196, **197–201**
  Lee, Arthur, 43
  Stamp Act, 9–10, 19–20, 27
  tax theory of, 21
  Townshend Revenue Act, 35
  Treaty of Paris, 123
Franklin stove, 74
Franklin, William, 77
Frederick II, 71, 72 (ill.)
Frederick the Great, 71, 72 (ill.)
French and Indian War, 2–3, 82
French Revolution, 99

G

Gage, Thomas
  governor of Massachusetts,
    44, 213
  Hutchinson, Thomas, 173
  Intolerable Acts, 46–47,
    200, 212
  Massachusetts Assembly, 31
  Quartering Acts, 39–40, 65
  Restraining Act, 26
  Townshend Revenue Act, 35
Gault, Charlayne Hunter, 105
George II, 7, 58
George III, 56 (ill.), 58–59 (box),
    112 (ill.)
  Continental Association,
    113, 122
  Declaration of
    Independence, 138
  Declaratory Act, 20
  end of American Revolutionary
    War, 241, 245, 247–48
  First Continental Congress, 51,
    108, 109, 212
  Grenville, George, 17
  health of, 16–17
  Henry, Patrick, 92
  Hutchinson letters affair, 44,
    173, 192, 200
  Indians, 3
  lead statue of, 22, 147
  North, Sir Frederick, 47
  Olive Branch Petition, 128, 130
  Proclamation of Rebellion,
    55–62
  Second Continental
    Congress, 127
  Stamp Act, 7
  *Summary View of the Rights of
    British America, A,* 82, 84,
    85–86
George IV, 59
Georgia, 16, 108, 122, 138
"Give me liberty, or give me
    death" speech, **89–96**, 217
Goddard, Mary Katherine, 147
Grant, Ulysses S., 42
Greene, Nathanael, 204
Grenville, George, 7–8, 16, 17, 42

H

Hallowell, Mr., 172
Hancock, John, 22, 147 (ill.),
    148 (box)
  British charge of treason, 87–88
  Declaration of
    Independence, 146
  Gage, Thomas, 213
  Hutchinson letters affair,
    174, 175
  Liberty (ship), 30, 126, 172, 178
Hawthorne, Nigel, 61

Henry, Patrick, 13–14, **89–96,**
      92–93 (box), 114 (box),
      214, 217
Hill, Wills, 30
Howe, William, 152, 153 (ill.)
Hughes, John, 10
Hutchinson, Anne, 173
Hutchinson letters affair, 44, 170,
      171–82, 183–89, 187 (box),
      191–96, 197–201
Hutchinson, Thomas, 32, 44,
      169–70, **171–82,** 173 (box),
      183–89, 191–96, 192 (ill.),
      197–201

I

Indians, 3, 164 (box), 165 (ill.)
Ingersoll, Jared, 10
Intolerable Acts, **37–48,** 200, 212

J

Jamestown, Virginia, 1
Jay, John, 123
Jefferson, Thomas, 137 (box),
      137 (ill.)
   Adams, Samuel, 17, 33
   Declaration of Independence,
      138, 146
   Declaration of the Causes
      and Necessity of Taking
      Up Arms, 128
   Lee, Arthur, 42
   Library of Congress, 154
   Randolph family, 114–15
   *Summary View of the Rights of
      British America, A,* **81–88**

K

King Charles II. *See* Charles II
King Frederick II. *See* Frederick II
King George II. *See* George II
King George III. *See* George III
King George IV. *See* George IV
King Louis XVI. *See* Louis XVI

L

Lake Champlain Maritime
      Museum, 209
Land Bank, 35
Lee, Arthur, 41, 42–43 (box)
Lee, Charles, 124, 224

Lee, Francis Lightfoot, 42
Lee, Henry "Light-Horse
      Harry," 42
Lee, Richard Bland, 43
Lee, Richard Henry, 42, 113, 114
      (box), 115 (ill.), 135, 151
Lee, Robert E., 42
Lennon, Sarah, 58
Letter to the Earl of Strafford
      about the Surrender of
      Cornwallis at Yorktown,
      241–45
*Letters from a Farmer in
      Pennsylvania to the
      Inhabitants of the British
      Colonies,* 42, **63–70,** 131, 132
Lewis, Anthony, 105
Liberty (ship), 30, 126, 172, 178
Library of Congress, 154, 155
Lightning rod, 74
Livingston, Robert, 135–36, 136
      (ill.), 146
London Magazine, 70
Louis XVI, 99
Louisiana Purchase, 137

M

McKean, Thomas, 131
Madness of King George, The,
      16–17, 61
Marquis of Rockingham, 20 (ill.),
      20, 49
Martin, Joseph Plumb, 214,
      221–27, 222 (box)
Maryland, 165–66
Massachusetts, 55, 171–82
Massachusetts Circular Letter,
      29–30, 31
Massachusetts Government Act,
      39, 46
Monroe, James, 99
Morris, Robert, 249
Murray, John. *See* Dunmore, Lord

N

*Narrative of Some of the Adventures,
      Dangers, and Sufferings of a
      Revolutionary Soldier, A,* 214,
      221–27
National Archives, 148
Native Americans, 3, 164 (box),
      165 (ill.)

New York Assembly, 26
North, Sir Frederick, 38–39, 47, 48, 51, 127

O

Olive Branch Petition, 57, **127–33**
Oliver, Andrew, 170, 191, 193, 194, 195, 197, 200
"On Conciliation," **49–54**

P

Paine, Thomas, 61, **97–106**, 98–99 (box), 214, **229–34**
Penn, Richard, 130
Penn, William, 130
Pennsylvania Gazette, 79
Pitt, William, 22–23
Plymouth Colony, 1
Poor Richard's Almanac, 79
Preston, Thomas, 35–36
Privy Council, 196, 197, 198, 200
Proclamation of Rebellion, **55–62**

Q

Quartering Act (1764), 65
Quartering Act (1765), 26, 40
Quartering Act (1766), 40, 65
Quartering Act (1774), 39–40, 45–46
Quebec, 117, 203
Queen Elizabeth II.
    See Elizabeth II

R

Randolph, Peyton, 108 (ill.), 108, 114–15
Randolph, Virginia, 137
Resolves of the House of Representatives . . ., **191–96**
Restraining Act, 26
Revere, Paul, 213
Revolutionary War. *See* American Revolutionary War
Rhode Island, 16
Rice, 116
Rights of Man, The, 99
Roanoke, Virginia, 1
Rules by Which a Great Empire May Be Reduced to a Small One, 78–79
Rutledge, Edward, 152

S

Second Continental Congress, 43, 109–11, **127–33**, **135–49**, **151–68**
Sherman, Roger, 135–36
Slavery, 87, 114–16, 218, 219–20, 235
Society of Friends, 69, 105
Sons of Liberty, 4, 33, 34
    Boston Tea Party, 179
    Hutchinson letters affair, 172, 178, 186
    Stamp Act, 15–16
South Carolina, 116
Spotswood, Alexander, 93
Stamp Act, 4, **7–18**, 9 (ill.), 14 (ill.), 23, 180 (ill.)
    Dickinson, John, 131
    Hancock, John, 148
Stamp Act Congress, 15
Strahan, William, 35, 78 (ill.), 79–80
Summary View of the Rights of British America, A, **81–88**, 137

T

Tarring and feathering, 30 (ill.), 30, 123
Tax acts
    Declaratory Act, 19–23
    Hutchinson letters affair, 171–82, 183–89, 191–96
    Intolerable Acts, 37–48
    Stamp Act, 7–18
    Townshend Revenue Act, 25–36
Tea Act of 1773, 37, 179
Temple, John, 197
Thomas Paine National Historical Association, 105
Thomson, Charles, 146
Townshend Acts of 1767, 63–64, 148, 172, 174
Townshend, Charles, 25, 26 (box), 27, 35
Townshend Revenue Act, **25–36**
Treaty of Paris, 123, 233, 249
Trudeau, Garry, 105

U

U.S. Constitution, 148, 251

V

Virginia delegates, 114–15 (box)
Virginia House of Burgesses, 81, 89, 108
Virginia, martial law in, **217–20**

W

Wallace, Mike, 105
Walpole, Horace, 215, **241–45**, 242 (ill.)
Ward, Samuel, 16
Washington, George, 93, 115 (box), 230 (ill.), 249 (ill.)
Arnold, Benedict, 204, 205, 206, 207
Continental Army, 139, 214, 215, 226–27, 238
farewell address to armies, **247–53**

Paine, Thomas, 98, 99, 101, 104, 229–31, 232
Second Continental Congress, 128–29
Stamp Act, 12–13
Washington, Martha Dandridge Custis, 12
Watson-Wentworth, Charles, 20 (ill.), 20, 49
Whately, Thomas, 171, 172, 187, 193, 197, 198
Whiting, John, 204, 205–6
Wilkinson, Eliza, 214, **235–39**
Wright, James, 108
Writs of assistance, 27–28

Y

"Yankee," 226
"Yankee Doodle," 226